A Unified Development Ordinance

LANDERS-ATKINS PLANNERS
838 Edward Ball Building
Jacksonville, Florida 32202

Michael B. Brough

A Unified Development Ordinance

Planners Press
American Planning Association
Washington, D.C.   Chicago, Illinois

Copyright 1985 by the American Planning Association
1313 E. 60th St., Chicago, IL 60637

All rights reserved
ISBN: 0-918286-39-5
Library of Congress Catalog Card Number: 85-70182
Printed in the United States of America

To My Father
Dr. Raymond D. Brough

Contents

Acknowledgments
Foreword
Introduction

Article I
General Provisions

§ 1   Short Title   1
§ 2   Authority   1
§ 3   Jurisdiction   1
§ 4   Effective Date   2
§ 5   Relationship to Existing Zoning, Subdivision and Flood Control Ordinances   2
§ 6   Relationship to Land-Use Plan   2
§ 7   No Use or Sale of Land or Buildings Except in Conformity With Chapter Provisions   2
§ 8   Fees   2
§ 9   Severability   3
§ 10 Computation of Time   3
§ 11 Miscellaneous
§ 12 through 14   Reserved   3

Article II
Basic Definitions and Interpretations

§ 15 Definitions   5
§ 16 Lots Divided by District Lines   18
§ 17 through 20   Reserved   18

Article III
Administrative Mechanisms

Part I. Planning Board

§ 21 Appointment and Terms of Planning Board Members   19
§ 22 Meetings of the Planning Board   20
§ 23 Quorum and Voting   21
§ 24 Planning Board Officers   21
§ 25 Powers and Duties of Planning Board   21
§ 26 Advisory Committees   22
§ 27 through 28   Reserved   22

Article III cont.
Administrative Mechanisms

Part II. Board of Adjustment

§ 29 Appointment and Terms of Board of Adjustment   22
§ 30 Meetings of the Board of Adjustment   23
§ 31 Quorum   24
§ 32 Voting   24
§ 33 Board of Adjustment Officers   25
§ 34 Powers and Duties of Board of Adjustment   26
§ 35 and 36   Reserved   26

Article III cont.
Administrative Mechanisms

Part III. Land-Use Administrator and Planning Director

§ 37 Land-Use Administrator   26
§ 38 Planning Director   26
§ 39 Reserved   26

Part IV. City Council

§ 40 The City Council   26
§ 41 through 45   Reserved   27

Article IV
Permits and Final Plat Approval

Part I. Zoning, Special-Use, and Conditional-Use Permits

- § 46 Permits Required 28
- § 47 No Occupancy, Use, or Sale of Lots Until Requirements Fulfilled 29
- § 48 Who May Submit Permit Applications 30
- § 49 Applications To Be Complete 30
- § 50 Staff Consultation Before Formal Application 31
- § 51 Staff Consultation After Application Submitted 32
- § 52 Zoning Permits 32
- § 53 Authorizing Use or Occupancy Before Completion of Development Under Zoning Permit 33
- § 54 Special-Use Permits and Conditional-Use Permits 34
- § 55 Burden of Presenting Evidence; Burden of Persuasion 35
- § 56 Recommendations on Special-Use Permit Applications 35
- § 57 Recommendations on Conditional-Use Permits 36
- § 58 Council Action on Conditional-Use Permits 36
- § 59 Board of Adjustment Action on Special-Use Permits 37

Article IV cont.
Permits and Final Plat Approval

Part I. Zoning, Special-Use, and Conditional-Use Permits

- § 60 Additional Requirements on Special-Use and Conditional-Use Permits 38
- § 61 Authorizing Use, Occupancy, or Sale Before Completion of Development Under Special-Use or Conditional-Use Permits 39
- § 62 Completing Developments in Phases 40
- § 63 Expiration of Permits 40
- § 64 Effect of Permit on Successors and Assigns 41
- § 65 Amendments to and Modifications of Permits 42
- § 66 Reconsideration of Board Action 43
- § 67 Applications to be Processed Expeditiously 44
- § 68 Maintenance of Common Areas, Improvements, and Facilities 44
- § 69 through 75 Reserved 44

Article IV cont.
Permits and Final Plat Approval

Part II. Major and Minor Subdivisions

- § 76 Regulation of Subdivisions 44
- § 77 No Subdivision Without Plat Approval 45
- § 78 Minor Subdivision Approval 45
- § 79 Major Subdivision Approval Process 46
- § 80 Endorsements on Major Subdivision Plats 49
- § 81 Plat Approval Not Acceptance of Dedication Offers 50
- § 82 Protection Against Defects 50
- § 83 Maintenance of Dedicated Areas Until Acceptance 51
- § 84 through 90 Reserved 51

Article V
Appeals, Variances, Interpretations

- § 91 Appeals 52
- § 92 Variances 52
- § 93 Interpretations 53
- § 94 Requests To Be Heard Expeditiously 54
- § 95 Burden of Proof in Appeals and Variances 54
- § 96 Board Action on Appeals and Variances 54
- § 97 through 100 Reserved 55

Article VI
Hearing Procedures for Appeals and Applications

- § 101 Hearing Required on Appeals and Applications 56
- § 102 Notice of Hearing 56
- § 103 Evidence 57
- § 104 Modification of Application at Hearing 57
- § 105 Record 58
- § 106 Written Decision 58
- § 107 through 110 Reserved 59

Article VII
Enforcement and Review

- § 111 Complaints Regarding Violations 60
- § 112 Persons Liable 60
- § 113 Procedures Upon Discovery of Violations 60
- § 114 Penalties and Remedies for Violations 60
- § 115 Permit Revocation 61
- § 116 Judicial Review 62
- § 117 through 120 Reserved 62

Article VIII
Nonconforming Situations

- § 121 Definitions 63
- § 122 Continuation of Nonconforming Situations and Completion of Nonconforming Projects 64
- § 123 Nonconforming Lots 64
- § 124 Extension or Enlargement of Nonconforming Situations 65
- § 125 Repair, Maintenance and Reconstruction 67
- § 126 Change In Use of Property Where a Nonconforming Situation Exists 68
- § 127 Abandonment and Discontinuance of Nonconforming Situations 69
- § 128 Completion of Nonconforming Projects 70
- § 129 through 134 Reserved 72

Article IX
Zoning Districts and Zoning Map

Part I. Zoning Districts

- § 135 Residential Districts Established 73
- § 136 Commercial Districts Established 73
- § 137 Manufacturing Districts Established 74
- § 138 Planned Unit Development Districts Established 74
- § 139 Floodplain and Floodway Districts 77
- § 140 and 141 Reserved 77

Part II. Zoning Map

- § 142 Official Zoning Map 77
- § 143 Amendments to Official Zoning Map 77
- § 144 and 145 Reserved 77

Article X
Permissible Uses

- § 146 Table of Permissible Uses 78
- § 147 Use of Designations Z, S, C in Table of Permissible Uses 86
- § 148 Board of Adjustment Jurisdiction Over Uses Otherwise Permissible With a Zoning Permit 87
- § 149 Permissible Uses and Specific Exclusions 87
- § 150 Accessory Uses 88
- § 151 Permissible Uses Not Requiring Permits 89
- § 152 Change in Use 89
- § 153 Developments in the B-5 Zoning District 91
- § 154 Combination Uses 91
- § 155 More Specific Use Controls 91
- § 156 and 157 Reserved 91

Article XI
Supplementary Use Regulations

Part I. General Provisions

- § 158 Planned Residential Developments 92
- § 159 Planned Unit Developments 92
- § 160 Temporary Emergency, Construction, or Repair Residences 93
- § 161 Special Events 93
- § 162 through 170 Reserved 94

Part II. Manufacturing/Processing Performance Standards

- § 171 Smoke 95
- § 172 Noise 95
- § 173 Vibration 96
- § 174 Odors 97
- § 175 Air Pollution 97
- § 176 Disposal of Liquid Wastes 98
- § 177 Water Consumption 98
- § 178 Electrical Disturbance or Interference 98
- § 179 and 180 Reserved 98

Article XII
Density and Dimensional Regulations

- § 181 Minimum Lot Size Requirements 99
- § 182 Residential Density 99
- § 183 Minimum Lot Widths 102
- § 184 Building Setback Requirements 103
- § 185 Accessory Building Setback Requirements 105
- § 186 Building Height Limitations 105
- § 187 Cluster Subdivisions 106
- § 188 Architecturally Integrated Subdivisions 107
- § 189 Density on Lots Where Portion Dedicated to City 107
- § 190 through 195 Reserved 108

Article XIII
Recreational Facilities and Open Space

- § 196 Miniparks Required 109
- § 197 Miniparks: Purpose and Standards 110
- § 198 Usable Open Space 111
- § 199 Ownership and Maintenance of Recreational Areas and Required Open Space 12
- § 200 Dedication of Open Space 112
- § 201 Homeowners Association 113
- § 202 Flexibility in Administration Authorized 113
- § 203 through 209 Reserved 114

Article XIV
Streets and Sidewalks

§ 210 Street Classification 115
§ 211 Access to Lots 116
§ 212 Access to Arterial Streets 116
§ 213 Entrances to Streets 116
§ 214 Coordination with Surrounding Streets 117
§ 215 Relationship of Streets to Topography 118
§ 216 Street Width, Sidewalk, and Drainage Requirements in Subdivisions 118
§ 217 General Layout of Streets 120
§ 218 Street Intersections 120
§ 219 Construction Standards and Specifications 121
§ 220 Public Streets and Private Roads in Subdivisions 121
§ 221 Road and Sidewalk Requirements in Unsubdivided Developments 124
§ 222 Attention to Handicapped in Street and Sidewalk Construction 125
§ 223 Street Names and House Numbers 125
§ 224 Bridges 125
§ 225 Utilities 125
§ 226 through 235 Reserved 125

Article XV
Utilities

§ 236 Utility Ownership and Easement Rights 126
§ 237 Lots Served by Governmentally Owned Water and Sewer Lines 126
§ 238 Sewage Disposal Facilities Required 126
§ 239 Determining Compliance with Section 238 127
§ 240 Water Supply System Required 129
§ 241 Determining Compliance With Section 240 129
§ 242 Lighting Requirements 132
§ 243 Excessive Illumination 132
§ 244 Electric Power 133
§ 245 Telephone Service 133
§ 246 Underground Utilities 133
§ 247 Utilities To Be Consistent With Internal and External Development 134
§ 248 As-Built Drawings Required 134
§ 249 Fire Hydrants 134
§ 250 Sites for and Screening of Dumpsters 134

Article XVI
Floodways, Floodplains, Drainage, and Erosion

Part I. Floodways and Floodplains

§ 251 Definitions 136
§ 252 Artificial Obstructions Within Floodways Prohibited 137
§ 253 Permissible Uses Within Floodways 137
§ 254 Construction Within Floodways and Floodplains Restricted 137
§ 255 Special Provisions for Subdivisions 139
§ 256 Water Supply and Sanitary Sewer Systems in Floodways and Floodplains 140
§ 257 Additional Duties of Administrator Related to Flood Insurance and Flood Control 140
§ 258 Location of Boundaries of Floodplain and Floodway Districts 141
§ 259 Setbacks from Streams Outside Designated Floodplains 141
§ 260 Reserved 141

Part II. Drainage, Erosion Control, Storm Water Management

§ 261 Natural Drainage System Utilized to Extent Feasible 141
§ 262 Developments Must Drain Properly 141
§ 263 Storm Water Management 142
§ 264 Sedimentation and Erosion Control 143
§ 265 through 269 Reserved 144

Article XVII
Signs

- § 270 Definitions 145
- § 271 Permit Required for Signs 146
- § 272 Signs Excluded From Regulation 147
- § 273 Certain Temporary Signs: Permit Exemptions and Additional Regulations 148
- § 274 Determining the Number of Signs 149
- § 275 Computation of Sign Area 150
- § 276 Total Sign Surface Area 150
- § 277 Freestanding Sign Surface Area 151
- § 278 Number of Freestanding Signs 152
- § 279 Subdivision and Multi-Family Development Entrance Signs 152
- § 280 Location and Height Requirements 152
- § 281 Sign Illumination and Signs Containing Lights 152
- § 282 Miscellaneous Restrictions and Prohibitions 153
- § 283 Maintenance of Signs 154
- § 284 Unlawful Cutting of Trees or Shrubs 154
- § 285 Nonconforming Signs 154
- § 286 Amortization of Nonconforming Signs 156
- § 287 through 289 Reserved 156

Article XVIII
Parking

- § 290 Definitions 157
- § 291 Number of Parking Spaces Required 157
- § 292 Flexibility in Administration Required 161
- § 293 Parking Space Dimensions 162
- § 294 Required Widths of Parking Area Aisles and Driveways 163
- § 295 General Design Requirements 163
- § 296 Vehicle Accommodation Area Surfaces 163
- § 297 Joint Use of Required Parking Spaces 164
- § 298 Satellite Parking 165
- § 299 Special Provisions For Lots With Existing Buildings 165
- § 300 Loading and Unloading Areas 166
- § 301 through 303 Reserved 167

Article XIX
Screening and Trees

Part I. Screening

- § 304 Council Findings Concerning the Need for Screening Requirements 168
- § 305 General Screening Standard 169
- § 306 Compliance With Screening Standard 169
- § 307 Descriptions of Screens 170
- § 308 Table of Screening Requirements 172
- § 309 Flexibility in Administration Required 174
- § 310 Combination Uses 174
- § 311 Subdivisions 174
- § 312 and 313 Reserved 174

Part II. Shading

- § 314 Council Findings and Declaration of Policy on Shade Trees 175
- § 315 Required Trees Along Dedicated Streets 175
- § 316 Retention and Protection of Large Trees 175
- § 317 Shade Trees in Parking Areas 176
- § 318 and 319 Reserved 177

Article XX
Amendments

- § 320 Amendments In General 178
- § 321 Initiation of Amendments 178
- § 322 Planning Board Consideration of Proposed Amendments 179
- § 323 Hearing Required; Notice 179
- § 324 Council Action on Amendments 180
- § 325 Ultimate Issue Before Council on Amendments 181
- § 326 Protests to Zoning District Changes 181

Appendixes

Appendix A
Information Required with Applications

A–1 In General 183
A–2 Written Application 183
A–3 Development Site Plans 184
A–4 Graphic Materials Required for Plans 184
A–5 Existing Natural, Man-Made, and Legal Features 185
A–6 Proposed Changes In Existing Features or New Features 186
A–7 Documents and Written Information in Addition to Plans 187
A–8 Number of Copies of Plans and Documents 188

Appendix B
Specifications on Driveway Entrances

Appendix C
Specifications for Street Design and Construction

C–1 Design Speed, Sight Distance, Centerline Radius 190
C–2 Cut and Fill Slopes 190
C–3 Sign Distances at Intersections 190
C–4 Radius at Street Intersections 191
C–5 Clearing and Grubbing 191
C–6 Grading and Compaction 191
C–7 Street Base 191
C–8 Street Surfaces 191
C–9 Pavement Section Variations 191
C–10 Street Cross Sections 191
C–11 Curb and Gutter 192
C–12 Sidewalks 192
C–13 Wheelchair Ramps 192
C–14 Storm Water Runoff Control 192
C–15 Sedimentation Control 192

Appendix C cont.
Standard Drawings

- No. 1 Sight Distance For No-Stop Condition 193
- No. 2 Sight Distance For Stop Condition (Secondary State Road) 193
- No. 3 Sight Distance For Stop Condition (Primary State Road) 194
- No. 4 Curb and Gutter 194
- No. 5 No Curb and Gutter 195
- No. 6 Residential Street—No Curb and Gutter 195
- No. 7 Residential Street—Curb and Gutter 196
- No. 8 Standard Curb and Gutter 196
- No. 9 Standard Wheelchair Ramp 197
- No. 10 Standard Catch Basin 198
- No. 11 Storm Water Manhole 199
- No. 12 Yard Inlet Cover 200
- No. 13 Yard Inlet 200
- No. 14 Sedimentation Control 201

Appendix D
Vehicle Accommodation Area Surfaces

- D–1 Paved Surfaces 202
- D–2 Unpaved Surfaces 202

Appendix E
Guide for Landscaping

- E–1 Guide for Protecting Existing Trees 203
- E–2 Standards for Street and Parking Lot Trees 203
- E–3 Formula for Calculating 20 Percent Shading of Paved Vehicle Accommodation Areas 204
- E–4 Typical Parking Lot Planting Islands 205
- E–5 Guide for Planting Trees 205
- E–6 Typical Opaque Screens 206
- E–7 Typical Semi-Opaque Screens 207
- E–8 Typical Broken Screens 207
- E–9 Guide for Planting Shrubs 208
- E–10 Lists of Recommended Trees and Shrubs 208
- E–11 Small Trees for Partial Screening 209
- E–12 Large Trees for Evergreen Screening 209
- E–13 Large Trees for Shading 210
- E–14 Small Shrubs for Evergreen Screening 210
- E–15 Large Shrubs for Evergreen Screening 211
- E–16 Assorted Shrubs for Broken Screens 211

Appendix F
Guide for Noise Levels

- F–1 Community Noise Measurement Data Sheet 212
- F–2 Computational Work Sheet 213

Appendix G
Worksheet

Acknowledgments

The material for this book is drawn primarily from my experience in drafting a unified development ordinance for several smaller but rapidly growing communities in North Carolina and in working with these local governments to interpret, administer, enforce, and revise this ordinance. Officials and administrators in all these communities have been helpful in critiquing and refining the ideas, concepts, and ordinance language that appear in this book, and I am grateful to all of them. However, I wish to acknowledge especially the assistance of the elected and appointed officials and administrators of the Town of Carrboro, where a unified ordinance similar to the one that appears in this book was first adopted; this work would never have been produced without their support. And I am particularly indebted to those Carrboro planning and zoning professionals who worked closely with me in developing the first ordinance: Sonna Loewenthal, Larry Belkin, Marc Weiss, Suellen Beaulieu, and David Broadwell.

Foreword

This book is designed to help local governments draft one land-use ordinance that combines the provisions more commonly found in separate zoning and subdivision ordinances. It is written in the belief that while any attempt to draft a "model ordinance" would be futile given the differences in state-to-state enabling legislation and the wide disparity in local needs and conditions, there are enough common elements in the types of concerns most local governments seek to address in their land-use ordinances that this guidebook approach may prove beneficial.

Specifically, this guidebook presents a mixture of ordinance language and commentary that focuses on the types of issues that should be addressed in a combined zoning/subdivision ordinance and illustrates one way to address those issues. General commentary precedes some articles, and commentary relating to the issues addressed in specific ordinance provisions follows those provisions. In many cases, ordinance provisions are not followed by any commentary where the problem or issue addressed by a particular provision or the objective it seeks to obtain is obvious. Again, it is emphasized that the ordinance text contained herein is proffered less as model language than to illustrate one way to address common problems. If the user finds particular language presented here appropriate in terms of local needs and laws, so much the better. However, the primary intent of this book is to assist the draftsman in asking the right questions rather than providing definitive answers.

The ordinance language and commentary in this text are derived from the author's experience in drafting a similar ordinance for several small cities (populations 2,000 to 20,000) in North Carolina and working on a daily basis with the officials administering such an ordinance. Because of its origins, this book has certain orientations that should be made explicit at the outset.

First, the issues addressed and the solutions proposed in this guidebook ordinance may not adequately meet the needs of communities at either end of the population spectrum because of the size of the cities for which it was written.[1] For example, the ordinance demands a higher level of administration than is required to enforce the most basic type of zoning ordinance, and this may diminish its usefulness for those very small towns that lack the necessary administrative capability. This is not to suggest that the guidebook ordinance is administratively complex. However, in contrast to the most elementary type of zoning ordinance, which allows the zoning enforcement officer little or no discretion and provides for precious little site plan review, this ordinance requires greater discretion and judgment by the administrator and more detailed analysis of development plans. Of course, engineering expertise (for review of utility and drainage plans) and even professional planning assistance (for general site plan review) need not necessarily be possessed in-house since it can be contracted and the costs can be included in the permit fee. But in any case, one or more capable people (depending on the volume of applications) must devote substantial, if not full-time, attention to administering and enforcing the type of ordinance proposed here. Communities that are too small to provide even the minimal level of administration needed may find this guidebook not entirely applicable to their situations.

On the other hand, because this ordinance was drafted to respond to the problems of smaller (although rapidly developing) cities, it should be recognized that the problems faced by much larger urban areas may demand an approach different than that presented here or solutions that are not addressed here. For example, larger jurisdictions with sophisticated administrative capabilities may prefer an approach that substitutes detailed performance standards for some of the more general design standards suggested in this guidebook. And some local governments will have need for provisions dealing with matters, such as the transfer of development rights or the control of solar access, that are not addressed in this text. Therefore, although the approach of combining zoning and subdivision regulations into one ordinance seems desirable for local governments of any size, draftsmen for larger jurisdictions need to review this guidebook with an awareness of its limitations.

A second orientation of this guidebook is that while many innovations are suggested, this work is more the product of an effort to revise, streamline, modernize, and improve familiar tools of development control than an attempt to develop radically different procedures or techniques. Those familiar with planning and zoning are aware that the literature in recent years abounds with criticisms of "traditional" zoning and calls for abandoning it or adopting new techniques.[2] Flexible and conditional zoning,[3] impact zoning,[4] development timing controls,[5] plan-based administrative review,[6] and performance zoning,[7] are among such techniques.

Given this criticism, it seems fair and perhaps imperative to offer a word of explanation and justification for a book that purports not to be a radical break with the past. To do this, it is necessary to explain very briefly how and where the approach taken in this text fits with the range of land-use control philosophies and techniques espoused and adopted over the years, particularly those discussed in recent literature.

At the risk, in fact the certainty, of gross oversimplification, it is possible to categorize zoning ordinances developed over the years according to the manner in which they deal with the following three potential subjects of local land-use regulation: *where* different types of land uses may be located, *when* land may be developed, and *how* development may take place (in terms of various design elements).

Very basic zoning ordinances, the type referred to by the critics when they speak of "traditional zoning," focus almost exclusively on the "where," although they typically include a few design-oriented provisions dealing with such matters as building height, setback limitations, and parking requirements.

Such "first generation" ordinances have simplicity and ease of administration to commend them, and they generally operate satisfactorily to protect existing development from encroachment by incompatible uses. However, traditional ordinances are criticized as being incapable of predicting or controlling the level, tempo, or direction of future growth, lacking the flexibility to allow creative or innovative design, and failing to exercise sufficient control over various project design elements, particularly those that concern aesthetics or the environment.

In response, "second generation" zoning ordinances include provisions covering a broader range of design elements such as signs, screening, landscaping, drainage, and flood control. They provide for greater flexibility through increased use of special- or conditional-use permits, floating zones, and other techniques designed to allow local governments to take a "wait and see" approach to land-use control and to approve projects on a case-by-case basis. Some ordinances also attempt to limit the total amount of growth, or at least the timing of development. This second generation of ordinances is criticized on the basis that the increased level of discretion and control that they lodge in local officials inevitably leads to gross abuses of authority that result in unwarranted delays in the approval process, approvals with onerous conditions, or even arbitrary rejections of legitimate projects.

Performance zoning, the "third generation" of ordinances, claims to provide for flexibility without arbitrariness by establishing objectively determinable criteria that measure a development's various impacts on the environment, neighboring properties, streets and utility systems, etc. In its purest form, performance zoning theoretically can respond to all of the "where, when, and how" concerns of land-use control. The criticisms of the more advanced forms of performance zoning are that: (i) it is extremely difficult and expensive to devise objectively measurable criteria to regulate many types of impacts, (ii) administering such an ordinance is beyond the capability of most jurisdictions, and (iii) even if the professionals understand such an ordinance, it is doubtful that the ordinance can be made comprehensible to the governing body that must adopt it or the general public that must abide by it.

This guidebook has a second generation orientation, with a bow to the first and some pilfering from the third. It takes a traditional approach to the "where" concerns to the extent that it anticipates the creation of zoning districts and the assignment of those districts to specified locations on a zoning map.[8] It also relies on performance zoning criteria to regulate the impacts of manufacturing/processing uses. But it is clearly most closely akin to the second generation of ordinances to the extent that it is oriented very heavily toward providing greater flexibility for the developer while maintaining local control over a wide range of design elements.

This guidebook does differ from many second generation ordinances, however, in that it attempts to balance the flexibility it gives to local administrative bodies with procedural safeguards that help ensure that the discretion granted is not used arbitrarily. In addition, it offers no solutions to the problems of controlling the tempo or timing of growth or limiting the maximum amount of growth (except through density controls). This "modified second generation" approach is set forth without undue criticism of other approaches or apologies for techniques not included. Rather, it represents the author's best effort to address the land-use control problems and needs of smaller and mid-size communities and to do so using terminology and concepts that those familiar with more traditional zoning and subdivision regulations can understand.

The third orientation of this guidebook is that it is designed as a working tool for the draftsman rather than a research source for the scholar. For this reason, while the ordinance provisions and commentary are based on research as well as experience, footnotes and citations have generally been omitted in the belief that they add more length than value to a work such as this.

---

[1] While this guidebook refers throughout to "cities," most of its provisions are also applicable to counties.

[2] Peter Atonna and Richard Counts, "New and Innovative Ideas in Land Use Controls—With or Without Zoning," *Proceedings of the Institute on Planning, Zoning, and Eminent Domain 1*, (1980).

[3] Robert H. Freilich, "Effectiveness of Flexible and Conditional Zoning Techniques—What They Can and Cannot Do For Our Cities," *Proceedings of the Institute on Planning, Zoning and Eminent Domain 167*, (1979).

[4] Roger Weils, "Impact Zoning: Incentive Land Use Management," *Management and Control of Growth*, Vol. 4 (1978): 43.

[5] Robert H. Freilich, "Development Timing, Morotoria and Controlling Growth," *Management and Control of Growth*, Vol. 2 (1975): 361.

[6] Paul H. Sedway, "Plan Based Administrative Review: A Planning and Zoning Detente," *Land Use and Zoning Digest,* Vol. 32, No. 10 (October 1980): 6. See also Wickersham, "The Permit System of Managing Land Use and Growth," *Management and Control of Growth*, Vol. 4 (1978): 184.

[7] Kendig, Connor, Byrd, and Heyman, *Performance Zoning* (1980); see also Thurow, Toner, Erley, "Performance Controls for Sensitive Lands," *PAS Report,* Nos. 307, 308 (1978).

[8] It goes without saying that careful planning, including an analysis of the carrying capacity of the land—or lack of it in terms of the natural environment and man-made systems—should precede the creation of zoning districts and the assignment of districts to a map.

Introduction
General Characteristics
of the Ordinance

This section offers an overview of the general characteristics that permeate each of the articles included in the guidebook.

The most striking general characteristic of this ordinance is that it treats in one unified text those areas of regulation more typically dealt with in separate zoning and subdivision ordinances.* This combined approach has several advantages. First, it conforms to the way that development, especially major residential development, tends to occur today; that is, in a manner that combines subdivided and unsubdivided elements or that blurs the distinctions between subdivisions and nonsubdivisions. For example, many residential developments today contain a mixture of housing types—single-family residences, duplexes, and multi-family (apartment) dwellings. In addition, and more recently, many developers seek to construct two-story, attached residential dwellings (commonly called "townhouses") and sell the units with the land under them—in essence building what is visually a multi-family project but what is technically and legally a subdivision. Under such circumstances, a regulatory system that requires separate ordinances for different phases of the same project or that fails to respond to market realities is at best cumbersome and at worst unworkable.

A second advantage of the combined zoning and subdivision ordinances is that it permits the land-use control system to be administered more efficiently because (i) the administrators and members of the various boards involved (planning board, board of adjustment, city council, appearance commission, etc.) need to become familiar with only one set of standards, and (ii) the approval processes for all types of development are covered in one ordinance.

Finally, a unified ordinance avoids the overlapping, conflicting, or inconsistent ordinance provisions found in land-use control systems consisting of separate zoning and subdivision ordinances, particularly when those ordinances were drafted by different individuals and adopted at different times.

A second general characteristic of this ordinance is that it seeks very deliberately to provide the developer with as much flexibility as possible, both in terms of the types of projects allowed and the design of those projects. Traditionally, zoning and subdivision regulations have concentrated on establishing minimum standards of development designed to prevent the construction of projects that are

---

*Also, because it is designed to be a comprehensive land-use ordinance, it deals with several subjects that sometimes are covered in zoning regulations but frequently are dealt with in separate ordinances—including signs, flood control, and sedimentation and erosion control.

undesirable or unsafe. But the danger is that in setting rigid standards that prevent the worst type of development, the ordinances can stifle creativity, preclude innovations in design, and thereby reduce all development to the lowest common denominator that accords with the public health and safety.

No ordinance can avoid this danger completely, but the ordinance provisions presented here do reflect the philosophy that developers should have as much flexibility as possible, consistent with the local government's need to retain sufficient authority to safeguard the public health, safety, and welfare. For example, the ordinance allows residential uses in commercial areas in recognition that, particularly in downtown commercial areas, residences are not only compatible with commercial uses but may be essential to the continued viability of those commercial areas. Another example is found in the provisions waiving all internal setback and minimum lot size requirements in "architecturally integrated subdivisions," which are subdivisions in which the developer is selling, according to an approved plan, not only the lot but the building located on it.

More generally, whenever appropriate and practicable, the ordinance establishes design standards by using broadly worded objectives (e.g., "parking lots shall be sufficiently illuminated to ensure the security of property and safety of persons using such . . . parking lots") rather than inflexible, numerical criteria. As a final illustration, in several areas (e.g., the parking requirements) the ordinance sets a general standard (adequate parking) and then establishes numerical ratios that are *presumptive* only. This leaves the permit-issuing authority enough flexibility to find, in particular cases, that some deviation from the presumptive numerical requirement provides better compliance with the basic standard than does the stated ratio. These and other illustrations of the emphasis placed on flexibility are explained more fully in the commentary to the text.

The third general characteristic of the ordinance presented, and a corollary to the second, is that it seeks to avoid excessive regulation. Ordinance draftsmen, perhaps because of excess enthusiasm and a natural desire to treat a subject comprehensively, occasionally fall victim to the temptation to be overinclusive both in terms of subject areas regulated and the detail of those regulations. However, the market imposes many constraints on developers, and such constraints need not be duplicated in local ordinances. In addition, since most major projects are subject to approval under a process that provides some discretion to the permit-issuing board to reject a project for reasons not *specifically* stated in the ordinance, it is unnecessary to anticipate and proscribe in the ordinance every conceivable design peccadillo. This approach does not reflect a regulatory timidity, but rather recognition of the wisdom of the colloquial saying, "If it ain't broke, don't fix it."

One final word on ordinance flexibility should be mentioned here. It is undeniable that the more flexibility an ordinance contains, the greater is the possibility that the ordinance can be arbitrarily administered—either to impose unwarranted hardships on developers or to allow favored developers to circumvent the purpose and intent of the ordinance's provisions. To a significant degree, the dangers of arbitrary administration are minimized by the careful attention to procedural provisions described in the following paragraph. Still, one must recognize that the trade-off between flexibility and the possibility of arbitrariness cannot be entirely avoided. But the author's experience is that far more problems are caused by an ordinance that provides too little rather than too much flexibility, and the ordinance presented in this guidebook therefore chooses to err, if at all, on the side of flexibility.

The fourth general characteristic of this ordinance is that it pays careful attention to and deals at some length with the problems of administering and enforcing a land-use ordinance. All too frequently, zoning and subdivision ordinances give short shrift to administrative provisions, leaving unanswered a host of important questions relating to matters such as approval of phased development, the effect of permits on successors and assigns, major and minor amendments of plans after permit approval, the treatment of various types of nonconforming situations, etc. The ordinance seeks to address as many of these issues as possible and to suggest ways in which the administrator may be given the necessary practical tools to administer and enforce the ordinance effectively and efficiently. In addition, because courts in recent years have increasingly focused on the procedural due process rights of parties affected by decisions made under zoning and subdivision ordinances, the ordinance deals more extensively than is traditionally the case with provisions relating to notice of hearings, hearing procedures, evidentiary requirements, written decisions (including findings), and procedures for appeals.

The substantive, as opposed to administrative, portions of the ordinance are contained in a series of separate articles dealing, respectively, with zoning districts, permissible uses, and supplementary use provisions (including industrial performance standards), followed by eight articles dealing with the following project design elements: (i) density and other dimensional aspects, (ii) recreational facilities and open space, (iii) streets and sidewalks, (iv) utilities, (v) floodways, floodplains, and drainage and erosion, (vi) signs, (vii) parking, and (viii) screening and trees.

Requirements concerning particular design elements are contained in those articles, regardless of whether the development is subdivided or unsubdivided or whether the permit-issuing body is the administrator, the board of adjustment, or the governing body. This approach facilitates two objectives.

First, it requires the governing body, in adopting the ordinance, to think comprehensively about each design element in the context of *all* types of development, and this increases the likelihood of a more consistent treatment of different types of development. This is not to say that, for example, the parking or sidewalk requirements should be the same for single-family subdivisions, apartments, and mobile home parks—only that, if and to the extent different standards are selected, these differences should be rationally justified.

Second, experience suggests that the separate treatment of different design elements makes it easier when later amending one ordinance provision to avoid unintentionally overlooking or affecting other related provisions.

The sixth general characteristic of the ordinance is that it is written with an awareness of the costs that regulations impose on development, and it seeks to ensure that the question is raised whether costs are justified by corresponding benefits. One way in which the ordinance demonstrates its cost consciousness has already been addressed: it provides developers with enough design flexibility to use imaginative, cost-cutting techniques. Other examples are found in the provisions allowing narrower pavement on less traveled public streets and authorizing, under some circumstances, streets constructed with shoulders and drainage swales rather than curbs and gutters.

Finally, a sincere attempt has been made to draft this ordinance in understandable English, free from obfuscatory legalisms or planning jargon. In a few cases, the need to draw fine distinctions has required that clarity be sacrificed to accuracy. It is hoped that such provisions are no more than exceptions that prove the rule.

Land-Use Ordinance

Article
- I. General Provisions
- II. Basic Definitions and Interpretations
- III. Administrative Mechanisms
- IV. Permits and Final Plat Approval
- V. Appeals, Variances, Interpretations
- VI. Hearing Procedures for Appeals and Applications
- VII. Enforcement and Review
- VIII. Nonconforming Situations
- IX. Zoning Districts and Zoning Map
- X. Permissible Uses
- XI. Supplementary Use Regulations
- XII. Density and Dimensional Regulations
- XIII. Recreational Facilities and Open Space
- XIV. Streets and Sidewalks
- XV. Utilities
- XVI. Floodways, Floodplains, Drainage and Erosion
- XVII. Signs
- XVIII. Parking
- XIX. Screening and Trees
- XX. Amendments

Article I — General Provisions

Commentary:

This ordinance is drafted to be included in a city's code of ordinances, and therefore various provisions refer to "this chapter" rather than "this ordinance." If included in such a code, it is likely that Sections 9 through 11 and Subsection 2(b) could be deleted to the extent that they duplicate provisions generally found in the first chapter of most city codes.

In places where it is obvious how a blank space should be filled in, only the space appears. In other places, an explanation of the required addition is stated in brackets.

Section 1: Short Title

This chapter shall be known and may be cited as the _____ Land-Use Ordinance.

Section 2: Authority

(a) This chapter is adopted pursuant to the authority contained in [here cite appropriate provisions of general enabling legislation for local charters].

Commentary:

No special statutory authority should be required in order to combine into a single ordinance those provisions more frequently found in separate zoning, subdivision, flood control, and other ordinances since this involves a change in form rather than substance.

(b) Whenever any provision of this chapter refers to or cites a section of the [relevant state or local law, e.g., North Carolina General Statutes] and that section is later amended or superseded, the chapter shall be deemed amended to refer to the amended section or the section that most nearly corresponds to the superseded section.

Section 3: Jurisdiction

(a) This chapter shall be effective throughout the city's planning jurisdiction. The city's planning jurisdiction comprises the area within the corporate boundaries of the city as well as the area described in that ordinance adopted by the city council on _____, entitled an "Ordinance Establishing Extraterritorial Jurisdiction," which ordinance is recorded in book _____, page _____ of the _____ County Registry. Such planning jurisdiction may be modified from time to time in accordance with Section _____ of the [applicable state law].

(b) In addition to other locations required by law, a copy of a map showing the boundaries of the city's planning jurisdiction shall be available for public inspection in the planning department.

Section 4:
Effective Date

The provisions in this chapter were originally adopted and became effective on _____.

Section 5:
Relationship to Existing Zoning, Subdivision and Flood Control Ordinances

To the extent that the provisions of this chapter are the same in substance as the previously adopted provisions that they replace in the city's zoning, subdivision, or flood control ordinances, they shall be considered as continuations thereof and not as new enactments unless otherwise specifically provided. In particular, a situation that did not constitute a lawful, nonconforming situation under the previously adopted zoning ordinance does not achieve lawful nonconforming status under this chapter merely by the repeal of the zoning ordinance.

Section 6:
Relationship to Land-Use Plan

It is the intention of the council that this chapter implement the planning policies adopted by the council for the city and its extraterritorial planning area, as reflected in the land-use plan and other planning documents. While the council reaffirms its commitment that this chapter and any amendment to it be in conformity with adopted planning policies, the council hereby expresses its intent that neither this chapter nor any amendment to it may be challenged on the basis of any alleged nonconformity with any planning document.

Commentary:

> Increasing attention is being paid today to the relationship between those documents that set forth a local government's formally adopted plans for its future and the ordinances that are, at least theoretically, designed to implement those plans. Several states have enacted legislation that requires a closer correlation between adopted plans and ordinances than traditionally has been legally required. The land-use ordinance should state what the relationship is or is intended to be. The language above exhorts the governing body to pay attention to its own plans but seeks to minimize the availability of a legal challenge to the ordinance based upon a purported lack of conformity with such plans.

Section 7:
No Use or Sale of Land or Buildings Except in Conformity With Chapter Provisions

(a) Subject to Article VIII of this chapter (Nonconforming Situations), no person may use, occupy, or sell any land or buildings or authorize or permit the use, occupancy, or sale of land or buildings under his control except in accordance with all of the applicable provisions of this chapter.

(b) For purposes of this section, the "use" or "occupancy" of a building or land relates to anything and everything that is done to, on, or in that building or land.

Section 8:
Fees

(a) Reasonable fees sufficient to cover the costs of administration, inspection, publication of notice and similar matters may be charged to applicants for zoning permits, sign permits, conditional-use permits, special-use permits, subdivision plat approval, zoning amendments, variances and other administrative relief. The amount of the fees charged shall be as set forth in the city's budget or as established by resolution of the council filed in the office of the city clerk.

(b) Fees established in accordance with Subsection (a) shall be paid upon submission of a signed application or notice of appeal.

3 General Provisions

Commentary:

Because fees are commonly subject to annual revision, it is generally advisable to include them only by reference in the ordinance text.

Section 9: Severability

It is hereby declared to be the intention of the council that the sections, paragraphs, sentences, clauses, and phrases of this ordinance are severable, and if any such section, paragraph, sentence, clause, or phrase is declared unconstitutional or otherwise invalid by any court of competent jurisdiction in a valid judgment or decree, such unconstitutionality or invalidity shall not affect any of the remaining sections, paragraphs, sentences, clauses, or phrases of this ordinance since the same would have been enacted without the incorporation into this ordinance of such unconstitutional or invalid section, paragraph, sentence, clause or phrase.

Section 10: Computation of Time

(a) Unless otherwise specifically provided, the time within which an act is to be done shall be computed by excluding the first and including the last day. If the last day is a Saturday, Sunday, or legal holiday, that day shall be excluded. When the period of time prescribed is less than seven days, intermediate Saturdays, Sundays, and holidays shall be excluded.

(b) Unless otherwise specifically provided, whenever a person has the right or is required to do some act within a prescribed period after the service of a notice or other paper upon him and the notice or paper is served by mail, three days shall be added to the prescribed period.

Section 11: Miscellaneous

(a) As used in this ordinance, words importing the masculine gender include the feminine and neuter.

(b) Words used in the singular in this ordinance include the plural and words used in the plural include the singular.

Sections 12 through 14: Reserved

Article II Basic Definitions and Interpretations

Commentary:

In general, definitions of terms should be placed in the ordinance as close as reasonably possible to the section in which such terms appear. Thus, if a term is used only in one section, it should be defined in that section, and if used only in one article, it should be defined at the beginning of that article. Terms used throughout the ordinance are defined in Section 15. In addition, for ease of reference, the definitions that appear at the beginning of various articles are also included in Section 15. These latter definitions may be dropped from this section to shorten it if the draftsman so chooses.

In drafting definitions, care should be taken to include only substantive criteria intended to be *definitional* and to avoid the inclusion of provisions intended to impose substantive requirements on the thing defined. Such extraneous substantive requirements are frequently found in two forms in the definitions section of ordinances, and both forms can create problems.

In the first form, a term is adequately defined and then at least one additional requirement follows the definition. For example, the definition of the term "street, cul-de-sac" might be followed by the additional requirement that "cul-de-sacs shall not exceed 550 feet in length." The obvious problem with including such requirements in a definitions section is that they are easily overlooked.

The second form in which extraneous substantive requirements are found in definitions creates a more subtle problem, usually one of interpretation. For example, if a cul-de-sac is defined as "a street not exceeding 550 feet in length that terminates in a vehicular turnaround," then a street 600 feet in length that terminates in a vehicular turnaround is not, by definition, a cul-de-sac, but neither is it prohibited by the ordinance (unless the 550-foot limitation is stated in another form elsewhere). To avoid such problems, definitions should contain only those provisions that specify what the thing *is*, leaving additional substantive requirements to the remaining provisions of the ordinance.

In some cases, the reason why a term is defined at all or defined in a particular way can best be understood in reference to the Table of Permissible Uses. In those cases, appropriate explanations are set forth in the commentary following that table.

If the land-use ordinance is included in a code of ordinances, it is likely the definitions of the terms "city," "council," and "person" can be deleted from this article as being unnecessarily duplicative of definitions usually contained in the introductory chapter of such a code.

Section 15: Definitions of Basic Terms

Unless otherwise specifically provided, or unless clearly required by the context, the words and phrases defined in this section shall have the meaning indicated when used in this chapter.

(1) *Accessory Use.* (See Section 150)

(2) *Administrator.* (See Section 37)

(3) *Antenna.* Equipment designed to transmit or receive electronic signals.

(4) *Base Flood.* The flood having a one percent chance of being equaled or exceeded in any given year. Also known as the 100-year flood.

(5) *Boarding House.* A residential use consisting of at least one dwelling unit together with more than two rooms that are rented or are designed or intended to be rented but which rooms, individually or collectively, do not constitute separate dwelling units. A rooming house or boarding house is distinguished from a tourist home in that the former is designed to be occupied by longer term residents (at least month-to-month tenants) as opposed to overnight or weekly guests.

(6) *Building.* A structure designed to be used as a place of occupancy, storage or shelter.

(7) *Building, Accessory.* A minor building that is located on the same lot as a principal building and that is used incidentally to a principal building or that houses an accessory use.

(8) *Building, Principal.* The primary building on a lot or a building that houses a principal use.

(9) *Certify.* Whenever this chapter requires that some agency certify the existence of some fact or circumstance to the city, the city may require that such certification be made in any manner that provides reasonable assurance of the accuracy of the certification. By way of illustration, and without limiting the foregoing, the city may accept certification by telephone from some agency when the circumstances warrant it, or the city may require that the certification be in the form of a letter or other document.

(10) *Child Care Home.* A home for not more than nine orphaned, abandoned, dependent, abused, or neglected children, together with not more than two adults who supervise such children, all of whom live together as a single housekeeping unit.

(11) *Child Care Institution.* An institutional facility housing more than nine orphaned, abandoned, dependent, abused, or neglected children.

(12) *Circulation Area.* That portion of the vehicle accommodation area used for access to parking or loading areas or other facilities on the lot. Essentially, driveways and other maneuvering areas (other than parking aisles) comprise the circulation area.

(13) *City.* The City of _____.

(14) *Combination Use.* A use consisting of a combination on one lot of two or more principal uses separately listed in the Table of Permissible Uses, Section 146. (Under some circumstances, a second principal use may be regarded as accessory to the first, and thus a combination use is not established. See Section 150. In addition, when two or more separately owned or separately operated enterprises occupy the same lot, and all such enterprises fall within the same principal use classification, this shall *not* constitute a combination use.)

(15) *Conditional-Use Permit.* A permit issued by the city council that authorizes the recipient to make use of property in accordance with the requirements of this chapter as well as any additional requirements imposed by the council.

(16) *Convenience Store.* A one-story, retail store containing less than 2,000 square feet of gross floor area that is designed and stocked to sell primarily food, beverages, and other household supplies to customers who purchase only a relatively few items (in contrast to a "supermarket"). It is designed to attract and depends upon a large volume of stop-and-go traffic. Illustrative examples of convenience stores are those operated by the "Fast Fare," "7-11" and "Pantry" chains.

(17) *Council.* The city council of the City of _____.

(18) *Day Care Center.* Any child care arrangement that provides day care on a regular basis for more than four hours per day for more than five children of preschool age.

(19) *Developer.* A person who is responsible for any undertaking that requires a zoning permit, special-use permit, conditional-use permit, or sign permit.

(20) *Development.* That which is to be done pursuant to a zoning permit, special-use permit, conditional-use permit, or sign permit.

(21) *Dimensional Nonconformity.* A nonconforming situation that occurs when the height, size, or minimum floor space of a structure or the relationship between an existing building or buildings and other buildings or lot lines does not conform to the regulations applicable to the district in which the property is located.

(22) *Driveway.* That portion of the vehicle accommodation area that consists of a travel lane bounded on either side by an area that is not part of the vehicle accommodation area.

(23) *Duplex.* See *Residence, Duplex.*

(24) *Dwelling Unit.* An enclosure containing sleeping, kitchen, and bathroom facilities designed for and used or held ready for use as a permanent residence by one family.

(25) *Expenditure.* A sum of money paid out in return for some benefit or to fulfill some obligation. The term also includes

7 Basic Definitions and Interpretations

binding contractual commitments to make future expenditures, as well as any other substantial changes in position.

(26) *Extraterritorial Planning Area.* That portion of the city's planning jurisdiction that lies outside the corporate limits of the city.

(27) *Family.* One or more persons living together as a single housekeeping unit.

Commentary: The definition of this seemingly simple word can be extremely controversial since the definition can determine whether, in areas zoned single-family, residences can be occupied by various types of groups of unrelated individuals. Two sorts of concerns are generally expressed in this regard: the first with the *number* of persons who can occupy a single-family residence, and the second with the *types* of persons who can occupy such residences. Both concerns are addressed from a definitional standpoint by defining a family in terms of a group related by blood or marriage. However, such definitions have been subject to a considerable amount of litigation, particularly to the extent that they exclude group homes for the handicapped from single-family districts. This ordinance attempts to deal with the foregoing concerns, not in the definition of the term family, but by drawing more refined distinctions between various types of uses that can loosely be categorized as group homes (see the Table of Permissible Uses, Classification 1.000) and by requiring larger lots for certain residential uses housing more than seven people (see Section 182).

(28) *Floodplain.* Any land area susceptible to be inundated by water from the base flood. As used in this chapter, the term refers to that area designated as subject to flooding from the base flood (100-year flood) on the "Flood Boundary and Floodway Map" prepared by the U.S. Department of Housing and Urban Development, a copy of which is on file in the planning department.

(29) *Floodway.* The channel of a river or other watercourse and the adjacent land areas that must be reserved in order to discharge the base flood without cumulatively increasing the water surface elevation more than one foot. As used in this chapter, the term refers to that area designated as a floodway on the "Flood Boundary and Floodway Map" prepared by the U.S. Department of Housing and Urban Development, a copy of which is on file in the planning department.

(30) *Gross Floor Area.* The total area of a building measured by taking the outside dimensions of the building at each floor level intended for occupancy or storage.

(31) *Habitable Floor.* Any floor usable for living purposes, which includes working, sleeping, eating, cooking, or recreation, or any combination thereof. A floor used only for storage is not a habitable floor.

(32) *Halfway House.* A home for not more than nine persons who have demonstrated a tendency toward alcoholism, drug abuse, mental illness, or antisocial or criminal conduct, together with

not more than two persons providing supervision and other services to such persons, eleven of whom live together as a single housekeeping unit.

(33) *Handicapped or Infirm Home.* A residence within a single dwelling unit for at least six but not more than nine persons who are physically or mentally handicapped or infirm, together with not more than two persons providing care or assistance to such persons, all living together as a single housekeeping unit. Persons residing in such homes, including the aged and disabled, principally need residential care rather than medical treatment.

(34) *Handicapped or Infirm Institution.* An institutional facility housing and providing care or assistance for more than nine persons who are physically or mentally handicapped or infirm. Persons residing in such homes, including the aged or disabled, principally need residential care rather than medical treatment.

(35) *High-Volume Traffic Generation.* All uses in the 2.000 classification other than low-volume traffic generation uses.

(36) *Home Occupation.* A commercial activity that: (i) is conducted by a person on the same lot (in a residential district) where such person resides, and (ii) is not so insubstantial or incidental or is not so commonly associated with the residential use as to be regarded as an accessory use (see Section 150), but that can be conducted without any significantly adverse impact on the surrounding neighborhood.

Without limiting the generality of the foregoing, a use may not be regarded as having an insignificantly adverse impact on the surrounding neighborhood if: (i) goods, stock in trade, or other commodities are displayed, (ii) any on-premises retail sales occur, (iii) more than one person not a resident on the premises is employed in connection with the purported home occupation, (iv) it creates objectionable noise, fumes, odor, dust or electrical interference, or (v) more than 25 percent of the total gross floor area of residential buildings plus other buildings housing the purported home occupation, or more than 500 square feet of gross floor area (whichever is less), is used for home occupation purposes.

The following is a nonexhaustive list of examples of enterprises that may be home occupations if they meet the foregoing definitional criteria: (i) the office or studio of a physician, dentist, artist, musician, lawyer, architect, engineer, teacher, or similar professional, (ii) workshops, greenhouses, or kilns, (iii) dressmaking or hairdressing studios.

(37) *Intermediate Care Home.* A facility maintained for the purpose of providing accommodations for not more than seven occupants needing medical care and supervision at a lower level than that provided in a nursing care institution but at a

higher level than that provided in institutions for the handicapped or infirm.

(38) *Intermediate Care Institution.* An institutional facility maintained for the purpose of providing accommodations for more than seven persons needing medical care and supervision at a lower level than that provided in a nursing care institution but at a higher level than that provided in institutions for the handicapped or infirm.

(39) *Kennel.* A commercial operation that: (i) provides food and shelter and care of animals for purposes not primarily related to medical care (a kennel may or may not be run by or associated with a veterinarian), or (ii) engages in the breeding of animals for sale.

(40) *Loading and Unloading Area.* That portion of the vehicle accommodation area used to satisfy the requirements of Section 300.

(41) *Lot.* A parcel of land whose boundaries have been established by some legal instrument such as a recorded deed or a recorded map and which is recognized as a separate legal entity for purposes of transfer of title.

If a public body or any authority with the power of eminent domain condemns, purchases, or otherwise obtains fee simple title to or a lesser interest in a strip of land cutting across a parcel of land otherwise characterized as a lot by this definition, or a private road is created across a parcel of land otherwise characterized as a lot by this definition, and the interest thus obtained or the road so created is such as effectively to prevent the use of this parcel as one lot, then the land on either side of this strip shall constitute a separate lot.

Subject to Section 123, the permit-issuing authority and the owner of two or more contiguous lots may agree to regard the lots as one lot if necessary or convenient to comply with any of the requirements of this ordinance.

(42) *Lot Area.* The total area circumscribed by the boundaries of a lot, except that: (i) when the legal instrument creating a lot shows the boundary of the lot extending into a public street right-of-way, then the lot boundary for purposes of computing the lot area shall be the street right-of-way line, or if the right-of-way line cannot be determined, a line running parallel to and 30 feet from the center of the traveled portion of the street, and (ii) in a residential district, when a private road that serves more than three dwelling units is located along any lot boundary, then the lot boundary for purposes of computing the lot area shall be the inside boundary of the traveled portion of that road.

(43) *Low-Volume Traffic Generation.* Uses such as furniture stores, carpet stores, major appliance stores, etc. that sell items that are large and bulky, that need a relatively large amount of

storage or display area for each unit offered for sale, and that therefore generate less customer traffic per square foot of floor space than stores selling smaller items.

(44) *Mobile Home.* A dwelling unit that: (i) is not constructed in accordance with the standards set forth in the [state or local building code applicable to site-built homes], and (ii) is composed of one or more components, each of which was substantially assembled in a manufacturing plant and designed to be transported to the home site on its own chassis, and (iii) exceeds 40 feet in length and eight feet in width.

Commentary:

The dwelling unit criterion, together with the length and width minimums, distinguish the mobile home from the travel trailer. Note also that the definition of a dwelling unit includes a requirement that the structure be used or held ready for use as a residence. Thus, a structure originally intended as a mobile *home* but used as a business office in a commercial district would not be a mobile home. If this result is not desired, the ordinance should contain a provision similar to the following: "Notwithstanding any other provisions of this ordinance, no building that (i) is composed of one or more components, each of which was substantially assembled in a manufacturing plant and designed to be transported on its own chassis, and (ii) is not constructed in accordance with the standards set forth in the [state or local building code applicable to site-built construction] may be located in the following zoning districts: _____."

(45) *Mobile Home, Class A.* A mobile home constructed after July 1, 1976, that meets or exceeds the construction standards promulgated by the U.S. Department of Housing and Urban Development that were in effect at the time of construction and that satisfies each of the following additional criteria:

(a) The home has a length not exceeding four times its width;

(b) The pitch of the home's roof has a minimum vertical rise of one foot for each five feet of horizontal run, and the roof is finished with a type of shingle that is commonly used in standard residential construction;

(c) The exterior siding consists of wood, hardboard, or aluminum (vinyl covered or painted, but in no case exceeding the reflectivity of gloss white paint) comparable in composition, appearance, and durability to the exterior siding commonly used in standard residential construction;

(d) A continuous, permanent masonry foundation, unpierced except for required ventilation and access, is installed under the home; and

(e) The tongue, axles, transporting lights, and removable towing apparatus are removed after placement on the lot and before occupancy.

(46) *Mobile Home, Class B.* A mobile home constructed after July 1, 1976, that meets or exceeds the construction standards

promulgated by the U.S. Department of Housing and Urban Development that were in effect at the time of construction but that does not satisfy the criteria necessary to qualify the house as a Class A mobile home.

(47) *Mobile Home, Class C.* Any mobile home that does not meet the definitional criteria of a Class A or Class B mobile home.

(48) *Mobile Home Park.* A residential use in which more than one mobile home is located on a single lot.

(49) *Modular Home.* A dwelling unit constructed in accordance with the standards set forth in the [state or local building code applicable to site-built homes] and composed of components substantially assembled in a manufacturing plant and transported to the building site for final assembly on a permanent foundation. Among other possibilities, a modular home may consist of two sections transported to the site in a manner similar to a mobile home (except that the modular home meets the [state or local building code applicable to site-built homes]), or a series of panels or room sections transported on a truck and erected or joined together on the site.

(50) *Nonconforming Lot.* A lot existing at the effective date of this chapter (and not created for the purposes of evading the restrictions of this chapter) that does not meet the minimum area requirement of the district in which the lot is located.

(51) *Nonconforming Project.* Any structure, development, or undertaking that is incomplete at the effective date of this chapter and would be inconsistent with any regulation applicable to the district in which it is located if completed as proposed or planned.

(52) *Nonconforming Situation.* A situation that occurs when, on the effective date of this chapter, any existing lot or structure or use of an existing lot or structure does not conform to one or more of the regulations applicable to the district in which the lot or structure is located. Among other possibilities, a non-conforming situation may arise because a lot does not meet minimum acreage requirements, because structures exceed maximum height limitations, because the relationship between existing buildings and the land (in such matters as density and setback requirements) is not in conformity with this chapter, or because land or buildings are used for purposes made unlawful by this chapter. Nonconforming signs shall not be regarded as nonconforming situations for purposes of Article VIII but shall be governed by the provisions of Sections 285 and 286.

(53) *Nonconforming Use.* A nonconforming situation that occurs when property is used for a purpose or in a manner made unlawful by the use regulations applicable to the district in which the property is located. (For example, a commercial office building in a residential district may be a nonconforming use.) The term also refers to the activity that constitutes the use made of the property. (For example, all the activity associated

with operating a retail clothing store in a residentially zoned area constitutes a nonconforming use.)

(54) *Nursing Care Home.* A facility maintained for the purpose of providing skilled nursing care and medical supervision at a lower level than that available in a hospital to not more than nine persons.

(55) *Nursing Care Institution.* An institutional facility maintained for the purpose of providing skilled nursing care and medical supervision at a lower level than that available in a hospital to more than nine persons.

(56) *Parking Area Aisles.* A portion of the vehicle accommodation area consisting of lanes providing access to parking spaces.

(57) *Parking Space.* A portion of the vehicle accommodation area set aside for the parking of one vehicle.

(58) *Person.* An individual, trustee, executor, other fiduciary, corporation, firm, partnership, association, organization, or other entity acting as a unit.

(59) *Planned Residential Development.* A development constructed on a tract of at least five acres under single ownership, planned and developed as an integral unit, and consisting of single-family detached residences combined with either two-family residences or multi-family residences, or both, all developed in accordance with Section 173.

(60) *Planned Unit Development (PUD).* A development constructed on a tract of at least 25 acres under single ownership, planned and developed as an integral unit, and consisting of a combination of residential and nonresidential uses on land within a PUD district (see Section 138) in accordance with Section 174.

(61) *Planning Jurisdiction.* The area within the city limits as well as the area beyond the city limits within which the city is authorized to plan for and regulate development, as set forth in Section 3.

(62) *Public Water Supply System.* Any water supply system furnishing potable water to 10 or more dwelling units or businesses or any combination thereof.

Commentary: This definition is taken from the North Carolina General Statutes. The distinction between a private or public water system becomes important in Article XV of this ordinance because, under the statutory scheme in North Carolina, different agencies have to approve different types of water supply systems.

(63) *Receive-Only Earth Station.* An antenna and attendant processing equipment for reception of electronic signals from satellites.

(64) *Residence, Duplex.* A two-family residential use in which the dwelling units share a common wall (including without

limitation the wall of an attached garage or porch) and in which each dwelling unit has living space on the ground floor and a separate, ground floor entrance.

(65) *Residence, Multi-Family.* A residential use consisting of a building containing three or more dwelling units. For purposes of this definition, a building includes all dwelling units that are enclosed within that building or attached to it by a common floor or wall (even the wall of an attached garage or porch).

(66) *Residence, Multi-Family Apartments.* A multi-family residential use other than a multi-family conversion or multi-family townhouse.

(67) *Residence, Multi-Family Conversion.* A multi-family residence containing not more than four dwelling units and results from the conversion of a single building containing at least 2,000 square feet of gross floor area that was in existence on the effective date of this provision and that was originally designed, constructed and occupied as a single-family residence.

(68) *Residence, Multi-Family Townhouses.* A multi-family resident use in which each dwelling unit shares a common wall (including without limitation the wall of an attached garage or porch) with at least one other dwelling unit and in which each dwelling unit has living space on the ground floor and a separate, ground floor entrance.

(69) *Residence, Primary with Accessory Apartment.* A residential use having the external appearance of a single-family residence but in which there is located a second dwelling unit that comprises not more than 25 percent of the gross floor area of the building nor more than a total of 750 square feet.

(70) *Residence, Single-Family Detached, More Than One Dwelling Per Lot.* A residential use consisting of two or more single-family detached dwelling units on a single lot.

(71) *Residence, Single-Family Detached, One Dwelling Unit Per Lot.* A residential use consisting of a single detached building containing one dwelling unit and located on a lot containing no other dwelling units.

(72) *Residence, Two-Family.* A residential use consisting of a building containing two dwelling units. If two dwelling units share a common wall, even the wall of an attached garage or porch, the dwelling units shall be considered to be located in one building.

(73) *Residence, Two-Family Apartment.* A two-family residential use other than a duplex, two-family conversion, or primary residence with accessory apartment.

(74) *Residence, Two-Family Conversion.* A two-family residence resulting from the conversion of a single building containing at least 2,000 square feet of gross floor area that was in existence on the effective date of this provision and that was originally

designed, constructed and occupied as a single-family residence.

(75) *Road.* All private ways used to provide motor vehicle access to (i) two or more lots or (ii) two or more distinct areas or buildings in unsubdivided developments.

(76) *Rooming House.* (See *Boarding House.*)

(77) *Sign.* Any device that (i) is sufficiently visible to persons not located on the lot where such device is located to accomplish either of the objectives set forth in subdivision (ii) of this definition; and (ii) is designed to attract the attention of such persons or to communicate information to them.

(78) *Sign, Freestanding.* A sign that is attached to, erected on, or supported by some structure (such as a pole, mast, frame, or other structure) that is not itself an integral part of or attached to a building or other structure having a principal function other than the support of a sign. A sign that stands without supporting elements, such as a "sandwich sign," is also a freestanding sign.

(79) *Sign, Nonconforming.* A sign that, on the effective date of this chapter, does not conform to one or more of the regulations set forth in this chapter, particularly Article XVII, Signs.

(80) *Sign, Off-Premises.* A sign that draws attention to or communicates information about a business, service, commodity, accommodation, attraction, or other activity that is conducted, sold, or offered at a location other than the premises on which the sign is located.

(81) *Sign Permit.* A permit issued by the land-use administrator that authorizes the recipient to erect, move, enlarge, or substantially alter a sign.

(82) *Sign, Temporary.* A sign that (i) is used in connection with a circumstance, situation, or event that is designed, intended or expected to take place or to be completed within a reasonably short or definite period after the erection of such sign, or (ii) is intended to remain on the location where it is erected or placed for a period of not more than 15 days. If a sign display area is permanent but the message displayed is subject to periodic changes, that sign shall not be regarded as temporary.

(83) *Special Events.* Circuses, fairs, carnivals, festivals, or other types of special events that (i) run for longer than one day but not longer than two weeks, (ii) are intended to or likely to attract substantial crowds, and (iii) are unlike the customary or usual activities generally associated with the property where the special event is to be located.

(84) *Special-Use Permit.* A permit issued by the board of adjustment that authorizes the recipient to make use of property in accordance with the requirements of this chapter as well as any additional requirements imposed by the board of adjustment.

(85) *Street*. A public street or a street with respect to which an offer of dedication has been made.

(86) *Street, Arterial*. A major street in the city's street system that serves as an avenue for the circulation of traffic onto, out, or around the city and carries high volumes of traffic.

(87) *Street, Collector*. A street whose principal function is to carry traffic between minor, local, and subcollector streets and arterial streets but that may also provide direct access to abutting properties. It serves or is designed to serve, directly or indirectly, more than 100 dwelling units and is designed to be used or is used to carry more than 800 trips per day.

(88) *Street, Cul-de-sac*. A street that terminates in a vehicular turnaround.

(89) *Street, Local*. A street whose sole function is to provide access to abutting properties. It serves or is designed to serve at least 10 but not more than 25 dwelling units and is expected to or does handle between 75 and 200 trips per day.

(90) *Street, Marginal Access*. A street that is parallel to and adjacent to an arterial street and that is designed to provide access to abutting properties so that these properties are somewhat sheltered from the effects of the through traffic on the arterial street and so that the flow of traffic on the arterial street is not impeded by direct driveway access from a large number of abutting properties.

(91) *Street, Minor*. A street whose sole function is to provide access to abutting properties. It serves or is designed to serve not more than nine dwelling units and is expected to or does handle up to 75 trips per day.

(92) *Street, Subcollector*. A street whose principal function is to provide access to abutting properties but is also designed to be used or is used to connect minor and local streets with collector or arterial streets. Including residences indirectly served through connecting streets, it serves or is designed to serve at least 26 but not more than 100 dwelling units and is expected to or does handle between 200 and 800 trips per day.

(93) *Structure*. Anything constructed or erected.

(94) *Subdivision*. The division of a tract of land into two or more lots, building sites, or other divisions for the purpose of sale or building development (whether immediate or future) and including all divisions of land involving the dedication of a new street or a change in existing streets; but the following shall not be included within this definition nor be subject to the regulations of this chapter applicable strictly to subdivisions: (i) the combination or recombination of portions of previously platted lots where the total number of lots is not increased and the resultant lots are equal to or exceed the minimum standards set forth in this chapter, (ii) the division of land into parcels

greater than 10 acres where no street right-of-way dedication is involved, or (iii) the public acquisition by purchase of strips of land for widening or opening streets, or (iv) the division of a tract in single ownership whose entire area is no greater than two acres into not more than three lots, where no street right-of-way dedication is involved and where the resultant lots are equal to or exceed the minimum standards set forth in this chapter.

Commentary: The foregoing definition is taken directly from the North Carolina General Statutes. Of course, the draftsman should consult the statutes of his own state for definitions that may be found in enabling legislation from that jurisdiction. If such enabling legislation leaves any discretion to the local government, then the principal issue to be considered is what exceptions to make to the basic definition set forth above in the language before the first semicolon. In the author's judgment, exceptions (i), (ii), and (iv) are ill advised; all three situations should at least be handled through the minor subdivision procedures (see Section 78). Note also that exception (ii) is too broad since it exempts from the review process the creation of 10-acre building sites served by private roads (dedication being a term of art referring to streets offered to and accepted by a government entity). Finally, the definition should make clear that even the division of property for purposes of financing (by the recording of a deed of trust) constitutes a subdivision.

(95) *Subdivision, Architecturally Integrated.* A subdivision in which approval is obtained not only for the division of land into lots but also for a configuration of principal buildings to be located on such lots. The plans for an architecturally integrated subdivision shall show the dimensions, height, and location of all such buildings to the extent necessary to comply with the purpose and intent of architecturally integrated subdivisions as set forth in Section 187.

(96) *Subdivision, Major.* Any subdivision other than a minor subdivision.

(97) *Subdivision, Minor.* A subdivision that does not involve any of the following: (i) the creation of more than a total of three lots; (ii) the creation of any new public streets, (iii) the extension of a public water or sewer system, or (iv) the installation of drainage improvements through one or more lots to serve one or more other lots.

(98) *Temporary Emergency, Construction, or Repair Residence.* A residence (which may be a mobile home) that is: (i) located on the same lot as a residence made uninhabitable by fire, flood, or other natural disaster and occupied by the persons displaced by such disaster, or (ii) located on the same lot as a residence that is under construction or undergoing substantial repairs or reconstruction and occupied by the persons intending to live in such permanent residence when the work is completed, or (iii) located on a nonresidential construction site and occupied by persons having construction or security responsibilities over such construction site.

(99) *Tower.* Any structure whose principal function is to support an antenna.

(100) *Tract.* A lot (see definition (41)). The term tract is used interchangeably with the term lot, particularly in the context of subdivisions, where one "tract" is subdivided into several "lots."

(101) *Travel Trailer.* A structure that (i) is intended to be transported over the streets and highways (either as a motor vehicle or attached to or hauled by a motor vehicle) and (ii) is designed for temporary use as sleeping quarters but that does not satisfy one or more of the definitional criteria of a mobile home.

(102) *Use.* The activity or function that actually takes place or is intended to take place on a lot.

(103) *Use, Principal.* A use listed in the Table of Permissible Uses.

(104) *Utility Facilities.* Any above-ground structures or facilities (other than buildings, unless such buildings are used as storage incidental to the operation of such structures or facilities) owned by a governmental entity, a nonprofit organization, a corporation, or any entity defined as a public utility for any purpose by [the appropriate provision of state law] and used in connection with the production, generation, transmission, delivery, collection, or storage of water, sewage, electricity, gas, oil, or electronic signals. Excepted from this definition are utility lines and supporting structures listed in Subsection 151(2).

(105) *Utility Facilities, Community or Regional.* All utility facilities other than neighborhood facilities.

(106) *Utility Facilities, Neighborhood.* Utility facilities that are designed to serve the immediately surrounding neighborhood and that must, for reasons associated with the purpose of the utility in question, be located in or near the neighborhood where such facilities are proposed to be located.

(107) *Variance.* A grant of permission by the board of adjustment that authorizes the recipient to do that which, according to the strict letter of this chapter, he could not otherwise legally do.

(108) *Vehicle Accommodation Area.* That portion of a lot that is used by vehicles for access, circulation, parking, and loading and unloading. It comprises the total of circulation areas, loading and unloading areas, and parking areas.

(109) *Wholesale Sales.* On-premises sales of goods primarily to customers engaged in the business of reselling the goods.

(110) *Wooded Area.* An area of contiguous wooded vegetation where trees are at a density of at least one six-inch or greater caliper tree per 325 square feet of land and where the branches and leaves form a contiguous canopy.

(111) *Zoning Permit.* A permit issued by the land-use administrator that authorizes the recipient to make use of property in accordance with the requirements of this chapter.

Section 16:
Lots Divided by District Lines

(a) Whenever a single lot two acres or less in size is located within two or more different zoning districts, the district regulations applicable to the district within which the larger portion of the lot lies shall apply to the entire lot.

(b) Whenever a single lot greater than two acres in size is located within two or more different zoning districts, each portion of that lot shall be subject to all the regulations applicable to the district in which it is located.

Sections 17 through 20:
Reserved

Article III Administrative Mechanisms

Commentary:

The provisions of this article illustrate clearly why it is impossible to draft a useful "model" land-use ordinance. However, every such ordinance should establish and prescribe the basic duties and operating procedures of the administrative entities responsible for administering and enforcing the ordinance. How extensive this article should be depends on where one draws the line between those matters that should be covered in the ordinance itself and those that should be covered in the bylaws of an administrative body. For example, the ordinance might establish the method for choosing the chairman of the planning board, or it might let the planning board decide this when it establishes its bylaws. The provisions that follow illustrate a middle-of-the-road course, establishing the administrative mechanisms and prescribing certain basic operating procedures but leaving many details to be filled in through bylaws.

Part I. Planning Board

**Section 21:
Appointment and Terms
of Planning Board Members**

(a) There shall be a planning board consisting of 10 members. Eight members, appointed by the city council, shall reside within the city. Two members, appointed by the county board of commissioners, shall reside within the city's extraterritorial planning area. If, despite good faith efforts, enough residents of the extraterritorial planning area cannot be found to fill the seats reserved for residents of such area, then the county board of commissioners may appoint other residents of the county (including residents of the city) to fill these seats. If the county board fails to make these appointments within 90 days after receiving a resolution from the city council requesting that they be made, the council may make them.

Commentary:

Assuming that the city has the authority to enforce the land-use ordinance within some prescribed area beyond its corporate boundaries, some mechanism should be found to allow people who reside within the "extraterritorial area" to have input into the decision-making process. The text illustrates the method that is probably most satisfactory—membership on the planning board. Extraterritorial membership is also provided for on the board of adjustment. See Section 29.

(b) Planning board members shall be appointed for three-year staggered terms, but members may continue to serve until their successors have been appointed. Initially, two in-town members and one extraterritorial area resident shall be appointed for three-year terms, three in-town members shall be appointed for two-year terms, and three in-town members and one extraterritorial area resident shall be appointed for one-year terms. Vacancies may be filled for the unexpired terms only.

Commentary: Staggered terms ensure a certain continuity and level of expertise on the board.

(c) Members may be appointed to successive terms without limitation.

(d) Planning board members may be removed by the council at any time for failure to attend three consecutive meetings or for failure to attend 30 percent or more of the meetings within any 12-month period or for any other good cause related to performance of duties. Upon request of the member proposed for removal the council shall hold a hearing on the removal before it becomes effective.

Commentary: Citizen boards frequently have difficulty obtaining a quorum. A requirement such as that set forth in this subsection helps ensure that only people willing to attend meetings can retain their membership on the board. The provision can be made stronger by providing for automatic termination of membership under specified circumstances, but in this event care must be taken that people whose memberships have expired are not inadvertently allowed to participate in decisions.

(e) If an in-town member moves outside the city or if an extraterritorial area member moves outside the planning jurisdiction, that shall constitute a resignation from the planning board, effective upon the date a replacement is appointed by the council.

Section 22: Meetings of the Planning Board

(a) The planning board shall establish a regular meeting schedule and shall meet frequently enough so that it can take action in conformity with Section 66 (Applications to be Processed Expeditiously).

(b) Since the board has only advisory authority, it need not conduct its meetings strictly in accordance with the quasi-judicial procedures set forth in Articles IV, V, and VI. However, it shall conduct its meetings so as to obtain necessary information and to promote the full and free exchange of ideas.

Commentary: Generally, planning boards act only in an advisory capacity, and thus there is less need for concern about the formalities of their meetings. However, if the planning board actually is the decision-making authority with respect to a permit application—e.g., a subdivision—then the ordinance should require the board to observe procedures similar to those followed by the board of adjustment as described in Articles IV, V, and VI.

(c) Minutes shall be kept of all board proceedings.

(d) All board meetings shall be open to the public, and whenever feasible the agenda for each board meeting shall be made available in advance of the meeting.

(e) Whenever the board is called upon to make recommendations concerning a conditional-use permit request, special-use permit request, or a minor zoning amendment proposal, the planning staff shall post on or near the subject property one or more notices that are sufficiently conspicuous in terms of size, location, and content to provide reasonably adequate notice to potentially interested persons of the matter that will appear on the board's agenda at a specified date and time. Such notice(s) shall be posted at least seven days prior to the meeting at which the matter is to be considered. The planning staff shall also send written notice to adjoining property owners if and to the extent required by any regulation or requirement of the planning board adopted under Subsection 25(b).

Commentary: When the planning board is asked to make recommendations concerning permit requests or minor zoning amendment applications, the type and extent of notice the ordinance requires to be provided to affected property owners depends upon what role the planning board is expected to play in the process. If one regards the planning board as a body that should base its recommendations strictly on "pure" planning concerns (whether a proposed project complies with the ordinance or a proposed amendment is in conformity with the comprehensive plan), then there is little need to notify affected property owners. However, if planning board consideration is also designed to bring to light the nature and extent of local opposition to a proposed permit or amendment before the final public hearing, then the type of notice indicated in this subsection is necessary.

**Section 23:
Quorum and Voting**

(a) A quorum for the planning board shall consist of a majority of the board membership (excluding vacant seats). A quorum is necessary for the board to take official action.

(b) All actions of the planning board shall be taken by majority vote, a quorum being present.

(c) A roll call vote shall be taken upon the request of any member.

(d) Extraterritorial planning area members may vote on all matters considered by the board, regardless of whether the property affected lies within or without the city.

Commentary: Some cities limit the participation of extraterritorial representatives to matters affecting only property outside the city. Apart from the ambiguities inherent in drawing such a distinction, it seems unrealistic to expect extraterritorial representatives to attend meetings faithfully if they can participate in only a portion of the board's deliberations.

**Section 24:
Planning Board Officers**

(a) At its first meeting in _____ of each year, the planning board shall, by majority vote of its membership (excluding vacant seats) elect one of its members to serve as chairman and preside over the board's meetings and one member to serve as vice-chairman. The people so designated shall serve in these capacities for terms of one year. Vacancies in these offices may be filled for the unexpired terms only by majority vote of the board membership (excluding vacant seats).

(b) The chairman and vice-chairman may take part in all deliberations and vote on all issues.

**Section 25:
Powers and Duties
of Planning Board**

(a) The planning board may:

(1) Make studies and recommend to the council plans, goals, and objectives relating to the growth, development, and redevelopment of the city and the surrounding extraterritorial planning area.

(2) Develop and recommend to the council policies, ordinances, administrative procedures, and other means for carrying out plans in a coordinated and efficient manner.

(3) Make recommendations to the council concerning proposed conditional-use permits and proposed zoning map changes, as provided by Sections 57 and 322.

(4) Perform any other duties assigned by the council.

Commentary:

Many planning boards spend so much of their time reviewing development proposals that they never get around to planning—especially long-range planning. One way to avoid this is to bypass the planning board completely in the development review and rezoning processes, or at least limit the planning board's review to the types of developments having the greatest impact on the community. Another technique is to have a "development review subcommittee" of the planning board. The important thing is to provide a mechanism whereby some citizen advisory group has an opportunity to focus on longer range planning concerns, free from political heat generated by particular development proposals.

(b) The planning board may adopt rules and regulations governing its procedures and operations not inconsistent with the provisions of the chapter.

Section 26:
Advisory Committees

(a) From time to time, the council may appoint one or more individuals to help the planning board carry out its planning responsibilities with respect to a particular subject area. By way of illustration, without limitation, the council may appoint advisory committees to consider the thoroughfare plan, bikeway plans, housing plans, economic development plans, etc.

(b) Members of such advisory committees shall sit as nonvoting members of the planning board when such issues are being considered and lend their talents, energies, and expertise to the planning board. However, all formal recommendations to the council shall be made by the planning board.

(c) Nothing in this section shall prevent the council from establishing independent advisory groups, committees, or commissions to make recommendations on any issue directly to the council.

Sections 27 through 28:
Reserved

Part II. Board of Adjustment

Section 29:
Appointment and Terms of Board of Adjustment

(a) There shall be a board of adjustment consisting of five regular members and two alternates. Four regular members and one alternate, appointed by the council, shall reside within the city. One regular member and one alternate, appointed by the county board of commissioners, shall reside within the city's extraterritorial planning area. If, despite good faith efforts, enough residents of the extraterritorial planning area cannot be found to fill the seats reserved for residents of such area, then the county board of commissioners may appoint other residents of the county (including residents of the city) to fill these seats. If the county board of commissioners fails to make these appointments within 90 days after receiving a resolution from the council requesting that they be made, the council may make them.

(b) Board of adjustment regular members and alternates shall be appointed for three-year staggered terms, but both regular members and alternates may continue to serve until their successors have been appointed. Initially, two regular in-town members and the extraterritorial area alternate member shall be appointed for three-year terms, one regular in-town member and the regular extraterritorial area member shall be appointed for two-year terms, and one regular in-town member and the in-town alternate shall be appointed for one-year terms. Vacancies may be filled for the unexpired terms only.

(c) Members may be reappointed to successive terms without limitation.

(d) Regular board of adjustment members may be removed by the council at any time for failure to attend three consecutive meetings or for failure to attend 30 percent or more of the meetings within any 12-month period or for any other good cause related to performance of duties. Alternate members may be removed for repeated failure to attend or participate in meetings when requested to do so in accordance with regularly established procedures. Upon request of the member proposed for removal, the council shall hold a hearing on the removal before it becomes effective.

(e) If a regular or alternate in-town member moves outside the city, or if an extraterritorial area regular or alternate member moves outside the planning jurisdiction, that shall constitute a resignation from the board, effective upon the date a replacement is appointed.

(f) Extraterritorial planning area members may vote on all matters coming before the board.

(g) The in-town alternate may sit only in lieu of a regular in-town member and the extraterritorial area alternate may sit only in lieu of the regular extraterritorial area member. When so seated, alternates shall have the same powers and duties as the regular member they replace.

Commentary:

The foregoing section describes the composition of a fairly typical board of adjustment. Alternate members are needed because of the four-fifths vote requirement described in Section 32. Much of the commentary under Section 21, dealing with the appointment and terms of the planning board, is also applicable to this section.

**Section 30:
Meetings of the Board of Adjustment**

(a) The board of adjustment shall establish a regular meeting schedule and shall meet frequently enough so that it can take action in conformity with Section 68 (Applications to be Processed Expeditiously).

(b) The board shall conduct its meetings in accordance with the quasi-judicial procedures set forth in Articles IV, V, and VI.

Commentary:

The reasons for these procedures are discussed in the commentary under the referenced articles.

(c) All meetings of the board shall be open to the public, and whenever feasible the agenda for each board meeting shall be made available in advance of the meeting.

Commentary:

Under the North Carolina open meetings law, all hearings and deliberations of the board of adjustment must be conducted in an open session. Before enactment of this statute, many boards went into executive session to conduct their deliberations on the issues before them, on the apparent theory that, being a "quasi-judicial body," they should, like a jury, decide cases free from public scrutiny. This analogy may have some merit in cases where the board is called upon to weigh the credibility of witnesses when there is conflicting testimony concerning material facts. However, in the experience of the author, this is seldom the case. Far more often the board is called upon to weigh the significance of facts that are undisputed, to make what are in effect legal or policy judgments. These are the very type of deliberations and judgments that should be made by a public body in full view of the concerned public. This increases public confidence in those decisions and helps reduce the possibility that they will be made arbitrarily.

There is another practical reason why it is inadvisable for boards of adjustment to close the deliberative portions of their meetings. Very often, in the course of those deliberations, it becomes apparent that additional input is needed from the applicant or others. For example, in considering the issuance of a special-use permit, the board may want to obtain the applicant's reaction before imposing certain conditions. This opportunity may be lost if the board has retired into executive session.

Section 31: Quorum

(a) A quorum for the board of adjustment shall consist of the number of members equal to four-fifths of the regular board membership (excluding vacant seats). A quorum is necessary for the board to take official action.

(b) A member who has withdrawn from the meeting without being excused as provided in Section 32 shall be counted as present for purposes of determining whether a quorum is present.

Section 32: Voting

(a) The concurring vote of four-fifths of the regular board membership (excluding vacant seats) shall be necessary to reverse any order, requirement, decision, or determination of the administrator or to decide in favor of the applicant any matter upon which it is required to pass under any ordinance (including the issuance of a special-use permit) or to grant any variance. All other actions of the board shall be taken by majority vote, a quorum being present.

Commentary:

The four-fifths vote is required by most zoning enabling legislation since such statutes generally follow the pattern established by the Standard State Zoning Enabling Act promulgated by the U.S. Department of Commerce in 1926. This extraordinary majority may be justifiable in the case of appeals, where a decision has already been made by the enforcement officer (although cases heard by appellate courts are decided by majority vote), or for variances, which by definition constitute an extraordinary form of relief. But in connection with the issuance of special-use permits, the four-fifths vote makes no sense at all, particularly if similar permits for many types of projects (called conditional-use permits in this ordinance) are issued by the governing body upon a simple majority vote. The requirement creates procedural problems (see Section

59) and seems generally unfair to the applicant. If legally possible, the four-fifths requirement should be avoided, at least in the case of special-use permits, and preferably in all cases.

(b) Once a member is physically present at a board meeting, any subsequent failure to vote shall be recorded as an affirmative vote unless the member has been excused in accordance with Subsection (c) or has been allowed to withdraw from the meeting in accordance with Subsection (d).

Commentary:

> This requirement is imposed in recognition of the natural tendency of board members to avoid deciding controversial cases by abstaining or simply leaving the meeting. Either of these courses of action severely prejudices an applicant because, under the four-fifths vote rule, the loss of one vote makes unanimity of the remaining members necessary to decide an issue in his favor, and the loss of two votes makes such a decision impossible.

(c) A member may be excused from voting on a particular issue by majority vote of the remaining members present under the following circumstances:

(1) If the member has a direct financial interest in the outcome of the matter at issue, or

(2) If the matter at issue involves the member's own official conduct, or

(3) If participation in the matter might violate the letter or spirit of a member's code of professional responsibility, or

(4) If a member has such close personal ties to the applicant that the member cannot reasonably be expected to exercise sound judgment in the public interest.

(d) A member may be allowed to withdraw from the entire remainder of a meeting by majority vote of the remaining members present for any good and sufficient reason other than the member's desire to avoid voting on matters to be considered at that meeting.

(e) A motion to allow a member to be excused from voting or excused from the remainder of the meeting is in order only if made by or at the initiative of the member directly affected.

(f) A roll call vote shall be taken upon the request of any member.

Section 33:
Board of Adjustment Officers

(a) At its first regular meeting in _____, the board of adjustment shall, by majority vote of its membership (excluding vacant seats) elect one of its members to serve as chairman and preside over the board's meetings and one member to serve as vice-chairman. The persons so designated shall serve in these capacities for terms of one year. Vacancies may be filled for the unexpired terms only by majority vote of the board membership (excluding vacant seats).

(b) The chairman or any member temporarily acting as chairman may administer oaths to witnesses coming before the board.

(c) The chairman and vice-chairman may take part in all deliberations and vote on all issues.

Section 34:
Powers and Duties of Board of Adjustment

(a) The board of adjustment shall hear and decide:

(1) Appeals from any order, decision, requirement, or interpretation made by the administrator, as provided in Section 91.

(2) Applications for special-use permits, as provided in Subsection 46(a).

(3) Applications for variances, as provided in Section 92.

(4) Questions involving interpretations of the zoning map, including disputed district boundary lines and lot lines, as provided in Section 93.

(5) Any other matter the board is required to act upon by any other city ordinance.

(b) The board may adopt rules and regulations governing its procedures and operations not inconsistent with the provisions of this chapter.

Sections 35 and 36:
Reserved

Part III. Land-Use Administrator and Planning Director

Section 37:
Land-Use Administrator

Except as otherwise specifically provided, primary responsibility for administering and enforcing this chapter may be assigned by the city manager to one or more individuals. The person or persons to whom these functions are assigned shall be referred to in this chapter as the "land-use administrator" or "administrator." The term "staff" or "planning staff" is sometimes used interchangeably with the term "administrator."

Commentary:
> For simplicity, this ordinance adheres to the convention of using the masculine pronoun to refer to the administrator, while fully recognizing that the ranks of zoning administrators contain many excellent female professionals.

Section 38:
Planning Director

The planning director is the administrative head of the planning department. As provided in Sections 78 and 79, the planning director is authorized to approve major and minor subdivision final plats.

Section 39:
Reserved

Part IV. City Council

Section 40:
The City Council

(a) The city council, in considering conditional-use permit applications, acts in a quasi-judicial capacity and, accordingly, is required to observe the procedural requirements set forth in Articles IV and VI of this chapter.

(b) In considering proposed changes in the text of this chapter or in the zoning map, the council acts in its legislative capacity and must proceed in accordance with the requirements of Article XX.

(c) Unless otherwise specifically provided in this chapter, in acting upon conditional-use permit requests or in considering amendments to this chapter or the zoning map, the council shall follow the regular, voting, and other requirements as set forth in other provisions of the city code, the city charter, or general law.

Commentary:

As indicated above, the role of the local governing body in this ordinance is twofold: not only does it act as a legislative body in adopting and amending the text of this ordinance and the accompanying map, it also acts in an administrative or quasi-judicial capacity in issuing conditional-use permits (see commentary following Section 46). It is important that the governing body understands the difference between these two roles since different rules of law and different procedures obtain, depending upon the function the council is performing.

In some jurisdictions, although still a minority, minor zoning map amendments are regarded as administrative rather than legislative decisions. In those jurisdictions, this distinction should be noted in this section.

Sections 41 through 45: Reserved

Article IV Permits and Final Plat Approval

Part I. Zoning, Special-Use, and Conditional-Use Permits

Section 46: Permits Required

(a) Subject to Section 271 (Sign Permits), the use made of property may not be substantially changed (see Section 152), substantial clearing, grading, or excavation may not be commenced, and buildings or other substantial structures may not be constructed, erected, moved, or substantially altered except in accordance with and pursuant to one of the following permits:

(1) A zoning permit issued by the administrator.

(2) A special-use permit issued by the board of adjustment.

(3) A conditional-use permit issued by the city council.

Commentary:

A zoning permit is often combined with a building permit (the latter signifying compliance with a state or local building code), but the permit or permits should make clear that two separate sets of regulations are involved and that there must be compliance with each before construction may begin.

The special- and conditional-use permits are similar to the zoning permit in that all three are issued only after a review of the submitted application reveals that the development, if constructed as proposed, will satisfy all the requirements of the ordinance. However, special- and conditional-use permits differ from zoning permits in two ways: (1) the boards that issue special- or conditional-use permits may turn down an application that meets the specific requirements of the ordinance for any of the generally stated reasons set forth in Section 54, and therefore these boards have greater discretion in deciding whether to issue a permit than does the administrator, and (2) in issuing special- or conditional-use permits, the board of adjustment or governing body may make the issue of such permits conditional upon the permit recipient's compliance with certain requirements over and above those stated in the ordinance (see Section 60).

The foregoing differences suggest the reasons why different types of development should be made permissible with a zoning permit as opposed to a special- or conditional-use permit. If the nature of a particular use—e.g., a day care center—is such that it might be appropriate in most areas within a residential zone but inappropriate in certain locations, the special- or conditional-use process provides the necessary flexibility to make a site-by-site determination. Or, if the external impacts of a particular use are sufficiently varied or indeterminable in advance, the special- or conditional-use process affords the community an opportunity to fine tune its requirements (in accordance with Section 60) to minimize or eliminate these externalities.

Apart from the fact that the board of adjustment is generally bound by a four-fifths vote requirement (see Section 32), the special- and conditional-use processes are identical, and different names are assigned to the two permits only to signify that one is issued by the board of adjustment and the other by the governing body. The determination as to which board should approve the particular type of use is usually based upon the extent of the impact the proposed project will have on the community; if the impact is localized, such as a day care center, the board of adjustment reviews the application, while projects such as major subdivisions, apartment complexes, and shopping centers are reviewed by the governing body.

(b) Zoning permits, special-use permits, conditional-use permits and sign permits are issued under this chapter only when a review of the application submitted, including the plans contained therein, indicates that the development will comply with the provisions of this chapter if completed as proposed. Such plans and applications as are finally approved are incorporated into any permit issued, and except as otherwise provided in Section 64, all development shall occur strictly in accordance with such approved plans and applications.

(c) Physical improvements to land to be subdivided may not be commenced except in accordance with a conditional-use permit issued by the council for major subdivisions or after final plat approval by the planning director for minor subdivisions (see Part II of this article).

Commentary:

Most subdivision ordinances establish a three-step approval process: preliminary sketch review, preliminary plat approval, and final plat approval. This ordinance follows this pattern. Preliminary sketch review is required by Section 50, the conditional-use permit process is the functional equivalent of preliminary plat review, and final plat approval is provided for in Part II of this article.

(d) A zoning permit, conditional-use permit, special-use permit, or sign permit shall be issued in the name of the applicant (except that applications submitted by an agent shall be issued in the name of the principal), shall identify the property involved and the proposed use, shall incorporate by reference the plans submitted, and shall contain any special conditions or requirements lawfully imposed by the permit-issuing authority. All such permits issued with respect to tracts of land in excess of one acre (except sign permits and zoning permits for single-family and two-family residential uses) shall be recorded in the _____ County Registry after execution by the record owner as provided in Section 63.

Commentary:

The reason for the recording requirement is stated in the commentary following Section 63.

Section 47:
No Occupancy, Use, or Sale
of Lots Until
Requirements Fulfilled

Issuance of a conditional-use, special-use, or zoning permit authorizes the recipient to commence the activity resulting in a change in use of the land or (subject to obtaining a building permit) to commence work designed to construct, erect, move, or substantially alter buildings or other substantial structures or to make necessary improvements to a subdivision. However, except as provided in Sections 53, 61, and 62, the intended use may not be commenced, no building may be occupied, and in the case of subdivisions, no lots may be sold until all of the requirements of this chapter and all additional requirements imposed pursuant to the issuance of a conditional-use or special-use permit have been complied with.

Commentary:
> The principal tool that the administrator has to ensure compliance with the land-use ordinance is the ability to prevent occupancy of buildings or sale of land until the development is in conformity with these regulations. Experience demonstrates that it is much more difficult to compel compliance once a structure is occupied or a business is in operation. In addition, if the applicable building code provides that a certificate of occupancy may not be given unless all local codes are met, this provides enormous enforcement leverage under circumstances where a development cannot obtain electricity without such a permit.

**Section 48:
Who May Submit
Permit Applications**

(a) Applications for zoning, special-use, conditional-use, or sign permits or minor subdivision plat approval will be accepted only from persons having the legal authority to take action in accordance with the permit or the minor subdivision plat approval. By way of illustration, in general this means that applications should be made by the owners or lessees of property, or their agents, or persons who have contracted to purchase property contingent upon their ability to acquire the necessary permits under this chapter, or the agents of such persons (who may make application in the name of such owners, lessees, or contract vendees).

(b) The administrator may require an applicant to submit evidence of his authority to submit the application in accordance with Subsection (a) whenever there appears to be a reasonable basis for questioning this authority.

Commentary:
> In some jurisdictions, the courts have mandated that a permit applicant have "standing" to apply for the permit. Even in the absence of such case law, the foregoing requirement commends itself as a way to prevent spending time and energy unnecessarily on purely speculative proposals.

**Section 49:
Applications To
Be Complete**

(a) All applications for zoning, special-use, conditional-use, or sign permits must be complete before the permit-issuing authority is required to consider the application.

(b) Subject to Subsection (c), an application is complete when it contains all of the information that is necessary for the permit-issuing authority to decide whether or not the development, if completed as proposed, will comply with all of the requirements of this chapter.

(c) In this chapter, detailed or technical design requirements and construction specifications relating to various types of improvements (streets, sidewalks, etc.) are set forth in one or more of the appendices to this chapter. It is not necessary that the application contain the type of detailed construction drawings that would be necessary to determine compliance with these appendices, so long as the plans provide sufficient information to allow the permit-issuing authority to evaluate the application in the light of the substantive requirements set forth in this text of this chapter.

However, whenever this chapter requires a certain element of a development to be constructed in accordance with the detailed requirements set forth in one or more of these appendices, then no construction work on such element may be commenced until detailed construction drawings have been submitted to and approved by the administrator. Failure to observe this requirement may result in permit revocation, denial of final subdivision plat approval, or other penalty as provided in Article VII.

Commentary:
> Developers, understandably, would prefer to know whether a project will be approved before they spend money on architects and engineers to design the project. Conversely, it would be to the local government's advantage to be able to review detailed plans concerning all aspects of the development before giving its approval. This subsection attempts to strike a happy medium, requiring the developer's permit application to contain plans showing the basic layout of the project, but not requiring detailed construction drawings until after the project is approved.

(d) The presumption established by this chapter is that all of the information set forth in Appendix A is necessary to satisfy the requirements of this section. However, it is recognized that each development is unique, and therefore the permit-issuing authority may allow less information or require more information to be submitted according to the needs of the particular case. For applications submitted to the city council or board of adjustment, the applicant may rely in the first instance on the recommendations of the administrator as to whether more or less information than that set forth in Appendix A should be submitted.

Commentary:
> This provision puts the administrator in the psychologically favorable position of being able, in certain cases, to waive the developer's presumptive obligation to provide specified information, rather than leaving the administrator in the less enviable position of having to impose on a developer the burden of providing necessary information.

(e) The administrator shall make every effort to develop application forms, instructional sheets, checklists, or other techniques or devices to assist applicants in understanding the application requirements and the form and type of information that must be submitted. In classes of cases where a minimal amount of information is necessary to enable the administrator to determine compliance with this chapter, such as applications for zoning permits to construct single-family or two-family houses, or applications for sign permits, the administrator shall develop standard forms that will expedite the submission of the necessary plans and other required information.

**Section 50:
Staff Consultation
Before Formal Application**

(a) To minimize development planning costs, avoid misunderstanding or misinterpretation, and ensure compliance with the requirements of this chapter, preapplication consultation between the developer and the planning staff is encouraged or required as provided in this section.

(b) Before submitting an application for a conditional-use permit authorizing a development that consists of or contains a major subdivision, the developer shall submit to the administrator a sketch plan of such subdivision, drawn approximately to scale (1 inch = 100 feet). The sketch plan shall contain:

(1) The name and address of the developer,

(2) The proposed name and location of the subdivision,

(3) The approximate total acreage of the proposed subdivision,

(4) The tentative street and lot arrangement,

(5) Topographic lines, and

(6) Any other information the developer believes necessary to obtain the informal opinion of the planning staff as to the proposed subdivision's compliance with the requirements of this chapter.

The administrator shall meet with the developer as soon as conveniently possible to review the sketch plan.

(c) Before submitting an application for any other permit, developers are strongly encouraged to consult with the planning staff concerning the application of this chapter to the proposed development.

Section 51: Staff Consultation After Application Submitted

(a) Upon receipt of a formal application for a zoning, special-use, or conditional-use permit, or minor plat approval, the administrator shall review the application and confer with the applicant to ensure that he understands the planning staff's interpretation of the applicable requirements of this chapter, that he has submitted all of the information that he intends to submit, and that the application represents precisely and completely what he proposes to do.

(b) If the application is for a special-use or conditional-use permit, the administrator shall place the application on the agenda of the appropriate board when the applicant indicates that the application is as complete as he intends to make it. However, as provided in Sections 56 and 57, if the administrator believes that the application is incomplete, he shall recommend to the appropriate board that the application be denied on that basis.

Commentary:

Of course, an application must be complete before the local government is compelled to review it, but this begs the question of when is an application complete and the even more important question of who should make that determination. In practice, the issue is never as simple as whether all the blanks on the application form have been filled in, but usually involves questions about whether the developer has provided sufficient information to allow a permit-issuing board to exercise its discretion (e.g., will the entrance to the project be safe, Section 213, or will the development be in harmony with the surrounding area, Section 54). This ordinance takes the position that the permit-issuing body should decide whether the application is complete. Therefore in the case of special- and conditional-use permits, it allows the developer to present his case to the permit-issuing board, even when the staff believes the information to be incomplete.

Section 52: Zoning Permits

(a) A completed application form for a zoning permit shall be submitted to the administrator by filing a copy of the application with the administrator in the planning department.

(b) The administrator shall issue the zoning permit unless he finds, after reviewing the application and consulting with the applicant as provided in Section 50, that:

(1) The requested permit is not within his jurisdiction according to the Table of Permissible Uses, or

(2) The application is incomplete, or

(3) If completed as proposed in the application, the development will not comply with one or more requirements of this chapter (not including those requirements concerning which a variance has been granted or those the applicant is not required to comply with under the circumstances specified in Article VIII, Nonconforming Situations).

(c) If the administrator determines that the development for which a zoning permit is requested will have or may have substantial impact on surrounding properties, he shall, at least 10 days before taking final action on the permit request, send a written notice to those persons who have listed for taxation real property any portion of which is within 150 feet of the lot that is the subject of the application, informing them that:

(1) An application has been filed for a permit authorizing identified property to be used in a specified way,

(2) All persons wishing to comment on the application should contact the administrator by a certain date, and

(3) Persons wishing to be informed of the outcome of the application should send a written request for such notification to the administrator.

Section 53: Authorizing Use or Occupancy Before Completion of Development Under Zoning Permit

In cases when, because of weather conditions or other factors beyond the control of the zoning-permit recipient (exclusive of financial hardship), it would be unreasonable to require the zoning-permit recipient to comply with all of the requirements of this chapter prior to commencing the intended use of the property or occupying any buildings, the administrator may authorize the commencement of the intended use or the occupancy of buildings (insofar as the requirements of this chapter are concerned) if the permit recipient provides a performance bond or other security satisfactory to the administrator to ensure that all of the requirements of this chapter will be fulfilled within a reasonable period (not to exceed 12 months) determined by the administrator.

Commentary:

As indicated, it is much easier to obtain compliance with the land-use ordinance before property is occupied or a business begun. However, in some cases, it would be unreasonable to insist upon total compliance before occupancy. The most obvious examples involve weather—it may be too cold or too wet to pave a parking lot or too hot and dry to plant screening. Under these circumstances, the local government's interests are protected by allowing the developer to post some sort of performance guarantee such as a bond, letter of credit, or cash in an escrow account.

Note that the above section excludes from consideration the circumstance most likely to prompt a request for "temporary" relief from the ordinance's requirements: the cost of complying with the land-use ordinance. This should be regarded as just another cost of doing business. If an enterprise is so marginal that it truly cannot afford to comply initially, the chances are very high that it never will be able to comply, and temporary relief will become permanent noncompliance.

**Section 54:
Special-Use Permits and
Conditional-Use Permits**

(a) An application for a special-use permit shall be submitted to the board of adjustment by filing a copy of the application with the administrator in the planning department.

(b) An application for a conditional-use permit shall be submitted to the council by filing a copy of the application with the administrator in the planning department.

(c) Subject to Subsection (d), the board of adjustment or the council, respectively, shall issue the requested permit unless it concludes, based upon the information submitted at the hearing, that:

(1) The requested permit is not within its jurisdiction according to the Table of Permissible Uses, or

(2) The application is incomplete, or

(3) If completed as proposed in the application, the development will not comply with one or more requirements of this chapter (not including those the applicant is not required to comply with under the circumstances specified in Article VIII, Nonconforming Situations), or

(d) Even if the permit-issuing board finds that the application complies with all other provisions of this chapter, it may still deny the permit if it concludes, based upon the information submitted at the hearing, that if completed as proposed, the development, more probably than not:

(1) Will materially endanger the public health or safety, or

(2) Will substantially injure the value of adjoining or abutting property, or

(3) Will not be in harmony with the area in which it is to be located, or

(4) Will not be in general conformity with the land-use plan, thoroughfare plan, or other plan officially adopted by the council.

Commentary:

As indicated in the commentary to Subsection 46(a), the ability of the permit-issuing authority to turn down a permit application for one of the generally stated reasons set forth above is one of the two principal characteristics that distinguish the special- or conditional-use permit process from the zoning permit process.

Note that the ordinance does not require the board, before issuing a permit, to find that the proposed development will *not* endanger the public health or safety or will *not* injure the value of adjoining property. Stated in the negative, such requirements impose on the applicant the almost impossible burden of imagining and disproving every possible negative impact of the development. In addition, the board is required to state its findings of fact in support of its conclusions; such a negative statement would complicate its job because it is very difficult to state why a development will *not* cause a problem. The way Subsection (d) is written avoids these problems since these general findings come into play only when a permit is rejected. If the development creates a problem, it should be a simple matter for the board to state exactly what the problem is as a finding of fact.

In drafting such general conditions, care must be taken (in those jurisdictions where the doctrine still has validity) to avoid a challenge on the constitutional basis that legislative power has been delegated without sufficient standards to guide the board's discretion. The standards set forth above have been approved several times by the North Carolina appellate courts.

**Section 55:
Burden of Presenting Evidence;
Burden of Persuasion**

(a) The burden of presenting a complete application (as described in Section 49) to the permit-issuing board shall be upon the applicant. However, unless the board informs the applicant at the hearing in what way the application is incomplete and offers the applicant an opportunity to complete the application (either at that meeting or at a continuation hearing), the application shall be presumed to be complete.

(b) Once a completed application has been submitted, the burden of presenting evidence to the permit-issuing board sufficient to lead it to conclude that the application should be denied for any reasons stated in Subdivisions 54(c)(1), 54(c)(3) or 54(d) shall be upon the party or parties urging this position, unless the information presented by the applicant in his application and at the public hearing is sufficient to justify a reasonable conclusion that a reason exists to so deny the application.

(c) The burden of persuasion on the issue of whether the development, if completed as proposed, will comply with the requirements of this chapter remains at all times on the applicant. The burden of persuasion on the issue of whether the application should be turned down for any of the reasons set forth in Subdivision 54(c)(4) rests on the party or parties urging that the requested permit should be denied.

Commentary:

> The foregoing section may appear to be somewhat technical. However, it is important that all parties understand who has the burden of bringing information to the permit-issuing board and who has the burden of persuasion. For example, this section makes clear that, if a development meeting the requirements of this ordinance is proposed and the neighbors object on the basis that the development would overburden an already heavily traveled road, the burden of producing evidence on the traffic impact lies with the neighbors, not the developer.

**Section 56:
Recommendations on
Special-Use Permit
Applications**

(a) When presented to the board of adjustment at the hearing, the application for a special-use permit shall be accompanied by a report setting forth the planning staff's proposed findings concerning the application's compliance with Section 49 (Application To Be Complete) and the other requirements of this chapter, as well as any staff recommendations for additional requirements to be imposed by the board of adjustment.

(b) If the staff proposes a finding or conclusion that the application fails to comply with Section 49 or any other requirement of this chapter, it shall identify the requirement in question and specifically state supporting reasons for the proposed findings or conclusions.

(c) The board of adjustment may, by general rule applicable to all cases or any class of cases, or on a case-by-case basis, refer applications to the planning board to obtain its recommendations.

Commentary:

> This ordinance provides that special-use permits, unlike conditional-use permits, need not be referred to the planning board for a recommendation. The theory behind this distinction is that the governing body has so many other responsibilities that it may not be able to give a

development all the consideration it warrants, and therefore the input of the planning board is of particular help. Presumably, however, the board of adjustment can devote as much attention to an application as the planning board, and therefore there is no need to refer all proposals to the planning board for its recommendation. Subsection (c) provides some flexibility in this regard.

Section 57: Recommendations on Conditional-Use Permit Applications

(a) Before being presented to the council, an application for a conditional-use permit shall be referred to the planning board for action in accordance with this section. The council may not hold a public hearing on a conditional-use permit application until the planning board has had an opportunity to consider the application pursuant to standard agenda procedures. In addition, at the request of the planning board, the council may continue the public hearing to allow the planning board more time to consider or reconsider the application.

Commentary:

> This ordinance anticipates that the planning board recommendations will be available to the governing body at the public hearing so that body can have all the information it needs to act upon the application on that occasion. The principal drawback to this approach is that the planning board does not have the benefit of the information presented at the public hearing when it makes its recommendations. The principal advantage of the approach suggested here is that it works more expeditiously than one in which the governing body holds a hearing, then refers the matter to the planning board, and then waits to receive a recommendation before acting.

(b) When presented to the planning board, the application shall be accompanied by a report setting forth the planning staff's proposed findings concerning the application's compliance with Section 49 and other requirements of this chapter, as well as any staff recommendations for additional requirements to be imposed by the council. If the planning staff report proposes a finding or conclusion that the application fails to comply with Section 49 or any other requirement of this chapter, it shall identify the requirement in question and specifically state supporting reasons for the proposed findings or conclusions.

(c) The planning board shall consider the application and the attached staff report in a timely fashion, and may, in its discretion, hear from the applicant or members of the public. (Notice to the adjoining property owners is provided for in Subsection 22(e).)

(d) After reviewing the application, the planning board shall report to the council whether it concurs in whole or in part with the staff's proposed findings and conditions, and to the extent there are differences the planning board shall propose its own recommendations and the reasons therefor.

(e) In response to the planning board's recommendations, the applicant may modify his application prior to submission to the council, and the planning staff may likewise revise its recommendations.

Section 58: Council Action on Conditional-Use Permits

In considering whether to approve an application for a conditional-use permit, the council shall proceed according to the following format:

(1) The council shall consider whether the application is complete. If no member moves that the application be found incomplete (specifying either the particular type of information lacking or the particular requirement with respect to which the application is incomplete) then this shall be taken as an affirmative finding by the council that the application is complete.

(2) The council shall consider whether the application complies with all of the applicable requirements of this chapter. If a motion to this effect passes, the council need not make further findings concerning such requirements. If such a motion fails or is not made then a motion shall be made that the application be found not in compliance with one or more of the requirements of this chapter. Such a motion shall specify the particular requirements the application fails to meet. Separate votes may be taken with respect to each requirement not met by the application. It shall be conclusively presumed that the application complies with all requirements not found by the council to be unsatisfied through this process.

(3) If the council concludes that the application fails to comply with one or more requirements of this chapter, the application shall be denied. If the council concludes that all such requirements are met, it shall issue the permit unless it adopts a motion to deny the application for one or more of the reasons set forth in Subsection 54(d). Such a motion shall propose specific findings, based upon the evidence submitted, justifying such a conclusion.

Commentary: This section requires the council to follow a step-by-step procedure that leads logically to the issuance or denial of a permit and allows the staff to prepare appropriate findings of fact as a necessary part of the record. See the forms that correspond to the requirements of this section, Appendix G.

Section 59:
Board of Adjustment Action on Special-Use Permits

In considering whether to approve an application for a special-use permit, the board of adjustment shall proceed in the same manner as the council when considering conditional-use permit applications (Section 58), except that the format of the board of adjustment's proceedings will differ as a result of the four-fifths voting requirement set forth in Subsection 32(a).

(1) The board shall consider whether the application is complete. If the board concludes that the application is incomplete and the applicant refuses to provide the necessary information, the application shall be denied. A motion to this effect shall specify either the particular type of information lacking or the particular requirement with respect to which the application is incomplete. A motion to this effect, concurred in by two members of the board, shall constitute the board's finding on this issue. If a motion to this effect is not made and concurred in by at least two members, this shall be taken as an affirmative finding by the board that the application is complete.

(2) The board shall consider whether the application complies with all of the applicable requirements of this chapter. If a motion to this effect passes by the necessary four-fifths vote, the board need not make further findings concerning such requirements. If such a motion fails to receive the necessary four-fifths vote or is not

made, then a motion shall be made that the application be found not in compliance with one or more requirements of this chapter. Such a motion shall specify the particular requirements the application fails to meet. A separate vote may be taken with respect to each requirement not met by the application, and the vote of the number of members equal to more than one-fifth of the board membership (excluding vacant seats) in favor of such a motion shall be sufficient to constitute such motion a finding of the board. It shall be conclusively presumed that the application complies with all requirements not found by the board to be unsatisfied through this process. As provided in Subsection 54(c), if the board concludes that the application fails to meet one or more of the requirements of this chapter, the application shall be denied.

(3) If the board concludes that all such requirements are met, it shall issue the permit unless it adopts a motion to deny the application for one or more of the reasons set forth in Subsection 54(d). Such a motion shall propose specific findings, based upon the evidence submitted, justifying such a conclusion. Since such a motion is not in favor of the applicant, it is carried by a simple majority vote.

Commentary:

The procedural peculiarities of this section are created by the four-fifths vote requirement (see Section 32(a) and commentary). Assuming for simplicity a five-member board, it is possible that a motion to issue a permit, grant a variance, or reverse the zoning administrator's decision could receive a majority vote of three members—not enough votes to pass the motion under the four-fifths rule but enough to prevent a majority vote in favor of a motion having the opposite effect. In the absence of the provisions of this section, the board might be unable to take dispositive action on an application or make findings of fact in support of its decision.

**Section 60:
Additional Requirements on Special-Use and Conditional-Use Permits**

(a) Subject to Subsection (b), in granting a special- or conditional-use permit, the board of adjustment or city council, respectively, may attach to the permit such reasonable requirements in addition to those specified in this chapter as will ensure that the development in its proposed location:

(1) Will not endanger the public health or safety,
(2) Will not injure the value of adjoining or abutting property,
(3) Will be in harmony with the area in which it is located, and
(4) Will be in conformity with the land-use plan, thoroughfare plan, or other plan officially adopted by the council.

(b) The permit-issuing board may not attach additional conditions that modify or alter the specific requirements set forth in this ordinance unless the development in question presents extraordinary circumstances that justify the variation from the specified requirements.

(c) Without limiting the foregoing, the board may attach to a permit a condition limiting the permit to a specified duration.

(d) All additional conditions or requirements shall be entered on the permit.

(e) All additional conditions or requirements authorized by this section are enforceable in the same manner and to the same extent as any other applicable requirement of this chapter.

(f) A vote may be taken on application conditions or requirements before consideration of whether the permit should be denied for any of the reasons set forth in Subsections 54(c) or (d).

Section 61:
Authorizing Use, Occupancy, or Sale Before Completion of Development Under Special-Use or Conditional-Use Permits

(a) In cases when, because of weather conditions or other factors beyond the control of the special-use or conditional-use permit recipient (exclusive of financial hardship) it would be unreasonable to require the permit recipient to comply with all of the requirements of this chapter before commencing the intended use of the property or occupying any buildings or selling lots in a subdivision, the permit-issuing board may authorize the commencement of the intended use or the occupancy of buildings or the sale of subdivision lots (insofar as the requirements of this chapter are concerned) if the permit recipient provides a performance bond or other security satisfactory to the board to ensure that all of these requirements will be fulfilled within a reasonable period (not to exceed 12 months).

Commentary:

See commentary to Section 53.

(b) When the board imposes additional requirements upon the permit recipient in accordance with Section 60 or when the developer proposes in the plans submitted to install amenities beyond those required by this chapter, the board may authorize the permittee to commence the intended use of the property or to occupy any building or to sell any subdivision lots before the additional requirements are fulfilled or the amenities installed if it specifies a date by which or a schedule according to which such requirements must be met or each amenity installed and if it concludes that compliance will be ensured as the result of any one or more of the following:

(1) A performance bond or other security satisfactory to the board is furnished,

(2) A condition is imposed establishing an automatic expiration date on the permit, thereby ensuring that the permit recipient's compliance will be reviewed when application for renewal is made,

(3) The nature of the requirements or amenities is such that sufficient assurance of compliance is given by Section 114 (Penalties and Remedies For Violations) and Section 115 (Permit Revocation).

(c) With respect to subdivisions in which the developer is selling only undeveloped lots, the council may authorize final plat approval and the sale of lots before all the requirements of this chapter are fulfilled if the subdivider provides a performance bond or other security satisfactory to the council to ensure that all of these requirements will be fulfilled within not more than 12 months after final plat approval.

Commentary:

Subsection (c) allows the sale of subdivision lots before subdivision improvements are completed upon the posting of security. This subsection is consistent with the procedures available in most subdivision ordinances. The theory justifying this exception to the basic requirement set forth in Subsection (a) is that, when undeveloped lots are sold, obviously the land must be developed before it can be used or occupied and so the purchaser is not prejudiced if all improvements are not completed at the time of sale as long as there is assurance that they will be within a reasonably short period of time.

**Section 62:
Completing Developments in Phases**

(a) If a development is constructed in phases or stages in accordance with this section, then, subject to Subsection (c), the provisions of Section 47 (No Occupancy, Use, or Sale of Lots Until Requirements Fulfilled) and Section 61 (exceptions to Section 47) shall apply to each phase as if it were the entire development.

(b) As a prerequisite to taking advantage of the provisions of Subsection (a), the developer shall submit plans that clearly show the various phases or stages of the proposed development and the requirements of this chapter that will be satisfied with respect to each phase or stage.

(c) If a development that is to be built in phases or stages includes improvements that are designed to relate to, benefit, or be used by the entire development (such as a swimming pool or tennis courts in a residential development) then, as part of his application for development approval, the developer shall submit a proposed schedule for completion of such improvements. The schedule shall relate completion of such improvements to completion of one or more phases or stages of the entire development. Once a schedule has been approved and made part of the permit by the permit-issuing authority, no land may be used, no buildings may be occupied, and no subdivision lots may be sold except in accordance with the schedule approved as part of the permit, provided that:

(1) If the improvement is one required by this chapter then the developer may utilize the provisions of Subsections 61(a) or 61(c),

(2) If the improvement is an amenity not required by this chapter or is provided in response to a condition imposed by the board, then the developer may utilize the provisions of Subsection 61(b).

**Section 63:
Expiration of Permits**

(a) Zoning, special-use, conditional-use, and sign permits shall expire automatically if, within one year after the issuance of such permits:

(1) The use authorized by such permits has not commenced, in circumstances where no substantial construction, erection, alteration, excavation, demolition, or similar work is necessary before commencement of such use, or

(2) Less than 10 percent of the total cost of all construction, erection, alteration, excavation, demolition, or similar work on any development authorized by such permits has been completed on the site. With respect to phased development (see Section 62), this requirement shall apply only to the first phase.

(b) If, after some physical alteration to land or structures begins to take place, such work is discontinued for a period of one year, then the permit authorizing such work shall immediately expire. However, expiration of the permit shall not affect the provisions of Section 64.

(c) The permit-issuing authority may extend for a period up to six months the date when a permit would otherwise expire pursuant to Subsections (a) or (b) if it concludes that (i) the permit has not yet expired, (ii) the permit recipient has proceeded with due diligence and in good faith, and (iii) conditions have not changed so substantially as to warrant a new application. Successive extensions may be granted for periods up to six months upon the same findings. All such extensions may be granted without resort to the formal processes and fees required for a new permit.

(d) For purposes of this section, the permit within the jurisdiction of the council or the board of adjustment is issued when such board votes to approve the application and issue the permit. A permit within the jurisdiction of the zoning administrator is issued when the earlier of the following takes place:

  (1) A copy of the fully executed permit is delivered to the permit recipient, and delivery is accomplished when the permit is hand-delivered or mailed to the permit applicant; or

  (2) The zoning administrator notifies the permit applicant that the application has been approved and that all that remains before a fully executed permit can be delivered is for the applicant to take certain specified actions, such as having the permit executed by the property owner so it can be recorded if required under [statutory citation].

(e) Notwithstanding any of the provisions of Article VIII (Nonconforming Situations), this section shall be applicable to permits issued prior to the date this section becomes effective.

Commentary:

The principal reason for having provisions such as those in the foregoing section is to enable the local government to evaluate a proposed development in the light of current conditions and ordinance requirements. A development may be appropriate and meet ordinance requirements one year, but be inappropriate five years later when conditions or the ordinance have changed. If the development has been constructed, nothing can be done. But if it has never been built, the local government should have the opportunity, ensured by this section, to reconsider its original approval. A secondary purpose of this provision is to discourage the submission of purely speculative proposals or proposals submitted solely to avoid the effects of possible subsequent ordinance amendments.

Section 64:
Effect of Permit on Successors and Assigns

(a) Zoning, special-use, conditional-use, and sign permits authorize the permittee to make use of land and structures in a particular way. Such permits are transferable. However, so long as the land or structures or any portion thereof covered under a permit continues to be used for the purposes for which the permit was granted, then:

  (1) No person (including successors or assigns of the person who obtained the permit) may make use of the land or structures covered under such permit for the purposes authorized in the permit except in accordance with all the terms and requirements of that permit, and

(2) The terms and requirements of the permit apply to and restrict the use of land or structures covered under the permit, not only with respect to all persons having any interest in the property at the time the permit was obtained, but also with respect to persons who subsequently obtain any interest in all or part of the covered property and wish to use it for or in connection with purposes other than those for which the permit was originally issued, so long as the persons who subsequently obtain an interest in the property had actual or record notice (as provided in Subsection (b)) of the existence of the permit at the time they acquired their interest.

Commentary:

It is sometimes said that permits "run with the land," but this phrase is misleading. It is true that the permission conferred by a permit to use land in a certain way should be independent of the ownership of the land, and therefore such permits are transferable. However, the restrictions they impose do not run with the land in the same way that covenants do. A restrictive covenant limiting the use of a lot to single-family residential purposes continues to bind that land, regardless of changes in the zoning or the desires of the owner to use it for other purposes. However, a zoning permit issued for a single-family residence would not bind a successor who wished to convert the home into a duplex (assuming that were a permissible use).

It is important, however, that the ordinance make clear that successors are bound by a permit issued to a predecessor so long as any portion of the property covered by a permit is being used for the purposes authorized under that permit. This is particularly significant with respect to open spaces which, in the absence of such a restriction, might be sold off and developed.

(b) Whenever a zoning, special-use, or conditional-use permit is issued to authorize development (other than single-family or two-family residences) on a tract of land in excess of one acre, nothing authorized by the permit may be done until the record owner of the property signs a written acknowledgement that the permit has been issued so that the permit may be recorded in the _____ County Registry and indexed under the record owner's name as grantor.

Commentary:

The recording requirement is imposed to ensure that a prospective purchaser of a tract has record notice that the land is restricted by the terms of a permit covering that property. In the absence of such record notice, it might be difficult to deny a good faith purchaser of a lot a permit to develop it on the basis that, for example, the property constitutes the required open space for another project.

Because recording involves additional procedural steps and expense, it is not required in all cases but only in those classes of cases where there appears to be a substantial likelihood that after the authorized development is completed there will remain an area of open space large enough to be developed. The foregoing section chooses one acre as the dividing line.

Section 65: Amendments to and Modifications of Permits

(a) Insignificant deviations from the permit (including approved plans) issued by the city council, the board of adjustment, or the administrator are permissible and the administrator may authorize such insignificant deviations. A deviation is insignificant if it has no discernible impact on neighboring properties, the general public, or those intended to occupy or use the proposed development.

(b) Minor design modifications or changes in permits (including approved plans) are permissible with the approval of the permit-issuing authority. Such permission may be obtained without a formal application, public hearing, or payment of any additional fee. For purposes of this section, minor design modifications or changes are those that have no substantial impact on neighboring properties, the general public, or those intended to occupy or use the proposed development.

(c) All other requests for changes in approved plans will be processed as new applications. If such requests are required to be acted upon by the council or board of adjustment, new conditions may be imposed in accordance with Section 60, but the applicant retains the right to reject such additional conditions by withdrawing his request for an amendment and may then proceed in accordance with the previously issued permit.

(d) The administrator shall determine whether amendments to and modifications of permits fall within the categories set forth above in Subsections (a), (b), and (c).

(e) A developer requesting approval of changes shall submit a written request for such approval to the administrator, and that request shall identify the changes. Approval of all changes must be given in writing.

Commentary:

It is almost inevitable that in any development of any significant size field conditions will necessitate some changes in approved plans. It would be a needless burden to require a developer to obtain a new permit for even the most minor modifications. On the other hand, neighboring property owners may have foregone objection to a project because of the level of screening shown on the plans or the modest density proposed, and if changes in these elements of the plans were approved without an opportunity for their input, they might well feel deceived.

This section attempts to cut a path through this thicket by establishing three classes of changes and giving the administrator the authority to determine in which class a requested change falls. The definitional distinctions between classes are not entirely precise, but that is the nature of the subject matter.

**Section 66:
Reconsideration of Board Action**

(a) Whenever (i) the city council disapproves a conditional-use permit application, or (ii) the board of adjustment disapproves an application for a special-use permit or a variance, on any basis other than the failure of the applicant to submit a complete application, such action may not be reconsidered by the respective board at a later time unless the applicant clearly demonstrates that:

  (1) Circumstances affecting the property that is the subject of the application have substantially changed, or
  (2) New information is available that could not with reasonable diligence have been presented at a previous hearing. A request to be heard on this basis must be filed with the administrator within the time period for an appeal to superior court (see Section 116). However, such a request does not extend the period within which an appeal must be taken.

(b) Notwithstanding Subsection (a), the council or board of adjustment may at any time consider a new application affecting the same property as an application previously denied. A new application is one that differs in some substantial way from the one previously considered.

Commentary:
This section is based on case law in North Carolina to the effect that the doctrine of *res judicata* applies to the decisions of boards of adjustment or governing bodies acting in their quasi-judicial, permit-issuing capacity.

Section 67:
Applications to be Processed Expeditiously

Recognizing that inordinate delays in acting upon appeals or applications may impose unnecessary costs on the appellant or applicant, the city shall make every reasonable effort to process appeals and permit applications as expeditiously as possible, consistent with the need to ensure that all development conforms to the requirements of this chapter.

Commentary:
Many ordinances establish rigid deadlines for various steps in the permit application process and provide that a failure to act upon an application within those deadlines constitutes approval by the administrative body involved. There are some advantages to this approach, and it may be necessary in jurisdictions where the administrative process would otherwise grind so slowly as to crush the developer. However, the author's experience has been that local governments are generally very conscious of the need to act expeditiously, and inordinate delays are usually the result of the failure of a developer to provide necessary information in a timely fashion. Where this is the case, the more flexible approach provided by the foregoing section is recommended.

Section 68:
Maintenance of Common Areas, Improvements, and Facilities

The recipient of any zoning, special-use, conditional-use, or sign permit, or his successor, shall be responsible for maintaining all common areas, improvements, or facilities required by this chapter or any permit issued in accordance with its provisions, except those areas, improvements, or facilities with respect to which an offer of dedication to the public has been accepted by the appropriate public authority. As illustrations, and without limiting the generality of the foregoing, this means that private roads and parking areas, water and sewer lines, and recreational facilities must be properly maintained so that they can be used in the manner intended, and required vegetation and trees used for screening, landscaping, or shading must be replaced if they die or are destroyed.

Sections 69 through 75:
Reserved

Part II. Major and Minor Subdivisions

Section 76:
Regulation of Subdivisions

Major subdivisions are subject to a two-step approval process. Physical improvements to the land to be subdivided are authorized by a conditional-use permit as provided in Part I of Article IV of this chapter, and sale of lots is permitted after final plat approval as provided in Section 79. Minor subdivisions only require a one-step approval process: final plat approval (in accordance with Section 78).

**Section 77:
No Subdivision Without Plat Approval**

(a) No person may subdivide his land except in accordance with all of the provisions of this chapter. In particular, no person may subdivide his land unless and until a final plat of the subdivision has been approved in accordance with the provisions of Section 78 or Section 79 and recorded in the _____ County Registry.

(b) The _____ County Register of Deeds may not record a plat of any subdivision within the city's planning jurisdiction unless the plat has been approved in accordance with the provisions of this chapter.

Commentary:

> The foregoing section establishes the chief enforcement tool that ensures compliance with this ordinance as it deals with subdivisions: a subdivision plat may not be recorded until it has been approved and approval is contingent upon compliance with the ordinance. Both subsections above merely restate what state law provides in North Carolina. Most local governments that have the authority to regulate subdivisions would be empowered to adopt a provision similar to Subsection (a), but since Subsection (b) is directed to a county official, this important enforcement mechanism will probably have to be provided by state law in most jurisdictions.

**Section 78:
Minor Subdivision Approval**

(a) The planning director shall approve or disapprove minor subdivision final plats in accordance with the provisions of this section.

Commentary:

> It is important for the sake of administrative efficiency and good public relations that there be established a quick and easy process for the review and approval of subdivisions that involve the creation of only a very few lots and no extension of public improvements. Where the dividing line between major and minor subdivisions is drawn—in terms of the number of lots involved—is a matter of local choice (see the definitions in Section 15 of this ordinance for one illustration).

(b) The applicant for minor subdivision plat approval, before complying with Subsection (c), shall submit a sketch plan to the planning director for a determination of whether the approval process authorized by this section can be and should be utilized. The planning director may require the applicant to submit whatever information is necessary to make this determination, including, but not limited to, a copy of the tax map showing the land being subdivided and all lots previously subdivided from that tract of land within the previous five years.

(c) Applicants for minor subdivision approval shall submit to the planning director a copy of a plat conforming to the requirements set forth in Subsections 79(b) and (c) (as well as two prints of such plat), except that a minor subdivision plat shall contain the following certificates in lieu of those required in Section 80:

  (1) Certificate of Ownership

  I hereby certify that I am the owner of the property described hereon, which property is within the subdivision regulation jurisdiction of the City of _____, and that I freely adopt this plan of subdivision.

  _____   _____
  Date   Owner

(2) Certificate of Approval

I hereby certify that the minor subdivision shown on this plat does not involve the creation of new public streets or any change in existing public streets, that the subdivision shown is in all respects in compliance with Chapter _____ of the _____ City Code, and that therefore this plat has been approved by the _____ planning director, subject to its being recorded in the _____ County Registry within 60 days of the date below.

_____ _____
Date   Planning Director

(3) A certificate of survey and accuracy, in the form stated in Subdivision 80(3).

Commentary: See commentary following Section 79.

(d) The planning director shall take expeditious action on an application for minor subdivision plat approval as provided in Section 67. However, either the planning director or the applicant may at any time refer the application to the major subdivision approval process.

Commentary: This provides an appeal process for the applicant in the form of *de novo* review by the planning board under the major subdivision approval process and also allows the planning director to assign an application to the more intensive major subdivision review process if he feels the proposed subdivision warrants it.

(e) Not more than a total of three lots may be created out of one tract using the minor subdivision plat approval process, regardless of whether the lots are created at one time or over an extended period of time.

(f) Subject to Subsection (d), the planning director shall approve the proposed subdivision unless the subdivision is not a minor subdivision as defined in Section 15 or the application or the proposed subdivision fails to comply with Subsection (e) or any other applicable requirement of this chapter.

(g) If the subdivision is disapproved, the planning director shall promptly furnish the applicant with a written statement of the reasons for disapproval.

(h) Approval of any plat is contingent upon the plat being recorded within 60 days after the date the Certificate of Approval is signed by the planning director or his designee.

Commentary: An automatic termination date for subdivision approval if the approved plat is not recorded is established for the same reasons that the ordinance provides for permit expiration dates. See the commentary to Section 63.

Section 79:
Major Subdivision Approval Process

Commentary: In many places, the planning board or governing body is made responsible for final plat approval. This is unnecessary since the process should be a purely technical one—making sure that the final plat contains the required information and that it corresponds to the plans approved in connection with the issuance of the conditional-use permit.

(a) The planning director shall approve or disapprove major subdivision final plats in accordance with the provisions of this section.

(b) The applicant for major subdivision plat approval shall submit to the administrator a final plat, drawn in waterproof ink on a sheet made of material that will be acceptable to the _____ County Register of Deed's Office for recording purposes, and having dimensions as follows: either 21" × 30", 12" × 18", or 18" × 24". When more than one sheet is required to include the entire subdivision, all sheets shall be made of the same size and shall show appropriate match marks on each sheet and appropriate references to other sheets of the subdivision. The scale of the plat shall be at one (1) inch equals not more than one hundred (100) feet. The applicant shall also submit two prints of the plat.

(c) In addition to the appropriate endorsements, as provided in Section 80, the final plat shall contain the following information:

(1) The name of the subdivision, which name shall not duplicate the name of any existing subdivision as recorded in the _____ County Registry,

(2) The name of the subdivision owner or owners,

(3) The township, county, and state where the subdivision is located,

(4) The name of the surveyor and his registration number and the date of survey,

(5) The scale according to which the plat is drawn in feet per inch or scale ratio in words or figures and bar graph, and

(6) All of the additional information required by [cite appropriate state statute].

Commentary:

It is probable that a state statute will govern what must be included on a final plat. Reproduced below is the appropriate provision of North Carolina law (G.S. 47-30). If the matters covered in this statute are not mandated by state law, then the draftsman should include them in the land use ordinance.

Every plat shall contain the following information:

(1) An accurately positioned north arrow coordinated with any bearings shown on the plat. Indication shall be made as to whether the north index is true, magnetic, North Carolina grid, or is referenced to old deed or plat bearings. If the north index is magnetic or referenced to old deed or plat bearings, the date and the source (if known) such index was originally determined shall be clearly indicated.

(2) The azimuth or courses and distances as surveyed of every line shall be shown. Distances shall be in feet or meters and decimals thereof. The number of decimal places shall be appropriate to the class of survey required.

(3) All plat lines shall be by horizontal (level) measurements. All information shown on the plat shall be correctly plotted to the scale shown. Enlargement of portions of a plat are acceptable

in the interest of clarity, where shown as inserts on the same sheet. Where the North Carolina grid is used the grid factor shall be shown on the face of the plat and a designation as to whether horizontal ground distances or grid distances were used.

(4) Where a boundary is formed by a curved line, the following data must be given: actual survey data from the point of curvature to the point of tangency shall be shown as standard curve data, or as a traverse of bearings and distances around the curve. If standard curve data is used the bearing and distance of the long chord (from point of curvature to point of tangency) must be shown on the face of the plat.

(5) Where a subdivision of land is set out on the plat, all streets and lots shall be carefully plotted with dimension lines indicating widths and all other information pertinent to reestablishing all lines in the field. This shall include bearings and distances sufficient to form a continuous closure of the entire perimeter.

(6) Where control corners have been established in compliance with G.S. 39-32.1, 39-32.2, 39-32.3, and 39-32.4, as amended, the location and pertinent information as required in the reference statute shall be plotted on the plat. All other corners which are marked by monument or natural object shall be so identified on all plats, and all corners of adjacent owners in the boundary lines of the subject tract which are marked by monument or natural object must be shown with a distance from one or more of the subject tract's corners.

(7) The names of adjacent landowners along with lot, block or parcel identifier and subdivision designations or other legal reference where applicable, shall be shown where they could be determined by the surveyor.

(8) All visible and apparent rights-of-way, watercourses, utilities, roadways, and other such improvements shall be accurately located where crossing or forming any boundary line of the property shown.

(9) Where the plat is the result of a survey, one or more corners shall, by a system of azimuths or courses and distances, be accurately tied to and coordinated with a monument of some United States or State Agency survey system, such as the National Geodetic Survey (formerly U.S. Coast and Geodetic Survey) system, where such monument is within 2,000 feet of said corner. Where the North Carolina Grid System coordinates of said monument are on file in the North Carolina Department of Natural Resources and Community Development, the coordinates of the referenced corner shall be computed and shown in X (easting) and Y (northing) ordinates on the map. In the absence of Grid Control, other appropriate natural monuments or landmarks shall be used.

(10) A vicinity map shall appear on the face of the plat.

(d) The planning director shall approve the proposed plat unless it finds that the plat or the proposed subdivision fails to comply with one or more of the requirements of this chapter or that the final plat differs substantially from the plans and specifications approved in conjunction with the conditional-use permit that authorized the development of the subdivision.

(e) If the final plat is disapproved by the planning director, the applicant shall be furnished with a written statement of the reasons for the disapproval.

(f) Approval of a final plat is contingent upon the plat being recorded within 60 days after the approval certificate is signed by the planning director or his designee.

Section 80:
Endorsements on Major Subdivision Plats

All major subdivision plats shall contain the endorsements listed in Subdivisions (1), (2), and (3) herein. The endorsements listed in Subdivision (4) shall appear on plats of all major subdivisions located outside the corporate limits of the city but within the planning jurisdiction.

(1) Certificate of Approval

I hereby certify that all streets shown on this plat are within the City of _____'s planning jurisdiction, all streets and other improvements shown on this plat have been installed or completed or that their installation or completion (within 12 months after the date below) has been assured by the posting of a performance bond or other sufficient surety, and that the subdivision shown on this plat is in all respects in compliance with Chapter _____ of the _____ City Code, and therefore this plat has been approved by the _____ planning director, subject to its being recorded in the _____ County Registry within 60 days of the date below.

_____ _____
Date   Planning Director

(2) Certificate of Ownership and Dedication

I hereby certify that I am the owner of the property described hereon, which property is located within the subdivision regulation jurisdiction of the City of _____, that I hereby freely adopt this plan of subdivision and dedicate to public use all areas shown on this plat as streets, alleys, walks, parks, open space, and easements, except those specifically indicated as private, and that I will maintain all such areas until the offer of dedication is accepted by the appropriate public authority. All property shown on this plat as dedicated for a public use shall be deemed to be dedicated for any other public use authorized by law when such other use is approved by the _____ City Council in the public interest.

_____ _____
Date   Owner

                                        (Notarized)

(3) Certificate of Survey and Accuracy

I hereby certify that this map (drawn by me) (drawn under my supervision) from (an actual survey made by me) (an actual survey made under my supervision) (a deed description recorded in Book _____, Page _____ of the _____ County Registry) (other); that the error of closure as calculated by latitudes and departures is 1: _____; that the boundaries not surveyed are shown as broken lines plotted from information found in Book _____, Page _____, and that this map was prepared in accordance with [*statutory citation*]. Witness my original signature, registration number and seal this _____ day of _____, 19____.

Seal or Stamp   Registered Land Surveyor

(Notarized)   Registration Number

(4) Division of Highways District Engineer Certificate

I hereby certify that the public streets shown on this plat have been completed, or that a performance bond or other sufficient surety has been posted to guarantee their completion, in accordance with at least the minimum specifications and standards of the State Department of Transportation for acceptance of subdivision streets on the state highway system for maintenance.

                                       District Engineer

Commentary: The endorsements required on the plat will vary from jurisdiction to jurisdiction according to differences in state laws and local practices. Endorsement (3) above is required by North Carolina law. Endorsement (4) is required because all streets outside cities in North Carolina are maintained by the State Department of Transportation.

Section 81:
Plat Approval Not Acceptance of Dedication Offers

Approval of a plat does not constitute acceptance by the city of the offer of dedication of any streets, sidewalks, parks, or other public facilities shown on a plat. However, the city may accept any such offer of dedication by resolution of the council or by actually exercising control over and maintaining such facilities.

Commentary: The recording of a plat constitutes an offer of dedication of the public facilities shown thereon. However, before such facilities become publicly owned, the local governing body must accept this offer, either explicitly by a formal resolution or implicitly by maintenance. The foregoing section also clarifies that plat approval does not constitute acceptance, a disclaimer that is particularly important in view of the fact that the one-year warranty provided for in Section 82 begins to run upon acceptance.

Section 82:
Protection Against Defects

(a) Whenever (pursuant to Section 61) occupancy, use or sale is allowed before the completion of all facilities or improvements intended for dedication, then the performance bond or the surety that is posted pursuant to Section 61 shall guarantee that any defects in such improvements or facilities that appear within one year after the dedication of such facilities or improvements is accepted shall be corrected by the developer.

(b) Whenever all public facilities or improvements intended for dedication are installed before occupancy, use, or sale is authorized, then the developer shall post a performance bond or other sufficient surety to guarantee that he will correct all defects in such facilities or improvements that occur within one year after the offer of dedication of such facilities or improvements is accepted.

(c) An architect or engineer retained by the developer shall certify to the city that all facilities and improvements to be dedicated to the city have been constructed in accordance with the requirements of this chapter. This certification shall be a condition precedent to acceptance by the city of the offer of dedication of such facilities or improvements.

(d) For purposes of this section, the term "defects" refers to any condition in publicly dedicated facilities or improvements that requires the city to make repairs in such facilities over and above the normal amount of maintenance that they would require. If such defects appear, the guaranty may be enforced regardless of whether the facilities or improvements were constructed in accordance with the requirements of this chapter.

Commentary:

Subsection (d) is necessary to avoid the defense of a developer that, for example, a particular street in which a defect has appeared was built according to city specifications and therefore should be the city's problem. This subsection is based upon the fact that the specifications of this chapter do not cover all aspects of construction and the assumption that, if properly constructed, streets and other facilities should not become defective within the first year.

Section 83:
Maintenance of Dedicated Areas Until Acceptance

As provided in Section 67, all facilities and improvements with respect to which the owner makes an offer of dedication to public use shall be maintained by the owner until such offer of dedication is accepted by the appropriate public authority.

Sections 84 through 90:
Reserved

Article V Appeals, Variances, Interpretations

Section 91: Appeals

(a) An appeal from any final order or decision of the administrator may be taken to the board of adjustment by any person aggrieved. An appeal is taken by filing with the administrator and the board of adjustment a written notice of appeal specifying the grounds therefor. A notice of appeal shall be considered filed with the administrator and the board of adjustment when delivered to the planning department, and the date and time of filing shall be entered on the notice by the planning staff.

(b) An appeal must be taken within 30 days after the date of the decision or order appealed from.

(c) Whenever an appeal is filed, the administrator shall forthwith transmit to the board of adjustment all the papers constituting the record relating to the action appealed from.

(d) An appeal stays all actions by the administrator seeking enforcement of or compliance with the order or decision appealed from, unless the administrator certifies to the board of adjustment that (because of facts stated in the certificate) a stay would, in his opinion, cause imminent peril to life or property. In that case, proceedings shall not be stayed except by order of the board of adjustment or a court, issued on application of the party seeking the stay, for due cause shown, after notice to the administrator.

(e) The board of adjustment may reverse or affirm (wholly or partly) or may modify the order, requirement or decision or determination appealed from and shall make any order, requirement, decision or determination that in its opinion ought to be made in the case before it. To this end, the board shall have all the powers of the officer from whom the appeal is taken.

Commentary:
> This language adheres very closely to that found in the Standard State Zoning Enabling Act.

Section 92: Variances

(a) An application for a variance shall be submitted to the board of adjustment by filing a copy of the application with the administrator in the planning department. Applications shall be handled in the same manner as applications for special-use permits in conformity with the provisions of Sections 48, 49, and 56.

(b) A variance may be granted by the board of adjustment if it concludes that strict enforcement of the ordinance would result in practical difficulties or unnecessary hardships for the applicant and that, by granting the variance, the spirit of the ordinance will be observed, public safety and welfare secured, and substantial justice done. It may reach these conclusions if it finds that:

(1) If the applicant complies strictly with the provisions of the ordinance, he can make no reasonable use of his property,

(2) The hardship of which the applicant complains is one suffered by the applicant rather than by neighbors or the general public,

(3) The hardship relates to the applicant's land, rather than personal circumstances,

(4) The hardship is unique, or nearly so, rather than one shared by many surrounding properties,

(5) The hardship is not the result of the applicant's own actions, and

(6) The variance will neither result in the extension of a nonconforming situation in violation of Article VIII nor authorize the initiation of a nonconforming use of land.

Commentary:

The language in the first part of this subsection restates the statutory authority to grant variances in North Carolina (it is closely patterned after the grant of authority contained in the Standard Zoning Enabling Act). The remaining subdivisions constitute an effort to restate judicial interpretations of this general language. The draftsman should consult the case law in his state to draft this section as accurately as possible. Note especially that Subdivision (b)(6) does not allow "use" variances. Of course, the law on this varies from jurisdiction to jurisdiction; some states require different degrees of hardship, depending on whether a use variance or dimensional variance is sought.

(c) In granting variances, the board of adjustment may impose such reasonable conditions as will ensure that the use of the property to which the variance applies will be as compatible as practicable with the surrounding properties.

(d) A variance may be issued for an indefinite duration or for a specified duration only.

(e) The nature of the variance and any conditions attached to it shall be entered on the face of the zoning permit, or the zoning permit may simply note the issuance of the variance and refer to the written record of the variance for further information. All such conditions are enforceable in the same manner as any other applicable requirement of this chapter.

Section 93: Interpretations

(a) The board of adjustment is authorized to interpret the zoning map and to pass upon disputed questions of lot lines or district boundary lines and similar questions. If such questions arise in the context of an appeal from a decision of the zoning administrator, they shall be handled as provided in Section 91.

(b) An application for a map interpretation shall be submitted to the board of adjustment by filing a copy of the application with the administrator in the planning department. The application shall contain sufficient information to enable the board to make the necessary interpretation.

(c) Where uncertainty exists as to the boundaries of districts as shown on the Official Zoning Map, the following rules shall apply:

(1) Boundaries indicated as approximately following the centerlines of alleys, streets, highways, streams, or railroads shall be construed to follow such centerlines,

(2) Boundaries indicated as approximately following lot lines, city limits or extraterritorial boundary lines, shall be construed as following such lines, limits or boundaries,

(3) Boundaries indicated as following shorelines shall be construed to follow such shorelines, and in the event of change in the shoreline shall be construed as following such shorelines,

(4) Where a district boundary divides a lot or where distances are not specifically indicated on the Official Zoning Map, the boundary shall be determined by measurement, using the scale of the Official Zoning Map,

(5) Where any street or alley is hereafter officially vacated or abandoned, the regulations applicable to each parcel of abutting property shall apply to that portion of such street or alley added thereto by virtue of such vacation or abandonment.

(d) Interpretations of the location of floodway and floodplain boundary lines may be made by the administrator as provided in Section 258.

Section 94: Requests to be Heard Expeditiously

As provided in Section 66, the board of adjustment shall hear and decide all appeals, variance requests, and requests for interpretations as expeditiously as possible, consistent with the need to follow regularly established agenda procedures, provide notice in accordance with Article VI, and obtain the necessary information to make sound decisions.

Commentary:

See commentary under Section 66.

Section 95: Burden of Proof in Appeals and Variances

(a) When an appeal is taken to the board of adjustment in accordance with Section 91, the administrator shall have the initial burden of presenting to the board sufficient evidence and argument to justify the order or decision appealed from. The burden of presenting evidence and argument to the contrary then shifts to the appellant, who shall also have the burden of persuasion.

(b) The burden of presenting evidence sufficient to allow the board of adjustment to reach the conclusions set forth in Subsection 92(b), as well as the burden of persuasion on those issues, remains with the applicant seeking the variance.

Section 96: Board Action on Appeals and Variances

(a) With respect to appeals, a motion to reverse, affirm, or modify the order, requirement, decision, or determination appealed from shall include, insofar as practicable, a statement of the specific reasons or findings of facts that support the motion. If a motion to reverse or modify is not made or fails to receive the four-fifths vote necessary for adoption (see Section 32), then a motion to uphold the decision appealed from shall be in order. This motion is adopted as the board's decision if supported by more than one-fifth of the board's membership (excluding vacant seats).

(b) Before granting a variance, the board must take a separate vote and vote affirmatively (by a four-fifths majority—see Section 32) on each of the six required findings stated in Subsection 92(b). Insofar as practicable, a motion to make an affirmative finding on each of the requirements set forth in Subsection 92(b) shall include a statement of the specific reasons or findings of fact supporting such motion.

(c) A motion to deny a variance may be made on the basis that any one or more of the six criteria set forth in Subsection 92(b) are not satisfied or that the application is incomplete. Insofar as practicable, such a motion shall include a statement of the specific reasons or findings of fact that support it. This motion is adopted as the board's decision if supported by more than one-fifth of the board's membership (excluding vacant seats).

Commentary: See commentary following Section 59.

Sections 97 through 100: Reserved

Article VI

Hearing Procedures for Appeals and Applications

Commentary:

The minimum hearing procedures provided for in this article will be dictated in each jurisdiction by a combination of statutory and case law. The trend is to require greater formality, making the proceedings more judicial in character. However, because the decision-making boards are not generally composed of people with legal training, there are limits to the extent to which the proceedings before these boards can or should be "judicialized." The provisions of this article attempt to set a middle course, requiring the observance of minimum due process standards without excessive formalities.

**Section 101:
Hearing Required on Appeals and Applications**

(a) Before making a decision on an appeal or an application for a variance, special-use permit, or conditional-use permit, or a petition from the planning staff to revoke a special-use permit or conditional-use permit, the board of adjustment or the city council, as the case may be, shall hold a hearing on the appeal or application.

(b) Subject to Subsection (c), the hearing shall be open to the public and all persons interested in the outcome of the appeal or application shall be given an opportunity to present evidence and arguments and ask questions of persons who testify.

(c) The board of adjustment or council may place reasonable and equitable limitations on the presentation of evidence and arguments and the cross-examination of witnesses so that the matter at issue may be heard and decided without undue delay.

(d) The hearing board may continue the hearing until a subsequent meeting and may keep the hearing open to take additional information up to the point a final decision is made. No further notice of a continued hearing need be published unless a period of six weeks or more elapses between hearing dates.

**Section 102:
Notice of Hearing**

The administrator shall give notice of any hearing required by Section 101 as follows:

(1) Notice shall be given to the appellant or applicant and any other person who makes a written request for such notice by mailing to such persons a written notice not later than 10 days before the hearing.

(2) Notice shall be given to neighboring property owners by mailing a written notice not later than 10 days before the hearing to those

persons who have listed for taxation real property any portion of which is located within 150 feet of the lot that is the subject of the application or appeal. Notice shall also be given by prominently posting signs in the vicinity of the property that is the subject of the proposed action. Such signs shall be posted not less than seven days prior to the hearing.

Commentary: The foregoing section, in effect, defines owners of adjacent property as those having listed the property for taxation. This is done for clarity and for ease of administration. The drawback is that there may be a substantial time lag between the date ownership of property changes and the date such change is reflected in the property tax listings. Obviously, each jurisdiction should choose the method most likely to notify the actual property owner, consistent with administrative feasibility.

(3) In the case of conditional-use permits, notice shall be given to other potentially interested persons by publishing a notice one time in a newspaper having general circulation in the area not less than seven nor more than fifteen days prior to the hearing.

Commentary: Newspaper notice is given of conditional-use permits only because projects requiring conditional-use permit approval are regarded as having more than neighborhood impact.

(4) The notice required by this section shall state the date, time, and place of the hearing, reasonably identify the lot that is the subject of the application or appeal, and give a brief description of the action requested or proposed.

Section 103: Evidence

(a) The provisions of this section apply to all hearings for which a notice is required by Section 101.

(b) All persons who intend to present evidence to the permit-issuing board, rather than arguments only, shall be sworn.

(c) All findings and conclusions necessary to the issuance or denial of the requested permit or appeal (crucial findings) shall be based upon reliable evidence. Competent evidence (evidence admissible in a court of law) shall be preferred whenever reasonably available, but in no case may crucial findings be based solely upon incompetent evidence unless competent evidence is not reasonably available, the evidence in question appears to be particularly reliable, and the matter at issue is not seriously disputed.

Commentary: The types of evidence that may be considered by the board depends upon the degree to which a particular jurisdiction requires local quasi-judicial bodies to adhere to the principles of evidence applicable in a court of law. In some jurisdictions, administrative procedure statutes may cover local boards, while in others case law alone may govern. The foregoing section illustrates a middle-of-the-road position, requiring some concern for the reliability of evidence but not slavish adherence to the rules of evidence that would be followed in court.

Section 104: Modification of Application at Hearing

(a) In response to questions or comments by persons appearing at the hearing or to suggestions or recommendations by the city council or board of adjustment, the applicant may agree to modify his application, including the plans and specifications submitted.

(b) Unless such modifications are so substantial or extensive that the board cannot reasonably be expected to perceive the nature and impact of the proposed changes without revised plans before it, the board may approve the application with the stipulation that the permit will not be issued until plans reflecting the agreed upon changes are submitted to the planning staff.

Commentary:

Frequently, in response to comments or concerns expressed at a public hearing by neighbors or board members, a developer will agree to modify his proposal. If such modifications are spelled out and their impact can be readily grasped, this section allows approval of the project as modified, instead of requiring the developer to come back to another meeting with revised plans. Of course, the developer must submit revised plans to the staff before the permit is issued. This is critical because the permit incorporates by reference approved plans, and those plans must reflect exactly what the developer proposed to do.

The foregoing process should be carefully distinguished from board approval that is conditioned upon approval of proposed changes by some administrative official. For example, the board may be inclined to issue a permit subject to the condition that screening be approved by the planning director, or that the entrance be relocated according to the directions of the public works director. If the ordinance establishes criteria relating to these things and specifies that the board is to issue the permit if the development meets all such requirements, then it would be impermissible for the board to delegate its responsibility for deciding whether the application meets the requirements of the ordinance. Rather, the applicant should be directed to show on the plans how the project will be screened or the entrance relocated, and these plans should be submitted to the board for approval.

**Section 105:
Record**

(a) A tape recording shall be made of all hearings required by Section 101, and such recordings shall be kept for at least two years. Accurate minutes shall also be kept of all such proceedings, but a transcript need not be made.

Commentary:

The minimum period that tapes should be kept is the period within which judicial review may be sought. However, it is useful to keep the tapes longer than the minimum period because, not infrequently, it becomes helpful to know exactly what was said at a meeting in order to interpret conditions imposed on the permit or to determine whether the project is in conformity with the representations made at the public hearing.

(b) Whenever practicable, all documentary evidence presented at a hearing as well as all other types of physical evidence shall be made a part of the record of the proceedings and shall be kept by the city for at least two years.

**Section 106:
Written Decision**

(a) Any decision made by the board of adjustment or city council regarding an appeal or variance or issuance or revocation of a conditional-use permit or special-use permit shall be reduced to writing and served upon the applicant or appellant and all other persons who make a written request for a copy.

(b) In addition to a statement of the board's ultimate disposition of the case and any other information deemed appropriate, the written decision shall state the board's findings and conclusions, as well as supporting reasons or facts, whenever this chapter requires the same as a prerequisite to taking action.

Commentary:

It is extremely difficult to get lay boards to make findings of fact and state legal conclusions as a trial court would generally do in issuing a decision. The formality with which this must be done will vary according to the law of the particular jurisdiction. However, as a general principle, a reviewing court must be able to determine what the board has done and why, and so the board should at least state the reasons why it has reached some general conclusion, particularly if a permit is denied. For example, if a permit is rejected on the basis that the project would endanger the public health and safety, the written decision should spell out the board's basis for reaching this conclusion.

Sections 107 through 110: Reserved

Article VII   Enforcement and Review

Section 111:
Complaints Regarding Violations

Whenever the administrator receives a written, signed complaint alleging a violation of this chapter, he shall investigate the complaint, take whatever action is warranted, and inform the complainant in writing what actions have been or will be taken.

Section 112:
Persons Liable

The owner, tenant, or occupant of any building or land or part thereof and any architect, builder, contractor, agent, or other person who participates in, assists, directs, creates, or maintains any situation that is contrary to the requirements of this chapter may be held responsible for the violation and suffer the penalties and be subject to the remedies herein provided.

Section 113:
Procedures Upon Discovery of Violations

(a) If the administrator finds that any provision of this chapter is being violated, he shall send a written notice to the person responsible for such violation, indicating the nature of the violation and ordering the action necessary to correct it. Additional written notices may be sent at the administrator's discretion.

(b) The final written notice (and the initial written notice may be the final notice) shall state what action the administrator intends to take if the violation is not corrected and shall advise that the administrator's decision or order may be appealed to the board of adjustment in accordance with Section 91.

(c) Notwithstanding the foregoing, in cases when delay would seriously threaten the effective enforcement of this chapter or pose a danger to the public health, safety, or welfare, the administrator may seek enforcement without prior written notice by invoking any of the penalties or remedies authorized in Section 114.

Section 114:
Penalties and Remedies for Violations

(a) Violations of the provisions of this chapter or failure to comply with any of its requirements, including violations of any conditions and safeguards established in connection with grants of variances or special-use or conditional-use permits, shall constitute a misdemeanor, punishable by a fine of up to $50, or a maximum 30 days imprisonment, or both.

Commentary:
> In some jurisdictions, a state statute may provide that a violation of an ordinance constitutes a misdemeanor and may prescribe the maximum penalties. In such cases, a statutory reference could be substituted for the foregoing language.

(b) Any act constituting a violation of the provisions of this chapter or a failure to comply with any of its requirements, including violations of any conditions and safeguards established in connection with the grants of variances or special-use or conditional-use permits, shall also subject the offender to a civil penalty of $25. If the offender fails to pay this penalty within 10 days after being cited for a violation, the penalty may be recovered by the city in a civil action in the nature of debt. A civil penalty may not be appealed to the board of adjustment if the offender was sent a final notice of violation in accordance with Section 113 and did not take an appeal to the board of adjustment within the prescribed time.

Commentary:

> Civil penalties, where authorized by statute, can be extremely useful tools in ordinance enforcement. Their principal virtue is that they constitute a sanction that can be applied without resort to the criminal process, where those seeking enforcement of zoning ordinances often encounter prosecutors' reluctance to prosecute and juries' reluctance to convict. But civil penalties (a "parking ticket" is probably the most familiar type of civil penalty) are enforced through the civil court system, and such penalties are regarded as obligations or debts of the violator, collectable in the same manner as other debts. In most jurisdictions, a rather informal but official process is available through some type of small claims court to hear such cases expeditiously. This saves time and minimizes expense.
>
> Civil penalties are not effective remedies for all types of violations. They work best against relatively minor violations that are not of a continuing nature—for example, where a person begins construction without obtaining a permit or installs a temporary or movable sign contrary to the requirements of the ordinance. They are least effective against serious, continuing violations such as a business that has opened in the wrong zoning district. In such cases, equitable relief (i.e., an injunction) is likely to be the only effective remedy.
>
> The last sentence of the foregoing subsection makes it clear that a violator does not have two opportunities to appeal to the board of adjustment.

(c) This chapter may also be enforced by any appropriate equitable action.

(d) Each day that any violation continues after notification by the administrator that such violation exists shall be considered a separate offense for purposes of the penalties and remedies specified in this section.

(e) Any one, all, or any combination of the foregoing penalties and remedies may be used to enforce this chapter.

Section 115: Permit Revocation

(a) A zoning, sign, special-use, or conditional-use permit may be revoked by the permit-issuing authority (in accordance with the provisions of this section) if the permit recipient fails to develop or maintain the property in accordance with the plans submitted, the requirements of this chapter, or any additional requirements lawfully imposed by the permit-issuing board.

(b) Before a conditional-use or special-use permit may be revoked, all of the notice and hearing and other requirements of Article VI shall be complied with. The notice shall inform the permit recipient of the alleged grounds for the revocation.

(1) The burden of presenting evidence sufficient to authorize the permit-issuing authority to conclude that a permit should be

revoked for any of the reasons set forth in Subsection (a) shall be upon the party advocating that position. The burden of persuasion shall also be upon that party.

(2) A motion to revoke a permit shall include, insofar as practicable, a statement of the specific reasons or findings of fact that support the motion.

(c) Before a zoning or sign permit may be revoked, the administrator shall give the permit recipient 10 days notice of intent to revoke the permit and shall inform the recipient of the alleged reasons for the revocation and of his right to obtain an informal hearing on the allegations. If the permit is revoked, the administrator shall provide to the permittee a written statement of the decision and the reasons therefor.

(d) No person may continue to make use of land or buildings in the manner authorized by any zoning, sign, special-use or conditional-use permit after such permit has been revoked in accordance with this section.

Commentary:

The permit revocation process is an important enforcement tool for two reasons. First, it provides for a sanction before court proceedings are initiated. While it may be true in theory that there is no more reason for a person to be concerned about violating the ordinance by operating without a permit than about violating the ordinance in some other way, experience demonstrates that permit revocation *does* have independent deterrent value. Second, if one is forced to go to court after a permit revocation proceeding, then the facts relating to the ordinance violation that justifies the permit revocation will be regarded by the court as having been established in that proceeding. In other words, review will be on the record rather than *de novo*, and the only factual issue before the courts will be whether the defendant is operating without a permit rather than whether the defendant is otherwise in violation of the ordinance.

**Section 116:
Judicial Review**

(a) Every decision of the city council granting or denying a conditional-use permit and every final decision of the board of adjustment shall be subject to review by the Superior Court of _____ County by proceedings in the nature of certiorari.

(b) The petition for the writ of certiorari must be filed with the _____ County Clerk of Court within 30 days after the later of the following occurrences:

(1) A written copy of the board's decision (see Section 106) has been filed in the office of the planning department, and

(2) A written copy of the board's decision (see Section 106) has been delivered by personal service or certified mail, return receipt requested, to the applicant or appellant and every other aggrieved party who has filed a written request for such copy at the hearing of the case.

(c) A copy of the writ of certiorari shall be served upon the City of _____.

**Sections 117 through 120:
Reserved**

Article VIII Nonconforming Situations

Commentary:

This article's coverage of nonconforming situations differs from that found in many ordinances in two ways. First, because much litigation in this area results from the failure of the ordinance to deal unambiguously with a wide variety of situations, this article attempts to deal more comprehensively and explicitly with this subject area than many ordinances. Second, this article takes a more liberal approach to nonconforming situations than is usually the case, providing for greater leeway in the renovation or repair of nonconforming uses and authorizing changes from one nonconforming use to another. This is done on the theory that, under more traditional ordinances, nonconforming uses generally do not fade away—they simply become more run-down and shabby looking. Therefore, the realistic choice is not between conformity and nonconformity but between a bad nonconformity and a better nonconformity.

Section 121: Definitions

Unless otherwise specifically provided or unless clearly required by the context, the words and phrases defined in this section shall have the meaning indicated when used in this article.

(1) *Dimensional Nonconformity.* A nonconforming situation that occurs when the height, size, or minimum floor space of a structure or the relationship between an existing building or buildings and other buildings or lot lines does not conform to the regulations applicable to the district in which the property is located.

(2) *Effective Date of This Chapter.* Whenever this article refers to the effective date of this chapter, the reference shall be deemed to include the effective date of any amendments to this chapter if the amendment, rather than this chapter as originally adopted, creates a nonconforming situation.

(3) *Expenditure.* A sum of money paid out in return for some benefit or to fulfill some obligation. The term also includes binding contractual commitments to make future expenditures, as well as any other substantial changes in position.

(4) *Nonconforming Lot.* A lot existing at the effective date of this chapter (and not created for the purposes of evading the restrictions of this chapter) that does not meet the minimum area requirement of the district in which the lot is located.

(5) *Nonconforming Project.* Any structure, development, or undertaking that is incomplete at the effective date of this chapter and would be inconsistent with any regulation applicable to the district in which it is located if completed as proposed or planned.

(6) *Nonconforming Sign.* A sign (see Section 270 for definition) that, on the effective date of this chapter does not conform to one or more of the regulations set forth in this chapter, particularly Article XVII, Signs.

(7) *Nonconforming Use.* A nonconforming situation that occurs when property is used for a purpose or in a manner made unlawful by the use regulations applicable to the district in which the property is located. (For example, a commercial office building in a residential district may be a nonconforming use.) The term also refers to the activity that constitutes the use made of the property. (For example, all the activity associated with running a bakery in a residentially zoned area is a nonconforming use.)

(8) *Nonconforming Situation.* A situation that occurs when, on the effective date of this chapter, an existing lot or structure or use of an existing lot or structure does not conform to one or more of the regulations applicable to the district in which the lot or structure is located. Among other possibilities, a nonconforming situation may arise because a lot does not meet minimum acreage requirements, because structures exceed maximum height limitations, because the relationship between existing buildings and the land (in such matters as density and setback requirements) is not in conformity with this chapter, or because land or buildings are used for purposes made unlawful by this chapter. Nonconforming signs shall not be regarded as nonconforming situations for purposes of this article but shall be governed by the provisions of Sections 285 and 286.

Section 122:
Continuation of Nonconforming Situations and Completion of Nonconforming Projects

(a) Unless otherwise specifically provided in this chapter and subject to the restrictions and qualifications set forth in Sections 123 through 128, nonconforming situations that were otherwise lawful on the effective date of this chapter may be continued.

(b) Nonconforming projects may be completed only in accordance with the provisions of Section 128.

Section 123:
Nonconforming Lots

(a) When a nonconforming lot can be used in conformity with all of the regulations applicable to the intended use, except that the lot is smaller than the required minimums set forth in Section 181, then the lot may be used as proposed just as if it were conforming. However, no use (e.g., a two-family residence) that requires a greater lot size than the established minimum lot size for a particular zone is permissible on a nonconforming lot.

(b) When the use proposed for a nonconforming lot is one that is conforming in all other respects but the applicable setback requirements (Section 184) cannot reasonably be complied with, then the entity authorized by this chapter to issue a permit for the proposed use (the administrator, board of adjustment, or council) may allow deviations from the applicable setback requirements if it finds that:

(1) The property cannot reasonably be developed for the use proposed without such deviations,

(2) These deviations are necessitated by the size or shape of the nonconforming lot, and

(3) The property can be developed as proposed without any significantly adverse impact on surrounding properties or the public health or safety.

(c) For purposes of Subsection (b), compliance with applicable building setback requirements is not reasonably possible if a building that serves the minimal needs of the use proposed for the nonconforming lot cannot practicably be constructed and located on the lot in conformity with such setback requirements. However, mere financial hardship does not constitute grounds for finding that compliance is not reasonably possible.

(d) This section applies only to undeveloped nonconforming lots. A lot is undeveloped if it has no substantial structures upon it. A change in use of a developed nonconforming lot may be accomplished in accordance with Section 126.

(e) Subject to the following sentence, if, on the date this section becomes effective, an undeveloped nonconforming lot adjoins and has continuous frontage with one or more other undeveloped lots under the same ownership, then neither the owner of the nonconforming lot nor his successors in interest may take advantage of the provisions of this section. This subsection shall not apply to a nonconforming lot if a majority of the developed lots located on either side of the street where such lot is located and within 500 feet of such lot are also nonconforming. The intent of this subsection is to require nonconforming lots to be combined with other undeveloped lots to create conforming lots under the circumstances specified herein, but not to require such combination when that would be out of character with the way the neighborhood has previously been developed.

Commentary:

The issue of how to treat contiguous nonconforming lots is a troublesome one, and legitimate pros and cons can be raised with respect to any alternative. The possibilities range from allowing all nonconforming lots to be developed to requiring that all contiguous, nonconforming lots under single ownership be combined into conforming lots. Subsection (e) sets forth a middle-of-the-road position. A more liberal approach would be to require the combination of nonconforming lots only in "paper" subdivisions, i.e., those where no lots have been sold and no improvements installed.

**Section 124:
Extension or Enlargement of Nonconforming Situations**

(a) Except as specifically provided in this section, no person may engage in any activity that causes an increase in the extent of nonconformity of a nonconforming situation. In particular, physical alteration of structures or the placement of new structures on open land is unlawful if such activity results in:

(1) An increase in the total amount of space devoted to a nonconforming use, or

(2) Greater nonconformity with respect to dimensional restrictions such as setback requirements, height limitations or density requirements or other requirements such as parking requirements.

(b) Subject to Subsection (d), a nonconforming use may be extended throughout any portion of a completed building that, when the use was made nonconforming by this chapter, was manifestly designed or arranged to accommodate such use. However, subject to Section 128 (authorizing the completion of nonconforming projects in certain circumstances), a nonconforming use may not be extended to additional buildings or to land outside the original building.

(c) Subject to Section 128 (authorizing the completion of nonconforming projects in certain circumstances), a nonconforming use of open land may not be extended to cover more land than was occupied by that use when it became nonconforming, except that a use that involves the removal of natural materials from the lot (e.g., a sand pit) may be expanded to the boundaries of the lot where the use was established at the time it became nonconforming if 10 percent or more of the earth products had already been removed on the effective date of this chapter.

Commentary: This subsection illustrates how this article attempts to deal specifically with a much litigated issue: whether the continued operation of a quarry (which by definition involves the continual expansion into new land) constitutes an unlawful expansion of a nonconforming use. From the point of view of the draftsman, it is less important how this question is answered than that it be answered.

(d) The volume, intensity, or frequency of use of property where a nonconforming situation exists may be increased and the equipment or processes used at a location where a nonconforming situation exists may be changed if these or similar changes amount only to changes in the degree of activity rather than changes in kind and no violations of other paragraphs of this section occur.

(e) Notwithstanding Subsection (a), any structure used for single-family residential purposes and maintained as a nonconforming use may be enlarged or replaced with a similar structure of a larger size, so long as the enlargement or replacement does not create new nonconformities or increase the extent of existing nonconformities with respect to such matters as setback and parking requirements. This paragraph is subject to the limitations stated in Section 127 (abandonment and discontinuance of nonconforming situations).

Commentary: This subsection also deals specifically with a frequently recurring question, i.e., whether a person may replace a smaller, nonconforming single-family residence (usually, a mobile home) with a larger one. The answer given here is consistent with the basic philosophy underlying this whole article, that since the nonconforming use (i.e., a mobile home) is not likely to be eliminated, it is better to allow it to be replaced with a more attractive home than to require that it be left in place to become more dilapidated and unsightly.

(f) Notwithstanding Subsection (a), whenever: (i) there exists a lot with one or more structures on it, and (ii) a change in use that does not involve any enlargement of a structure is proposed for such lot, and (iii) the parking or loading requirements of Article XVIII that would be applicable as a result of the proposed change cannot be satisfied on such lot because there is not sufficient area available on the lot that can practicably be used for parking or loading, then the proposed use shall not be regarded as resulting in an impermissible extension or enlargement of a nonconforming situation. However, the applicant shall be required to comply with all applicable parking and loading requirements that can be satisfied without acquiring additional land, and shall also be required to obtain satellite parking in accordance with Section 297 if: (i) parking requirements cannot be satisfied on the lot with respect to which the permit is required; and (ii) such satellite parking is reasonably available. If such satellite parking is not reasonably available at the time the zoning or special- or conditional-use permit is granted, then the permit recipient shall be required to obtain it if and when it does become reasonably available. This requirement shall be a continuing condition of the permit.

Commentary:

This subsection is also written from the lesser of evils point of view. Particularly in older sections of town, there may exist buildings on lots that are too small in relation to the building to provide adequate parking. If one use moves out and another requiring even more parking proposes to move in, this would constitute an illegal increase in a nonconforming situation in the absence of this subsection. The problem is that the proposed use may be the only tenant for the building. Therefore, one may have to make a choice between allowing the creation of a more nonconforming situation with respect to parking or requiring the building to remain vacant. This subsection accepts the former as the lesser of evils.

Section 125: Repair, Maintenance and Reconstruction

(a) Minor repairs to and routine maintenance of property where nonconforming situations exist are permitted and encouraged. Major renovation, i.e., work estimated to cost more than 25 percent of the appraised valuation of the structure to be renovated may be done only in accordance with a zoning permit issued pursuant to this section.

(b) If a structure located on a lot where a nonconforming situation exists is damaged to an extent that the costs of repair or replacement would exceed 25 percent of the appraised valuation of the damaged structure, then the damaged structure may be repaired or replaced only in accordance with a zoning permit issued pursuant to this section. This subsection does not apply to structures used for single-family residential purposes, which structures may be reconstructed pursuant to a zoning permit just as they may be enlarged or replaced as provided in Subsection 124(e).

(c) For purposes of Subsections (a) and (b):

  (1) The "cost" of renovation or repair or replacement shall mean the fair market value of the materials and services necessary to accomplish such renovation, repair, or replacement.

  (2) The "cost" of renovation or repair or replacement shall mean the total cost of all such intended work, and no person may seek to avoid the intent of Subsections (a) or (b) by doing such work incrementally.

  (3) The "appraised valuation" shall mean either the appraised valuation for property tax purposes, updated as necessary by the

increase in the consumer price index since the date of the last valuation, or the valuation determined by a professionally recognized property appraiser.

(d) The administrator shall issue a permit authorized by this section if he finds that, in completing the renovation, repair or replacement work:

(1) No violation of Section 124 will occur, and

(2) The permittee will comply to the extent reasonably possible with all provisions of this chapter applicable to the existing use (except that the permittee shall not lose his right to continue a nonconforming use).

Compliance with a requirement of this chapter is not reasonably possible if compliance cannot be achieved without adding additional land to the lot where the nonconforming situation is maintained or moving a substantial structure that is on a permanent foundation. Mere financial hardship caused by the cost of meeting such requirements as paved parking does not constitute grounds for finding that compliance is not reasonably possible.

Section 126: Change in Use of Property Where a Nonconforming Situation Exists

(a) A change in use of property (where a nonconforming situation exists) that is sufficiently substantial to require a new zoning, special-use, or conditional-use permit in accordance with Section 46 may not be made except in accordance with Subsections (b) through (d). However, this requirement shall not apply if only a sign permit is needed.

(b) If the intended change in use is to a principal use that is permissible in the district where the property is located, and all of the other requirements of this chapter applicable to that use can be complied with, permission to make the change must be obtained in the same manner as permission to make the initial use of a vacant lot. Once conformity with this chapter is achieved, the property may not revert to its nonconforming status.

(c) If the intended change in use is to a principal use that is permissible in the district where the property is located, but all of the requirements of this chapter applicable to that use cannot reasonably be complied with, then the change is permissible if the entity authorized by this chapter to issue a permit for that particular use (the administrator, board of adjustment, or council) issues a permit authorizing the change. This permit may be issued if the permit-issuing authority finds, in addition to any other findings that may be required by this chapter, that:

(1) The intended change will not result in a violation of Section 124, and

(2) All of the applicable requirements of this chapter that can reasonably be complied with will be complied with. Compliance with a requirement of this chapter is not reasonably possible if compliance cannot be achieved without adding additional land to the lot where the nonconforming situation is maintained or moving a substantial structure that is on a permanent foundation. Mere financial hardship caused by the cost of meeting such requirements as paved parking does not constitute grounds for finding that compliance is not reasonably possible. And in no case may an applicant be given permission pursuant to this

subsection to construct a building or add to an existing building if additional nonconformities would thereby be created.

(d) If the intended change in use is to another principal use that is also nonconforming, then the change is permissible if the entity authorized by this chapter to issue a permit for that particular use (administrator, board of adjustment, or council) issues a permit authorizing the change. The permit-issuing authority may issue the permit if it finds, in addition to other findings that may be required by this chapter, that:

(1) The use requested is one that is permissible in some zoning district with either a zoning, special-use, or conditional-use permit, and

(2) All of the conditions applicable to the permit authorized in Subsection (c) of this section are satisfied, and

(3) The proposed development will have less of an adverse impact on those most affected by it and will be more compatible with the surrounding neighborhood than the use in operation at the time the permit is applied for.

Section 127: Abandonment and Discontinuance of Nonconforming Situations

(a) When a nonconforming use is (i) discontinued for a consecutive period of 180 days, or (ii) discontinued for any period of time without a present intention to reinstate the nonconforming use, the property involved may thereafter be used only for conforming purposes.

(b) If the principal activity on property where a nonconforming situation other than a nonconforming use exists is (i) discontinued for a consecutive period of 180 days, or (ii) discontinued for any period of time without a present intention of resuming that activity, then that property may thereafter be used only in conformity with all of the regulations applicable to the preexisting use unless the entity with authority to issue a permit for the intended use issues a permit to allow the property to be used for this purpose without correcting the nonconforming situations. This permit may be issued if the permit-issuing authority finds that eliminating a particular nonconformity is not reasonably possible (i.e., cannot be accomplished without adding additional land to the lot where the nonconforming situation is maintained or moving a substantial structure that is on a permanent foundation). The permit shall specify which nonconformities need not be corrected.

(c) For purposes of determining whether a right to continue a nonconforming situation is lost pursuant to this section, all of the buildings, activities, and operations maintained on a lot are generally to be considered as a whole. For example, the failure to rent one apartment in a nonconforming apartment building for 180 days shall not result in a loss of the right to rent that apartment or space thereafter so long as the apartment building as a whole is continuously maintained. But if a nonconforming use is maintained in conjunction with a conforming use, discontinuance of a nonconforming use for the required period shall terminate the right to maintain it thereafter.

(d) When a structure or operation made nonconforming by this chapter is vacant or discontinued at the effective date of this chapter, the 180-day period for purposes of this section begins to run on the effective date of this chapter.

Section 128: Completion of Nonconforming Projects

(a) All nonconforming projects on which construction was begun at least 180 days before the effective date of this chapter as well as all nonconforming projects that are at least 10 percent completed in terms of the total expected cost of the project on the effective date of this chapter may be completed in accordance with the terms of their permits, so long as these permits were validly issued and remain unrevoked and unexpired. If a development is designed to be completed in stages, this subsection shall apply only to the particular phase under construction.

(b) Except as provided in Subsection (a), all work on any nonconforming project shall cease on the effective date of this chapter, and all permits previously issued for work on nonconforming projects may begin or may be continued only pursuant to a zoning, special-use, conditional-use, or sign permit issued in accordance with this section by the individual or board authorized by this chapter to issue permits for the type of development proposed. The permit-issuing authority shall issue such a permit if it finds that the applicant has in good faith made substantial expenditures or incurred substantial binding obligations or otherwise changed his position in some substantial way in reasonable reliance on the land-use law as it existed before the effective date of this chapter and thereby would be unreasonably prejudiced if not allowed to complete his project as proposed. In considering whether these findings may be made, the permit-issuing authority shall be guided by the following, as well as other relevant considerations:

(1) All expenditures made to obtain or pursuant to a validly issued and unrevoked building, zoning, sign, or special- or conditional-use permit shall be considered as evidence of reasonable reliance on the land-use law that existed before this chapter became effective.

(2) Except as provided in Subdivision (b)(1), no expenditures made more than 180 days before the effective date of this chapter may be considered as evidence of reasonable reliance on the land-use law that existed before this chapter became effective. An expenditure is made at the time a party incurs a binding obligation to make that expenditure.

(3) To the extent that expenditures are recoverable with a reasonable effort, a party shall not be considered prejudiced by having made those expenditures. For example, a party shall not be considered prejudiced by having made some expenditure to acquire a potential development site if the property obtained is approximately as valuable under the new classification as it was under the old, for the expenditure can be recovered by a resale of the property.

(4) To the extent that a nonconforming project can be made conforming and that expenditures made or obligations incurred can be effectively utilized in the completion of a conforming project, a party shall not be considered prejudiced by having made such expenditures.

(5) An expenditure shall be considered substantial if it is significant both in dollar amount and in terms of (i) the total estimated cost of the proposed project, and (ii) the ordinary business practices of the developer.

(6) A person shall be considered to have acted in good faith if actual knowledge of a proposed change in the land-use law affecting the proposed development site could not be attributed to him.

(7) Even though a person had actual knowledge of a proposed change in the land-use law affecting a development site, the permit-issuing authority may still find that he acted in good faith if he did not proceed with his plans in a deliberate attempt to circumvent the effects of the proposed ordinance. The permit-issuing authority may find that the developer did not proceed in an attempt to undermine the proposed ordinance if it determines that (i) at the time the expenditures were made, either there was considerable doubt about whether any ordinance would ultimately be passed, or it was not clear that the proposed ordinance would prohibit the intended development, and (ii) the developer had legitimate business reasons for making expenditures.

(c) When it appears from the developer's plans or otherwise that a project was intended to be or reasonably could be completed in phases, stages, segments, or other discrete units, the developer shall be allowed to complete only those phases or segments with respect to which the developer can make the showing required under Subsection (b). In addition to the matters and subject to the guidelines set forth in Subdivisions (1) through (6) of Subsection (b), the permit-issuing authority shall, in determining whether a developer would be unreasonably prejudiced if not allowed to complete phases or segments of a nonconforming project, consider the following in addition to other relevant factors:

(1) Whether any plans prepared or approved regarding uncompleted phases constitute conceptual plans only or construction drawings based upon detailed surveying, architectural, or engineering work.

(2) Whether any improvements, such as streets or utilities, have been installed in phases not yet completed.

(3) Whether utilities and other facilities installed in completed phases have been constructed in such a manner or location or such a scale, in anticipation of connection to or interrelationship with approved but uncompleted phases, that the investment in such utilities or other facilities cannot be recouped if such approved but uncompleted phases are constructed in conformity with existing regulations.

(d) The permit-issuing authority shall not consider any application for the permit authorized by Subsection (b) that is submitted more than 60 days after the effective date of this chapter. The permit-issuing authority may waive this requirement for good cause shown, but in no case may it extend the application deadline beyond one year.

(e) The administrator shall send copies of this section to the persons listed as owners for tax purposes (and developers, if different from the owners) of all properties in regard to which permits have been issued for nonconforming projects or in regard to which a nonconforming project is otherwise known to be in some stage of development. This notice shall be sent by certified mail not less than 15 days before the effective date of this chapter.

(f) The permit-issuing authority shall establish expedited procedures for hearing applications for permits under this section. These applications shall be heard, whenever possible, before the effective date of this chapter, so that construction work is not needlessly interrupted.

Commentary:

The foregoing section deals with the extremely difficult issue of when does a developer achieve a vested right to complete a project despite a change in the ordinance that would make some element or aspect of the project nonconforming. The law on this varies considerably from jurisdiction to jurisdiction. However the important point to be made here is that the ordinance should establish in the first instance the circumstances under which a vested right is obtained (within the guidelines of established precedent) just as it does with respect to other nonconforming situations. If the ordinance fails to do this, then a court is set free to fashion its own vested rights doctrine. However, if the ordinance itself establishes the guidelines, then the court's role is the much more limited one of deciding (i) whether the ordinance exceeds constitutional limitations and (ii) whether the ordinance has been correctly applied. In addition, if an administrative or quasi-judicial proceeding is established to determine the existence of vested rights on a case-by-case basis (as is done in this section), then a court's role is restricted to one of determining whether the administrative body acted arbitrarily or unlawfully, because the finding of facts by the administrative body will be binding on the court if supported by evidence in the record.

Sections 129 through 134: Reserved

Article IX Zoning Districts and Zoning Map

Part I. Zoning Districts

Section 135: Residential Districts Established

(a) The following residential districts are hereby established: R-40, R-15, R-11, R-7, and R-3. Each of these districts is designed and intended to secure for the persons who reside there a comfortable, healthy, safe, and pleasant environment in which to live, sheltered from incompatible and disruptive activities that properly belong in nonresidential districts. Other objectives of some of these districts are explained in the remainder of this section.

(b) The R-40 district is designed to accommodate single-family residential development in areas within the city's planning jurisdiction that are not served by public water or sewer facilities and that are not yet appropriate for development at higher densities. Some types of mobile homes are allowed to be used for single-family residential purposes in this district.

(c) The R-15 and R-11 districts are designed primarily to accommodate single-family detached residential uses (other than mobile homes) at medium densities in areas served by public water and sewer facilities. Two-family and multi-family residences are allowed in these districts only in the context of planned residential developments (see Section 158).

(d) The R-7 district is designed to accommodate single-family detached, two-family, and multi-family dwelling units, as well as some types of mobile homes used as single-family residences and mobile home parks.

(e) The R-3 zone is designed primarily to accommodate higher density multi-family developments.

Commentary:
> The types of zoning districts that each community will need will obviously depend upon the unique characteristics and circumstances of that community. The districts that are described in this section illustrate the kinds of districts that might be appropriate for a "typical" small city or town.

Section 136: Commercial Districts Established

(a) The following commercial districts are hereby established: B-1, B-2, B-2H, B-3, B-4, and B-5. These districts are created to accomplish the purposes and serve the objectives set forth in the remainder of this section.

(b) The B-1 (central business) district is designed to accommodate a wide variety of commercial activities (particularly those that are pedestrian oriented) that will result in the most intensive and attractive use of the city's central business district.

(c) The B-2 and B-2H (community business) districts are designed to accommodate commercial development on a scale that is less intensive than that permitted in a B-1 district. A lesser intensity of development is achieved through setback, height, and minimum lot size requirements that are more restrictive than those applicable to the B-1 zone. The types of uses permissible in these zones are generally similar to the types permissible in a B-1 zone, except that additional automobile-oriented businesses (e.g., drive-in banks and restaurants) not allowed in the B-1 zone are permissible in these zones. The B-2 and B-2H thus may provide a transition in some areas between a B-1 zone and a residential zone or may provide for a smaller scale shopping center that primarily serves one neighborhood or area of the city (as opposed to a regional shopping center). The dimensional restrictions in the zone are also designed in appropriate areas to encourage the renovation for commercial purposes of buildings that formerly were single-family residences. The only difference between the B-2 and B-2H zones is the difference in height limitations spelled out in Section 186. Therefore all other references in this chapter to the B-2 district shall be deemed to include the B-2H district.

(d) The B-3 (office/residential) district is designed to accommodate a mixture of residential uses and uses that fall primarily within the 3.000 classification in the Table of Permissible Uses (office, clerical, research, services, etc.). It is intended that this zoning classification be applied primarily in areas that no longer are viable as single-family residential areas because of high traffic volumes on adjacent streets or because of other market factors but remain viable as locations for multi-family residential developments or offices. Such areas will also generally constitute transition or buffer zones between major arterials or more intensively developed commercial areas and residential districts.

(e) The B-4 (general commercial) district is designed to accommodate the widest range of commercial activities.

(f) The B-5 (highway service) is designed to accommodate commercial activities that draw business primarily from and provide services primarily to [the interstate highway].

Section 137: Manufacturing Districts Established

The following districts are hereby established primarily to accommodate enterprises engaged in the manufacturing, processing, creating, repairing, renovating, painting, cleaning, or assembling of goods, merchandise, or equipment: M-1 and M-2. The performance standards set forth in Part 1 of Article XI place limitations on the characteristics of uses located in these districts. The limitations in the M-1 district are more restrictive than those in the M-2 district.

Section 138: Planned Unit Development Districts Established

(a) There are hereby established 24 different planned unit development (PUD) districts as described in this section. Each PUD district is designed to combine the characteristics of at least three and possibly four zoning districts.

(1) One element of each PUD district shall be the medium-density residential element. Here there are two possibilities, each one corresponding either to the R-15 or R-11 residential districts

described in Subsection 135(c). Within that portion of the PUD zone that is developed for medium density residential purposes, all development must be in accordance with the regulations applicable to the medium density residential district to which the particular PUD zoning district corresponds (except that planned residential developments shall not be permissible).

(2) A second element of each PUD district shall be the higher density residential element. Here there are two possibilities, each one corresponding either to the R-7 or R-3 zoning districts described in Subsections 135(d) and (e), respectively. Within that portion of the PUD district that is developed for higher density residential purposes, all development must be in accordance with the regulations applicable to the higher density residential district to which the PUD district corresponds.

(3) A third element of each PUD district shall be the commercial element. Here there are three possibilities, each one corresponding to one of the following commercial districts identified in Section 136: B-1, B-2, or B-3. Within that portion of a PUD district that is developed for purposes permissible in a commercial district, all development must be in accordance with the regulations applicable to the commercial district to which the PUD district corresponds.

(4) A manufacturing/processing element may be a fourth element of any PUD district. Here there are two alternatives. The first is that uses permitted within the M-1 district would be permitted within the PUD district. The second alternative is that uses permitted only within the M-1 or M-2 zoning districts would not be permitted. If an M-1 element is included, then within that portion of the PUD district that is developed for purposes permissible in an M-1 district, all development must be in accordance with the regulations applicable to the M-1 district.

(b) In accordance with the description set forth in Subsection (a), the 24 PUD districts shall carry the following designations to indicate their component elements:

(1) R-15, R-7, B-1, M-1
(2) R-15, R-7, B-1
(3) R-15, R-7, B-2, M-1
(4) R-15, R-7, B-2
(5) R-15, R-7, B-3, M-1
(6) R-15, R-7, B-3
(7) R-15, R-3, B-1, M-1
(8) R-15, R-3, B-1
(9) R-15, R-3, B-2, M-1
(10) R-15, R-3, B-2
(11) R-15, R-3, B-3, M-1
(12) R-15, R-3, B-3
(13) R-11, R-7, B-1, M-1

(14) R-11, R-7, B-1
(15) R-11, R-7, B-2, M-1
(16) R-11, R-7, B-2
(17) R-11, R-7, B-3, M-1
(18) R-11, R-7, B-3
(19) R-11, R-3, B-1, M-1
(20) R-11, R-3, B-1
(21) R-11, R-3, B-2, M-1
(22) R-11, R-3, B-2
(23) R-11, R-3, B-3, M-1
(24) R-11, R-3, B-3

(c) No area of less than 25 contiguous acres may be zoned as a PUD district, and then only upon the request of the owner or owners of all the property intended to be covered by such zone.

(d) As indicated in the Table of Permissible Uses (Section 146), a planned unit development (use classification 30.000) is the only permissible use of a PUD zone and planned unit developments are permissible only in such zones.

(e) Planned unit developments are subject to the requirements set forth in Section 159.

Commentary:

At this point, the reader should refer to Article II and note the definitional distinctions between planned unit developments, planned residential developments, and combination uses. In a B-2 zoning district, a development that combine single-family residences, multi-family residences, offices, and retail shops would be a combination use, not a planned unit development, since all four of these uses are permissible in a B-2 zoning district. But if a developer proposed such a project in an area zoned R-40 or R-15, he would have to first secure the appropriate PUD zoning.

Note that under this ordinance PUD approval is a two-step process: first, the property is rezoned and then a PUD conditional-use permit is issued. The reason this approach is suggested is that in most jurisdictions a local government has much more discretion in deciding whether to rezone property than it does in deciding whether to issue a permit for a proposed development that the ordinance makes conditionally permissible on a tract of land already zoned for that purpose.

Many ordinances spell out a whole series of use, density, and design requirements for PUDs that are separate and different from those applicable to other developments. This ordinance treats a PUD as if the tract on which it is developed were divided into various residential, commercial, and perhaps even industrial zoning districts. (Were it not for the concern about "spot zoning," the tract might actually be divided into various zoning districts. The approach taken here achieves the same objectives while reducing the dangers of a spot zoning challenge.) Then the tract may be developed in accordance with the use, density, and design regulations spelled out elsewhere in the ordinance.

**Section 139:
Floodplain and Floodway Districts**

The floodplain and floodway districts are hereby established as "overlay" districts, meaning that these districts are overlaid upon other districts and the land so encumbered may be used in a manner permitted in the underlying district only if and to the extent such use is also permitted in the applicable overlay district. The floodplain and floodway districts are further described in Part I of Article XVI of this chapter.

**Sections 140 and 141:
Reserved**

Part II. Zoning Map

**Section 142:
Official Zoning Map**

(a) There shall be a map known and designated as the Official Zoning Map, which shall show the boundaries of all zoning districts within the city's planning jurisdiction. This map shall be drawn on acetate or other durable material from which prints can be made, shall be dated, and shall be kept in the planning department.

(b) The Official Zoning Map dated _____ is adopted and incorporated herein by reference. Amendments to this map shall be made and posted in accordance with Section 143.

(c) Should the Official Zoning Map be lost, destroyed, or damaged, the administrator may have a new map drawn on acetate or other durable material from which prints can be made. No further council authorization or action is required so long as no district boundaries are changed in this process.

**Section 143:
Amendments to Official Zoning Map**

(a) Amendments to the Official Zoning Map are accomplished using the same procedures that apply to other amendments to this chapter, as set forth in Article XX.

(b) The administrator shall update the Official Zoning Map as soon as possible after amendments to it are adopted by the council. Upon entering any such amendment on the map, the administrator shall change the date of the map to indicate its latest revision. New prints of the updated map may then be issued.

(c) No unauthorized person may alter or modify the Official Zoning Map.

(d) The planning department shall keep copies of superseded prints of the zoning map for historical reference.

Commentary:

> It is vitally important that the local government take measures to ensure both that the zoning map is kept current and that copies of outdated maps are available for historical reference. Although the importance of the former is more obvious than the latter, accurate historical records are frequently necessary to determine the legitimacy of claims that lawful nonconforming use status has been achieved.

**Sections 144 and 145:
Reserved**

Article X Permissible Uses

Section 146:
Table of Permissible Uses

Commentary:

The Table of Permissible Uses (see pages 79-85) should be read in close conjunction with the definitions of terms set forth in Section 15 and the other interpretative provisions set forth in this article.

> The Table of Permissible Uses attempts to list separately those uses that have impacts that can be differentiated from other uses. In other words, uses are categorized according to their impacts rather than by naming the type of enterprise involved. Thus, for example, where more traditional ordinances list separately different types of retail stores (drug stores, grocery stores, florist shops, etc.), uses involving retail sales are categorized in this ordinance according to whether the enterprise tends to generate a higher or lower volume of traffic per square foot of floor space and whether goods are displayed outside enclosed buildings.
>
> The use classification numbers assigned to the different categories of uses provide a convenient, shorthand means of referencing use types in other parts of the ordinance, particularly in the articles dealing with parking and screening requirements.
>
> The commentary following the Table of Permissible Uses helps to explain many of the use classifications, and the numbered paragraphs of the commentary are keyed into the table with footnote references. The assignment of different types of uses to different types of districts in the table is done for illustrative purposes only. Each community must make its own choices based upon local needs and circumstances.

Table of Permissible Uses*

USES DESCRIPTION	ZONES											
	R40	R15	R11	R7	R3	B1	B2	B3	B4	B5	M1	M2
1.000 RESIDENTIAL[1]												
1.100 Single-Family Residences												
1.110 Single-family detached, one dwelling unit per lot[2]												
1.111 Site-built and modular structures	Z	Z	Z	Z	Z	Z	Z	Z				
1.112 Class "A" mobile home	Z			Z								
1.113 Class "B" mobile home	S											
1.114 Class "C" mobile home												
1.120 Single-family detached, more than one dwelling unit per lot												
1.121 Site-built and modular structures	ZSC	ZSC	ZSC	ZSC	ZSC	ZSC	ZSC	ZSC				
1.122 Class A, B, or C mobile homes (mobile home park)	ZSC			ZSC								
1.200 Two-Family Residences												
1.210 Two-family conversion				Z	Z	Z	Z	Z				
1.220 Primary residence with accessory apartment				ZSC	ZSC	ZSC	ZSC	ZSC				
1.230 Duplex				ZSC	ZSC	ZSC	ZSC	ZSC				
1.240 Two-family apartment				ZSC	ZSC	ZSC	ZSC	ZSC				
1.300 Multi-Family Residences												
1.310 Multi-family conversion				Z	Z	Z	Z	Z				
1.320 Multi-family townhomes				ZSC	ZSC	ZSC	ZSC	ZSC				
1.330 Multi-family apartments				ZSC	ZSC	ZSC	ZSC	ZSC				
1.400 Homes emphasizing special services, treatment, or supervision[3]												
1.410 Homes for handicapped or infirm		Z	Z	Z	Z			Z				
1.420 Nursing care, intermediate care homes		S	S	S	S			S				
1.430 Child care homes		S	S	S	S			S				
1.440 Halfway houses						S	S	S	S			
1.500 Miscellaneous, rooms for rent situations												
1.510 Rooming houses, boarding houses				S	S	S	S	S				
1.520 Tourist homes and other temporary residences renting by the day or week				S	S	S	S	S				
1.530 Hotels, motels, and similar businesses or institutions providing overnight accommodations						C	C	C	C	C		
1.600 Temporary emergency, construction, and repair residences	Z	Z	Z	Z	Z	Z	Z	Z	Z	Z	Z	Z
1.700 Home Occupations[4]	Z	Z	Z	Z	Z	Z	Z	Z				
1.800 Planned residential developments[5]		C	C									
2.000 SALES AND RENTAL OF GOODS, MERCHANDISE AND EQUIPMENT												

*See Section 147 for explanations of Z, S, C designations in Table of Permissible Uses.

Table of Permissible Uses

USES DESCRIPTION	R40	R15	R11	R7	R3	B1	B2	B3	B4	B5	M1	M2
2.100 No storage or display of goods outside fully enclosed building												
2.110 High-volume[6] traffic generation												
2.111 Miscellaneous						ZC	ZC		ZC	ZC		
2.112 Convenience stores							S		S	S		
2.120 Low-volume traffic generation						ZC	ZC		ZC	ZC		
2.130 Wholesale sales									ZC			
2.200 Storage and display of goods outside fully enclosed building allowed												
2.210 High-volume traffic generation									ZC	ZC	ZC	ZC
2.220 Low-volume traffic generation									ZC	ZC	ZC	ZC
2.230 Wholesale sales									ZC		ZC	ZC
3.000 OFFICE, CLERICAL, RESEARCH AND SERVICES NOT PRIMARILY RELATED TO GOODS OR MERCHANDISE												
3.100 All operations conducted entirely within fully enclosed building												
3.110 Operations designed to attract and serve customers or clients on the premises, such as the offices of attorneys, physicians, other professions, insurance and stock brokers, travel agents, government office buildings, etc.[6]						ZC	ZC	ZC	ZC	ZC	ZC	ZC
3.120 Operations designed to attract little or no customer or client traffic other than employees of the entity operating the principal use						ZC	ZC	ZC	ZC	ZC	ZC	ZC
3.130 Office or clinics of physicians or dentists with not more than 10,000 square feet of gross floor area						ZC	ZC	ZC	ZC			
3.200 Operations conducted within or outside fully enclosed building												
3.210 Operations designed to attract and serve customers or clients on the premises									ZC	ZC	ZC	ZC
3.220 Operations designed to attract little or no customer or client traffic other than the employees of the entity operating the principal use									ZC	ZC	ZC	ZC
3.230 Banks with drive-in windows						S	S	S				
4.000 MANUFACTURING, PROCESSING, CREATING, REPAIRING, RENOVATING, PAINTING, CLEANING, ASSEMBLING OF GOODS, MERCHANDISE AND EQUIPMENT[7]												
4.100 All operations conducted entirely within fully enclosed building												
4.110 Majority of dollar volume of business done with walk-in trade						ZC	ZC		ZC	ZC	ZC	ZC
4.120 Majority of dollar volume of business not done with walk-in trade							ZC		ZC	ZC	ZC	ZC

Table of Permissible Uses

USES DESCRIPTION		R40	R15	R11	R7	R3	B1	B2	B3	B4	B5	M1	M2
4.200	Operations conducted within or outside fully enclosed building									ZC	ZC	ZC	ZC
5.000	**EDUCATIONAL, CULTURAL, RELIGIOUS, PHILANTHROPIC, SOCIAL, FRATERNAL USES**												
5.100	**Schools**												
5.110	Elementary and secondary (including associated grounds and athletic and other facilities)	C	C	C	C	C							
5.120	Trade or vocational schools						S	S		S		S	S
5.130	Colleges, universities, community colleges (including associated facilities such as dormitories, office buildings, athletic fields, etc.)	C	C	C	C	C				C		C	C
5.200	Churches, synagogues, and temples (including associated residential structures for religious personnel and associated buildings but not including elementary school or secondary school buildings)	Z	Z	Z	Z	Z	Z	Z	Z	Z			
5.300	**Libraries, museums, art galleries, art centers, and similar uses (including associated educational and instructional activities)**												
5.310	Located within a building designed and previously occupied as a residence or within a building having a gross floor area not exceeding 3,500 square feet	S	S	S	S	S	Z	Z	Z	Z			
5.320	Located within any permissible structure						Z	Z	Z	Z			
5.400	Social, fraternal clubs and lodges, union halls, and similar uses						Z	Z		Z			
6.000	**RECREATION, AMUSEMENT, ENTERTAINMENT**												
6.100	**Activity conducted entirely within building or substantial structure**												
6.110	Bowling alleys, skating rinks, indoor tennis and squash courts, billiard and pool halls, indoor athletic and exercise facilities and similar uses						ZS	ZS		ZS	ZS		
6.120	Movie theatres												
6.121	Seating capacity of not more than 300						Z	Z		Z	Z		
6.122	Unlimited seating capacity						Z	Z		Z	Z		
6.130	Coliseums, stadiums, and all other facilities listed in the 6.100 classification designed to seat or accommodate simultaneously more than 1,000 people									C		C	C

Table of Permissible Uses

USES DESCRIPTION	ZONES											
	R40	R15	R11	R7	R3	B1	B2	B3	B4	B5	M1	M2
6.200 Activity conducted primarily outside enclosed buildings or structures												
6.210 Privately owned outdoor recreational facilities such as golf and country clubs, swimming or tennis clubs, etc., not constructed pursuant to a permit authorizing the construction of some residential development	S	S	S	S	S							
6.220 Publicly owned and operated outdoor recreational facilities such as athletic fields, golf courses, tennis courts, swimming pools, parks, etc., not constructed pursuant to a permit authorizing the construction of another use such as a school	C	C	C	C	C			C	C	C	C	C
6.230 Golf driving ranges not accessory to golf courses, par 3 golf courses, miniature golf courses, skateboard parks, water slides, and similar uses									ZS	ZS		
6.240 Horseback riding; stables (not constructed pursuant to permit authorizing residential development)	S											
6.250 Automobile and motorcycle racing tracks											S	S
6.260 Drive-in movie theatres									S		S	S
7.000 INSTITUTIONAL RESIDENCE OR CARE OR CONFINEMENT FACILITIES												
7.100 Hospitals, clinics, other medical (including mental health) treatment facilities in excess of 10,000 square feet of floor area									C			
7.200 Nursing care institutions, intermediate care institutions, handicapped or infirm institutions, child care institutions									S			
7.300 Institutions (other than halfway houses) where mentally ill persons are confined												
7.400 Penal and correctional facilities											C	C
8.000 RESTAURANTS, BARS, NIGHT CLUBS												
8.100 No substantial carry-out or delivery service, no drive-in service, no service or consumption outside fully enclosed structure						Z	Z		Z	Z		
8.200 No substantial carry-out or delivery service, no drive-in service, service or consumption outside fully enclosed structure allowed						Z	Z		Z	Z		
8.300 Carry-out and delivery service, consumption outside fully enclosed structure allowed								Z	Z	Z		
8.400 Carry-out and delivery service, drive-in service, service or consumption outside fully enclosed structure allowed									Z	Z		

Table of Permissible Uses

USES DESCRIPTION	ZONES											
	R40	R15	R11	R7	R3	B1	B2	B3	B4	B5	M1	M2
9.000 MOTOR VEHICLE-RELATED SALES AND SERVICE OPERATIONS												
9.100 Motor vehicle sales or rental; mobile home sales									Z			
9.200 Sales with installation of motor vehicle parts or accessories (e.g., tires, mufflers, etc.)							S		Z	Z		
9.300 Motor vehicle repair and maintenance, not including substantial body work							S		Z	Z	Z	Z
9.400 Motor vehicle painting and body work											Z	Z
9.500 Gas sales							Z		Z	Z		
9.600 Car wash							Z		Z	Z		
10.000 STORAGE AND PARKING												
10.100 Automobile parking garages or parking lots not located on a lot on which there is another principal use to which the parking is related						Z	Z	Z	Z			
10.200 Storage of goods not related to sale or use of those goods on the same lot where they are stored												
10.210 All storage within completely enclosed structures							Z		Z		Z	Z
10.220 Storage inside or outside completely enclosed structures									S		Z	Z
10.300 Parking of vehicles or storage of equipment outside enclosed structures where: (i) vehicles or equipment are owned and used by the person making use of lot, and (ii) parking or storage is more than a minor and incidental part of the overall use made of the lot									S		S	S
11.000 SCRAP MATERIALS SALVAGE YARDS, JUNKYARDS, AUTOMOBILE GRAVEYARDS											S	S
12.000 SERVICES AND ENTERPRISES RELATED TO ANIMALS												
12.100 Veterinarian	S								S			
12.200 Kennel	S								S			
13.000 EMERGENCY SERVICES												
13.100 Police Stations	C	C	C	C	C	C	C	C	C	C	C	C
13.200 Fire Stations	C	C	C	C	C	C	C	C	C	C	C	C
13.300 Rescue squad, ambulance service	C	C	C	C	C	C	C	C	C	C	C	C
13.400 Civil defense operation						S	S	S	S		S	S

Table of Permissible Uses

USES DESCRIPTION	R40	R15	R11	R7	R3	B1	B2	B3	B4	B5	M1	M2
14.000 AGRICULTURAL, SILVICULTURAL, MINING, QUARRYING OPERATIONS												
14.110 Agricultural operations, farming												
14.100 Excluding livestock	Z	Z	Z	Z	Z				Z	Z	Z	Z
14.120 Including livestock												
14.200 Silvicultural operations	Z	Z	Z						Z	Z	Z	Z
14.300 Mining or quarrying operations, including on-site sales of products											S	S
14.400 Reclamation landfill	Z	Z	Z	Z	Z	Z	Z	Z	Z	Z	Z	Z
15.000 MISCELLANEOUS PUBLIC AND SEMI-PUBLIC FACILITIES												
15.100 Post office						S	S		S			
15.200 Airport											C	C
15.300 Sanitary landfill	C											C
15.400 Military Reserve, National Guard Centers											S	S
16.000 DRY CLEANER, LAUNDROMAT							S		Z			
17.000 UTILITY FACILITIES												
17.100 Neighborhood	S	S	S	S	S	S	S	S	S	S	S	S
17.200 Community or Regional											S	S
18.000 TOWERS AND RELATED STRUCTURES												
18.100 Towers and antennas 50 feet tall or less	Z	Z	Z	Z	Z	Z	Z	Z	Z	Z	Z	Z
18.200 Towers and antennas more than 50 feet tall and receive-only earth station	S										Z	Z
19.000 OPEN AIR MARKETS AND HORTICULTURAL SALES												
19.100 Open air markets (farm and craft markets, flea markets, produce markets)										S		
19.200 Horticultural sales with outdoor display										Z		
20.000 FUNERAL HOME							Z	Z	Z			
21.000 CEMETERY AND CREMATORIUM												
21.100 Cemetery	C								C		C	C
21.200 Crematorium											S	S
22.000 NURSERY SCHOOLS; DAY CARE CENTERS	S	S	S	S	S		S	S	S			

85 Permissible Uses

Table of Permissible Uses

USES DESCRIPTION	ZONES											
	R40	R15	R11	R7	R3	B1	B2	B3	B4	B5	M1	M2
23.000 TEMPORARY STRUCTURES USED IN CONNECTION WITH THE CONSTRUCTION OF A PERMANENT BUILDING OR FOR SOME NON-RECURRING PURPOSE	Z	Z	Z	Z	Z	Z	Z	Z	Z	Z	Z	Z
24.000 BUS STATION, TRAIN STATION						S	S		S			
25.000 COMMERCIAL GREENHOUSE OPERATIONS												
25.100 No on-premises sales	S	S					Z		Z	Z	Z	Z
25.200 On-premise sales permitted							Z		Z	Z	Z	Z
26.000 SPECIAL EVENTS	C	C	C	C	C	C	C	C	C	C	C	C
27.000 OFF PREMISES SIGNS										Z	Z	Z
28.000 SUBDIVISIONS												
28.100 Major	C	C	C	C	C	C	C	C	C	C	C	C
28.200 Minor	Z	Z	Z	Z	Z	Z	Z	Z	Z	Z	Z	Z
29.000 COMBINATION USES	ZSC	ZSC	ZSC	ZSC	ZSC	ZSC	ZSC	ZSC	ZSC	ZSC	ZSC	ZSC
30.000 PLANNED UNIT DEVELOPMENTS	Permissible only in planned unit development districts with a conditional-use permit.											

[1] The ordinance must carefully distinguish between types of residential uses so the governing body can make deliberate policy choices about where different types of residential uses ought to be allowed. (See Section 15 for definitions of the types of residential uses listed in the table.) Once the "where" question is answered, the density issue can be addressed (see Sections 181 and 182).

The definitions of residential types in Section 15 are written in such a way that whether a development is subdivided or unsubdivided or whether the units are intended for rent or sale has no definitional significance. Neither should such factors have any bearing on where the different types of residential uses are allowed.

The term "condominium" does not appear in the definition section or the table because this term refers to a type of ownership—not a type of residence. The condominium form of ownership can be applied to all types of residential types—including single-family detached residences. (Not infrequently, mobile home parks are condominiums.)

[2] The issue of where mobile homes should be allowed is one of the most controversial and difficult questions faced by the local governing body. This ordinance distinguishes between modular and mobile homes and further distinguishes between types of mobile homes which may enable the governing body to devise a more satisfactory solution to the mobile home problem than is possible if all types of manufactured homes are lumped in one category.

[3] This ordinance attempts to distinguish between homes emphasizing special services, treatment, or supervision and institutions providing similar services on a much larger scale. The latter are listed under use classification 7.000. See Section 15 for the definitional distinctions between the uses in classification 1.400 and those in classification 7.000.

Particularly with respect to homes for the handicapped (often called "group homes"), the issue of whether and to what degree such homes may be treated differently than other single-family residences under zoning ordinances has been frequently litigated, and a fair amount of state legislation has also been enacted on this subject. Local law should be checked before completing the Table of Permissible Uses with respect to this type of use.

[4] This ordinance takes a three-tier approach to the issue of the extent to which residents may use their own homes for business purposes. At the least intrusive level, business activities may be regarded as part of an accessory use for which no additional permit is needed. See Section 150 for a more detailed explanation of an accessory use. A home occupation

constitutes the second tier, and a zoning permit is required for commercial activities that rise to this level (as defined in Secton 15). Business activities that are more extensive than those permitted as home occupations fall in the third category—nonpermitted uses.

[5]In most communities, areas that have been developed primarily with single-family detached residences continue to resist vociferously any intrusion into the neighborhood of multi-family developments. Of course, there is no inherent incompatibility between single-family and multi-family residential uses, as is demonstrated often by the successful marketing of planned residential developments in which both types of units are sold. However, in such planned developments, the purchasers of the single-family units are aware of the inclusion within the development of multi-family units, and, by definition, all types of residences are properly oriented and designed to be compatible with the rest of the development. But when new multi-family developments seek to locate next to preexisting single-family residential subdivisions, the residents of such subdivisions very often are understandably less accommodating toward what they perceive as an intrusion that may adversely affect their property.

The planned residential development use classification seeks to address this problem by allowing multi-family residences in single-family zoning districts only in the context of a well-planned development containing both single-and multi-family dwellings, with the single-family units acting as a "buffer" between the development and preexisting single-family neighborhoods.

[6]The high volume/low volume traffic generation dichotomy is drawn so that different parking standards can be applied to uses that tend to generate different parking needs per unit of floor area. For the same reason, a distinction is drawn within the 3.000 classification between the types of offices that attract persons other than employees and those that do not.

[7]Manufacturing/processing uses are allowed in specified business districts, but only where there is no adverse impact on adjacent properties. See the performance standards set forth in Article XI, Part 1. If such uses were entirely forbidden in all business districts, this would preclude the butcher, the baker, and the candlestick maker.

Section 147: Use of the Designations Z, S, C in Table of Permissible Uses

(a) Subject to Section 148, when used in connection with a particular use in the Table of Permissible Uses (Section 146), the letter "Z" means that the use is permissible in the indicated zone with a zoning permit issued by the administrator. The letter "S" means a special-use permit must be obtained from the board of adjustment, and the letter "C" means a conditional-use permit must be obtained from the city council.

(b) When used in connection with residential uses (use classification 1.000), the designation "ZSC" means that such developments of less than five dwelling units must be pursuant to a zoning permit, developments of five or more but less than 13 dwelling units need a special-use permit, and developments of 13 or more dwelling units require a conditional-use permit.

(c) When used in connection with nonresidential uses, the designation "ZS" or "ZC" means that such developments require a zoning permit if the lot to be developed is less than one acre in size and a special- or conditional-use permit, respectively, if the lot is one acre or larger in area.

(d) Use of the designation ZSC for combination uses is explained in Section 154.

Commentary:

The commentary following Section 46 describes the differences between the types of permits and explains why a particular project should be required to obtain one type of permit rather than another. In general, the type of permit required depends upon the perceived impact of the development. Because the Table of Permissible Uses classifies uses into general categories, some technique is needed to separate those uses within a particular classification that have little impact (and therefore need only a zoning permit) from those whose impact is more substantial

87 Permissible Uses

(thereby requiring a special- or conditional-use permit). This ordinance chooses to do this according to the size of the development. Thus, for example, a small retail store or group of stores occupying less than one acre would require only a zoning permit, while a shopping center greater than one acre would need a conditional-use permit.

**Section 148:
Board of Adjustment Jurisdiction Over Uses Otherwise Permissible With a Zoning Permit**

Notwithstanding any other provisions of this article, whenever the Table of Permissible Uses (interpreted in the light of Section 147 and the other provisions of this article) provides that a use in a nonresidential zone or a nonconforming use in a residential zone is permissible with a zoning permit, a special-use permit shall nevertheless be required if the administrator finds that the proposed use would have an extraordinary impact on neighboring properties or the general public. In making this determination, the administrator shall consider, among other factors, whether the use is proposed for an undeveloped or previously developed lot, whether the proposed use constitutes a change from one principal use classification to another, whether the use is proposed for a site that poses peculiar traffic or other hazards or difficulties, and whether the proposed use is substantially unique or is likely to have impacts that differ substantially from those presented by other uses that are permissible in the zoning district in question.

Commentary:

The foregoing section represents an attempt to provide the local government with enough flexibility so that projects that would ordinarily fall within a category requiring only a zoning permit can be subjected to the greater scrutiny inherent in the special-use permit process if the project is perceived to have an extraordinary impact. The governing body is likely to feel more secure in providing for approval of more types of projects with only a zoning permit if the ordinance provides this type of flexibility to deal with the unusual case.

**Section 149:
Permissible Uses and Specific Exclusions**

(a) The presumption established by this chapter is that all legitimate uses of land are permissible within at least one zoning district in the city's planning jurisdiction. Therefore, because the list of permissible uses set forth in Section 146 (Table of Permissible Uses) cannot be all inclusive, those uses that are listed shall be interpreted liberally to include other uses that have similar impacts to the listed uses.

(b) Notwithstanding Subsection (a), all uses that are not listed in Section 146 (Table of Permissible Uses), even given the liberal interpretation mandated by Subsection (a), are prohibited. Nor shall Section 146 (Table of Permissible Uses) be interpreted to allow a use in one zoning district when the use in question is more closely related to another specified use that is permissible in other zoning districts.

(c) Without limiting the generality of the foregoing provisions, the following uses are specifically prohibited in all districts:

(1) Any use that involves the manufacture, handling, sale, distribution, or storage of any highly combustible or explosive materials in violation of the city's fire prevention code.

(2) Stockyards, slaughterhouses, rendering plants.

(3) Use of a travel trailer as a temporary or permanent residence. (Situations that do not comply with this subdivision on the

effective date of this chapter are required to conform within one year. See Section 130.)

(4) Use of a motor vehicle parked on a lot as a structure in which, out of which, or from which any goods are sold or stored, any services are performed, or other business is conducted. (Situations that do not comply with this subdivision on the effective date of this chapter are required to conform within 30 days. See Section 130.)

Commentary:

Subsection (a) attempts to deal with the reality that not even the most prescient of draftsmen can anticipate and describe all types of permissible uses. It authorizes the administrator to treat a proposed use that does not neatly fit into any specified use classification in the same manner as the use that is most similar in terms of impacts. However, Subsection (b) seeks to guard against the possibility that some unanticipated and undesirable use could claim permissible standing. It provides that uses that do not have impacts similar to listed uses are not allowed, at least until the ordinance is amended to deal with them.

Section 150: Accessory Uses

(a) The Table of Permissible Uses (Section 146) classifies different principal uses according to their different impacts. Whenever an activity (which may or may not be separately listed as a principal use in this table) is conducted in conjunction with another principal use and the former use (i) constitutes only an incidental or insubstantial part of the total activity that takes place on a lot, or (ii) is commonly associated with the principal use and integrally related to it, then the former use may be regarded as accessory to the principal use and may be carried on underneath the umbrella of the permit issued for the principal use. For example, a swimming pool/tennis court complex is customarily associated with and integrally related to a residential subdivision or multi-family development and would be regarded as accessory to such principal uses, even though such facilities, if developed apart from a residential development, would require a special-use permit (use classification 6.210).

(b) For purposes of interpreting Subsection (a):

(1) A use may be regarded as incidental or insubstantial if it is incidental or insubstantial in and of itself or in relation to the principal use,

(2) To be "commonly associated" with a principal use it is not necessary for an accessory use to be connected with such principal use more times than not, but only that the association of such accessory use with such principal use takes place with sufficient frequency that there is common acceptance of their relatedness.

(c) Without limiting the generality of Subsections (a) and (b), the following activities, so long as they satisfy the general criteria set forth above, are specifically regarded as accessory to residential principal uses:

(1) Offices or studios within an enclosed building and used by an occupant of a residence located on the same lot as such building to carry on administrative or artistic activities of a commercial nature, so long as such activities do not fall within the definition of a home occupation.

(2) Hobbies or recreational activities of a noncommercial nature.

(3) The renting out of one or two rooms within a single-family residence (which one or two rooms do not themselves constitute a separate dwelling unit) to not more than two persons who are not part of the family that resides in the single-family dwelling.

(4) Yard sales or garage sales, so long as such sales are not conducted on the same lot for more than three days (whether consecutive or not) during any 90-day period.

(**d**) Without limiting the generality of Subsections (a) and (b), the following activities shall not be regarded as accessory to a residential principal use and are prohibited in residential districts.

(1) Storage outside of a substantially enclosed structure of any motor vehicle that is neither licensed nor operational.

(2) Parking outside a substantially enclosed structure of more than four motor vehicles between the front building line of the principal building and the street on any lot used for purposes that fall within the following principal use classifications: 1.100, 1.200, or 1.400.

Commentary:

The accessory use, like the nonconforming use, often presents interpretative problems. Subsections (a) and (b) above attempt to distinguish between principal uses and accessory uses. Subsection (c) deals with several recurring situations and clarifies that they are to be regarded as accessory to residential principle uses. Subsection (d) illustrates how the land-use ordinance may be used to deal with some commonly encountered problems in residential areas.

Section 151: Permissible Uses Not Requiring Permits

Notwithstanding any other provisions of this chapter, no zoning, special-use, or conditional-use permit is necessary for the following uses:

(1) Streets.

(2) Electric power, telephone, telegraph, cable television, gas, water, and sewer lines, wires or pipes, together with supporting poles or structures, located within a public right-of-way.

(3) Neighborhood utility facilities located within a public right-of-way with the permission of the owner (state or town) of the right-of-way.

Commentary:

This section makes clear that governmental bodies and public utilities need not obtain permits under the land-use ordinance before enlarging, installing, or extending public streets or utility facilities. Of course, if such facilities are constructed within new subdivisions or other types of developments, they would be reviewed in that context.

Section 152: Change in Use

(a) A substantial change in use of property occurs whenever the essential character or nature of the activity conducted on a lot changes. This occurs whenever:

(1) The change involves a change from one principal use category to another.

(2) If the original use is a combination use (29.000) or planned unit development (30.000), the relative proportion of space devoted to the individual principal uses that comprise the combination use or planned unit development use changes to such an extent that the parking requirements for the overall use are altered.

(3) If the original use is a combination use or planned unit development use, the mixture of *types* of individual principal uses that comprise the combination use or planned unit development use changes.

(4) If the original use is a planned residential development, the relative proportions of different types of dwelling units change.

(5) If there is only one business or enterprise conducted on the lot (regardless of whether that business or enterprise consists of one individual principal use or a combination use), that business or enterprise moves out and a different type of enterprise moves in (even though the new business or enterprise may be classified under the same principal use or combination use category as the previous type of business). For example, if there is only one building on a lot and a florist shop that is the sole tenant of that building moves out and is replaced by a clothing store, that constitutes a change in use even though both tenants fall within principal use classification 2.111. However, if the florist shop were replaced by another florist shop, that would not constitute a change in use since the type of business or enterprise would not have changed. Moreover, if the florist shop moved out of a rented space in a shopping center and was replaced by a clothing store, that would not constitute a change in use since there is more than one business on the lot and the essential character of the activity conducted on that lot (shopping center—combination use) has not changed.

(b) A mere change in the status of property from unoccupied to occupied or vice versa does not constitute a change in use. Whether a change in use occurs shall be determined by comparing the two active uses of the property without regard to any intervening period during which the property may have been unoccupied, unless the property has remained unoccupied for more than 180 consecutive days or has been abandoned.

(c) A mere change in ownership of a business or enterprise or a change in the name shall not be regarded as a change in use.

Commentary:

The definition of change in use is critical because apart from physical alteration to buildings or land it is the change from one use to another that triggers the need to obtain a permit under this ordinance (see Section 46). The broader this definition is written, the more circumstances there will be that require a developer to seek a permit. It is a policy question how broadly this definition should sweep, and the foregoing section illustrates one approach to this issue.

Note that, because of Subdivision (a)(2) and (3), it is important that the developers of office buildings and shopping centers apply for the types of combination uses that will accommodate the full range of likely future tenants. Otherwise, a new permit for the entire development would have to be obtained before a tenant engaged in an anticipated use could occupy the property.

Section 153:
Developments in the
B-5 Zoning District

The 2.000, 3.000, and 4.000 classifications in the Table of Permissible Uses are written in very broad terms. However, it is the intention of this chapter that uses described in those classifications are permissible in an area zoned B-5 only when the particular use is in accordance with the objectives of the B-5 zoning district set forth in Section 136. Thus, tourist-oriented retail stores or outlet stores that are oriented toward interstate traffic are permitted, while major grocery stores that are primarily oriented toward and draw their business mostly from area residents are not.

Section 154:
Combination Uses

(a) When a combination use comprises two or more principal uses that require different types of permits (zoning, special-use, or conditional-use), then the permit authorizing the combination use shall be:

(1) A conditional-use permit if any of the principal uses combined requires a conditional-use permit.

(2) A special-use permit if any of the principal uses combined requires a special-use permit but none requires a conditional-use permit.

(3) A zoning permit in all other cases.

This is indicated in the Table of Permissible Uses by the designation ZSC in each of the columns adjacent to the 29.000 classification.

(b) When a combination use consists of a single-family detached residential subdivision that is not architecturally integrated (see Section 188) and two-family or multi-family uses, the total density permissible on the entire tract shall be determined by having the developer indicate on the plans the portion of the total lot that will be developed for each purpose and calculating the density for each portion as if it were a separate lot.

(c) When a combination use consists of a single-family detached, architecturally integrated subdivision and two-family or multi-family uses, then the total density permissible on the entire tract shall be determined by dividing the area of the tract by the minimum square footage per dwelling unit specified in Section 182.

Commentary:

> For clarification of Subsections (b) and (c), see the discussion on density in the commentary following Section 182.

Section 155:
More Specific Use Controls

Whenever a development could fall within a more than one use classification in the Table of Permissible Uses (Section 146), the classification that most closely and most specifically describes the development controls. For example, a small doctor's office or clinic clearly falls within the 3.110 classification (office and service operations conducted entirely indoors and designed to attract customers or clients to the premises). However, classification 3.130, "office or clinics of physicians or dentists with not more than 10,000 square feet of gross floor area" more specifically covers this use and therefore is controlling.

Sections 156 and 157:
Reserved

Article XI Supplementary Use Regulations

Part I. General Provisions

Commentary:
As the name suggests, this article contains additional regulations applicable to specific types of uses that supplement the requirements found in other articles. Part I deals with miscellaneous uses and Part II sets forth performance requirements applicable to 4.000 classification uses. Sections in Part I will tend to be added over time as a community has experience with particular types of uses and sees the need to develop regulations applicable just to those uses.

**Section 158:
Planned Residential Developments**

(a) Planned residential developments (PRDs) are permissible only on tracts of at least five acres located within an R-11 or R-15 zoning district.

(b) The overall density of a tract developed by a PRD shall be determined as provided in Section 182.

(c) Permissible types of residential uses within a PRD include single-family detached dwellings (use classification 1.111), two-family residences (1.200), and multi-family residences (1.300). At least 50 percent of the total number of dwelling units must be single-family detached residences on lots of at least 7,000 square feet.

(d) A PRD shall be an architecturally integrated subdivision.

(e) To the extent practicable, the two-family and multi-family portions of a PRD shall be developed more toward the interior rather than the periphery of the tract so that the single-family detached residences border adjacent properties.

(f) In a planned residential development, the screening requirements that would normally apply where two-family or multi-family development adjoins a single-family development shall not apply within the tract developed as a planned residential development, but all screening requirements shall apply between the tract so developed and adjacent lots.

Commentary:
See the Table of Permissible Uses, Footnote 5.

**Section 159:
Planned Unit Developments**

(a) In a planned unit development, the developer may make use of the land for any purpose authorized in a particular PUD zoning district in which the land is located, subject to the provisions of this chapter. Section 138 describes the various types of PUD zoning districts.

(b) Within any lot developed as a planned unit development, not more than 35 percent of the total lot area may be developed for higher density residential puposes (R-7 or R-3, as applicable), not more than 10 percent of the total lot area may be developed for purposes that are permissible only in a B-1, B-2, or B-3 zoning district (whichever corresponds to the PUD zoning district in question), and not more than 5 percent of the total lot area may be developed for uses permissible only in the M-1 zoning district (assuming the PUD zoning district allows such uses at all).

(c) The plans for the proposed planned unit development shall indicate the particular portions of the lot that the developer intends to develop for higher density residential purposes, lower density residential purposes, purposes permissible in a commercial district (as applicable), and purposes permissible only in an M-1 district (as applicable). For purposes of determining the substantive regulations that apply to the planned unit development, each portion of the lot so designated shall then be treated as if it were a separate district, zoned to permit, respectively, higher density residential (R-7 or R-3), lower density residential (R-15 or R-11), commercial or M-1 uses. However, only one permit—a planned unit development permit—shall be issued for the entire development.

(d) The nonresidential portions of any planned unit development may not be occupied until all of the residential portions of the development are completed or their completion is assured by any of the mechanisms provided in Article IV to guarantee completion. The purpose and intent of this provision is to ensure that the planned unit development procedure is not used, intentionally or unintentionally, to create nonresidential uses in areas generally zoned for residential uses except as part of an integrated and well-planned, primarily residential development.

Commentary: See the commentary following Section 138.

Section 160: Temporary Emergency, Construction, or Repair Residences

(a) Temporary residences used on construction sites of nonresidential premises shall be removed immediately upon the completion of the project.

(b) Permits for temporary residences to be occupied pending the construction, repair, or renovation of the permanent residential building on a site shall expire within six months after the date of issuance, except that the administrator may renew such permit for one additional period not to exceed three months if he determines that such renewal is reasonably necessary to allow the proposed occupants of the permanent residential building to complete the construction, repair, renovation, or restoration work necessary to make such building habitable.

Section 161: Special Events

(a) In deciding whether a permit for a special event should be denied for any reason specified in Subsection 54(d), or in deciding what additional conditions to impose under Section 60, the council shall ensure that, (if the special event is conducted at all):

(1) The hours of operation allowed shall be compatible with the uses adjacent to the activity.

(2) The amount of noise generated shall not disrupt the activities of adjacent land uses.

(3) The applicants shall guarantee that all litter generated by the special event be removed at no expense to the city.

(4) The council shall not grant the permit unless it finds that the parking generated by the event can be accommodated without undue disruption to or interference with the normal flow of traffic or with the right of adjacent and surrounding property owners.

(b) In cases where it is deemed necessary, the council may require the applicant to post a bond to ensure compliance with the conditions of the conditional-use permit.

(c) If the permit applicant requests the city to provide extraordinary services or equipment or if the city manager otherwise determines that extraordinary services or equipment should be provided to protect the public health or safety, the applicant shall be required to pay to the city a fee sufficient to reimburse the city for the costs of these services. This requirement shall not apply if the event has been anticipated in the budget process and sufficient funds have been included in the budget to cover the costs incurred.

Sections 162 through 170: Reserved

Part II. Manufacturing/Processing Performance Standards

Commentary:

All zoning ordinances are concerned with the impacts of development and seek to ensure that the way one person uses his property does not unreasonably interfere with another person's use of his property. Control of negative impacts can be achieved indirectly by regulating where types of uses can go, and directly by regulating the impacts themselves through performance standards. Performance standards fall into two general categories: subjective and quantitative.

To illustrate the foregoing, consider noise regulation. If a community is concerned about protecting its residential areas from obnoxious noise, it can accomplish this in large part through zoning by limiting the permissible uses in such areas to residential uses. This controls the noise impacts indirectly. Alternatively, the zoning ordinance might allow a wider variety of uses, subject to the condition that such uses not generate "offensive noise." This would be an example of a subjective performance standard. Finally, the ordinance might specify a quantitative standard—in this case, a decibel limit.

It would be ideal if quantitative performance standards could be developed for all types of impacts because then zoning ordinances could do away with permissible use tables and measure all impacts directly. Unfortunately for reasons discussed in the foreword, that approach is not yet practical is most jurisdictions. However, this guidebook does present illustrative performance standards to regulate manufacturing/processing uses for two reasons. First, the need for performance standards is greater with respect to these types of uses than it is for other uses such as commercial, residential, and office where the impacts are commonly known and where indirect regulation therefore makes more sense. The various types of enterprises that fall within the 4.000 use classification differ so widely in terms of impacts that the alternative to a performance approach would be an enormous laundry list of types of uses. Second, "industrial" performance standards have been included in zoning ordinances for years and therefore it is possible for draftsmen to draw upon the experience of other communities to develop standards that are workable and enforceable.

Sections 171 through 178, like all other sections of this guidebook, are presented to stimulate thinking concerning the types of provisions a land-use ordinance might contain. The reader will note that both subjective and quantitative performance standards are illustrated.

Section 171: Smoke

(a) For the purpose of determining the density of equivalent opacity of smoke, the Ringlemann Chart, as adopted and published by the United States Department of Interior, *Bureau of Mines Information Circular 8333*, May 1967, shall be used. The Ringlemann number referred to in this section refers to the number of the area of the Ringlemann Chart that coincides most nearly with the visual density of equivalent opacity of the emission of smoke observed. For example, a reading of Ringlemann No. 1 indicates a 20 percent density of the smoke observed.

(b) All measurements shall be taken at the point of emission of the smoke.

(c) In the B-1, B-2, B-3, B-4, B-5, and all PUD districts, no 4.000 classification use may emit from a vent, stack, chimney, or combustion process any smoke that is visible to the naked eye.

(d) In the M-1 district, no 4.000 classification use may emit from a vent, stack, chimney, or combustion process any smoke that exceeds a density or equivalent capacity of Ringlemann No. 1, except that an emission that does not exceed a density or equivalent capacity of Ringlemann No. 2 is permissible for a duration of not more than four minutes during any eight-hour period if the source of such emission is not located within 250 feet of a residential district.

(e) In the M-2 district, no 4.000 classification use may emit from a vent, stack, chimney, or combustion process any smoke that exceeds a density or equivalent capacity of Ringlemann No. 2, except that an emission that does not exceed a density or equivalent capacity of Ringlemann No. 3 is permissible for a duration not more than four minutes during any eight-hour period if the source of emission is not located within 500 feet of a residential district.

Section 172: Noise

(a) No 4.000 classification use in any permissible business district may generate noise that tends to have an annoying or disruptive effect upon (i) uses located outside the immediate space occupied by the 4.000 use if that use is one of several located on a lot, or (ii) uses located on adjacent lots.

(b) Except as provided in Subsection (f), the table set forth in Subsection (e) establishes the maximum permissible noise levels for 4.000 classification uses in the M-1 and M-2 districts. Measurements shall be taken at the boundary line of the lot where the 4.000 classification use is located, and, as indicated, the maximum permissible noise levels vary according to the zoning of the lot adjacent to the lot on which the 4.000 classification use is located.

(c) A decibel is a measure of a unit of sound pressure. Since sound waves having the same decibel level "sound" louder or softer to the human ear depending upon the frequency of the sound wave in cycles-per-second (i.e., whether the pitch of the sound is high or low) an A-weighted filter constructed in accordance with the specifications of the American National Standards Institute, which automatically takes account of the varying effect on the human ear of different pitches, shall be used on any sound level meter taking measurements required by this section. And accordingly, all measurements are expressed in dB(A) to reflect the use of his A-weighted filter.

(d) The standards established in the table set forth in Subsection (e) are expressed in terms of the Equivalent Sound Level (Leq), which must be calculated by taking 100 instantaneous A-weighted sound levels at 10-second intervals (see Appendix F–1) and computing the Leq in accordance with the table set forth in Appendix F–2.

(e) Table of Maximum Permitted Sound Levels, dB(A).

	(re: 0.0002 Microbar) Zoning of Adjacent Lot				
Zoning of Lot Where 4,000 Use Located	Residential and PUD 7 a.m.–7 p.m.	7 p.m.–7 a.m.	B1, B2 B3, B4, B5	M1	M2
M-1	50	45	55	60	65
M-2	50	45	60	65	70

(f) Impact noises are sounds that occur intermittently rather than continuously. Impact noises generated by sources that do not operate more than one minute in any one-hour period are permissible up to a level of 10 dB(A) in excess of the figures listed in Subsection (e), except that this higher level of permissible noise shall not apply from 7 p.m. to 7 a.m. when the adjacent lot is zoned residential. The impact noise shall be measured using the fast response of the sound level meter.

(g) Noise resulting from temporary construction activity that occurs between 7 a.m. and 7 p.m. shall be exempt from the requirements of this section.

Section 173: Vibration

(a) No 4.000 classification use in any permissible business district may generate any ground-transmitted vibration that is perceptible to the human sense of touch measured at (i) the outside boundary of the immediate space occupied by the enterprise generating the vibration if the enterprise is one of several located on a lot, or (ii) the lot line if the enterprise generating the vibration is the only enterprise located on a lot.

(b) No 4.000 classification use in an M-1 or M-2 district may generate any ground-transmitted vibration in excess of the limits set forth in Subsection (e). Vibration shall be measured at any adjacent lot line or residential district line as indicated in the table set forth in Subsection (d).

(c) The instrument used to measure vibrations shall be a three-component measuring system capable of simultaneous measurement of vibration in three mutually perpendicular directions.

(d) The vibration maximums set forth in Subsection (e) are stated in terms of particle velocity, which may be measured directly with suitable instrumentation or computed on the basis of displacement and frequency. When computed, the following formula shall be used:

$$PV = 6.28\, F \times D$$

Where:
PV = Particle velocity, inches-per-second
F = Vibration frequency, cycles-per-second
D = Single amplitude displacement of the vibration, inches.

The maximum velocity shall be the vector sum of the three components recorded.

(e) Table of Maximum Ground-Transmitted Vibration

Zoning District	Particle Velocity, Inches-Per-Second	
	Adjacent Lot Line	Residential District
M-1	0.10	0.02
M-2	0.20	0.02

(f) The values stated in Subsection (e) may be multiplied by two for impact vibrations, i.e., discrete vibration pulsations not exceeding one second in duration and having a pause of at least one second between pulses.

(g) Vibrations resulting from temporary construction activity that occurs between 7 a.m. and 7 p.m. shall be exempt from the requirements of this section.

Section 174: Odors

(a) For purposes of this section, the "odor threshold" is defined as the minimum concentration in air of a gas, vapor, or particulate matter that can be detected by the olfactory systems of a panel of healthy observers.

(b) No 4.000 classification use in any district may generate any odor that reaches the odor threshold, measured at:

(1) The outside boundary of the immediate space occupied by the enterprise generating the odor.

(2) The lot line if the enterprise generating the odor is the only enterprise located on a lot.

Section 175: Air Pollution

(a) Any 4.000 classification use that emits any "air contaminant" as defined in [the appropriate state statute] shall comply with applicable state standards concerning air pollution, as set forth in [the state air pollution control law].

(b) No zoning, special-use, or conditional-use permit may be issued with respect to any development covered by Subsection (a) until the [state agency with jurisdiction] has certified to the permit-issuing authority that the appropriate state permits have been received by the developer, or that the developer will be eligible to receive such permits and that the development is otherwise in compliance with applicable air pollution laws.

**Section 176:
Disposal of Liquid Wastes**

(a) No 4.000 classification use in any district may discharge any waste contrary to the provisions of [the state law governing discharges of radiological, chemical, or biological wastes into surface or subsurface waters].

(b) No 4.000 classification use in any district may discharge into the city sewage treatment facilities any waste that cannot be adequately treated by biological means.

**Section 177:
Water Consumption**

No 4.000 classification use that requires for its operation a daily average of more than _____ gallons of water per employee is permissible in any district.

**Section 178:
Electrical Disturbance or Interference**

No 4.000 classification use may:

(a) Create any electrical disturbance that adversely affects any operations or equipment other than those of the creator of such disturbance, or

(b) Otherwise cause, create, or contribute to the interference with electronic signals (including television and radio broadcasting transmissions) to the extent that the operation of any equipment not owned by the creator of such disturbance is adversely affected.

**Sections 179 and 180:
Reserved**

Article XII Density and Dimensional Regulations

Section 181: Minimum Lot Size

Subject to the provisions of Sections 187 (Cluster Subdivisions) and 188 (Architecturally Integrated Subdivisions), all lots in the following zones shall have at least the amount of square footage indicated in the following table:

Zone	Minimum Square Feet
R-3	3,000
R-7	7,000
R-11	11,000
R-15	15,000
R-20	20,000
R-40	40,000
B-1	3,000*
B-2	5,000*
B-3	7,000
B-4	No Minimum
B-5	No Minimum
M-1	No Minimum
M-2	No Minimum

*If used for residential purposes, otherwise no minimum.

Commentary:

As the commentary following Section 182 explains, a minimum lot size requirement is often used to regulate residential density. Even in ordinances that allow deviation from established minimum lot sizes for greater design flexibility—as this one does through its cluster subdivision and architecturally integrated subdivision provisions—a minimum lot size is still necessary to control density when land is subdivided without using these techniques.

There is less need to establish minimum lot sizes in nonresidential zones unless one is pursuaded that market forces may not be sufficient to prevent the division of land into lots that are too small to be developed.

Section 182: Residential Density

(a) Subject to Subsection (b) and the provisions of Section 187 (Cluster Subdivisions) and Section 188 (Architecturally Integrated Subdivisions), every lot developed for residential purposes shall have the number of square feet per dwelling unit indicated in the following table. In determining the number of dwelling units permissible on a tract of land, fractions shall be rounded to the nearest whole number.

Zone	Minimum Square Feet Per Dwelling Unit
R-3	3,000
R-7	7,000
R-11	11,000
R-15	15,000
R-20	20,000
R-40	40,000
B-1	3,000
B-2	5,000
B-3	7,000

(b) Two-family conversions and primary residences with an accessory apartment shall be allowed only on lots having at least 150 percent of the minimum square footage required for one dwelling unit on a lot in such district. With respect to multi-family conversions into three- or four-dwelling units, the minimum lot size shall be 200 percent and 250 percent respectively of the minimum required for one dwelling unit.

Commentary:

There are several different ways to regulate residential density, and the draftsman will have to investigate each to determine which will best meet the community's needs. Careful attention should be paid to the possible market bias that each technique introduces. The standard residential density control techniques are as follows:

Minimum lot size. With respect to standard single-family residential subdivisions, a minimum lot size requirement controls density. Obviously, the greater the minimum lot size, the lower the density. However note that for two reasons a minimum lot size does not translate readily into a dwelling-units-per-acre equivalent. First, a substantial portion (usually 10 to 20 percent) of the lot will be consumed by street rights-of-way. And second, unless the shape of the tract and its topography cooperate perfectly, many of the lots will have to exceed the minimum lot size. The significance of this is twofold. First, it is impossible to know how many single-family lots can actually be created out of a parcel of a given size until sufficient planning work has been done to sketch out road locations and potential lot configurations. Second, if both single-family and multi-family residences are permitted on a tract of a given size, and if the minimum lot size is 10,000 square feet and the multi-family density is established by a requirement of 10,000 square feet per dwelling unit, the multi-family density (determined by dividing the total square footage of the lot by 10,000) will be substantially higher than the actual single-family density.

The latter two consequences can be avoided by providing for "architecturally integrated subdivisions" (see definition in Section 15, and Section 188). In these subdivisions, minimum lot sizes are waived and the overall density is determined by dividing the total square footage of the tract (without first subtracting street rights-of-way) by the minimum square footage per dwelling unit. The density would thus be the same as the density for multi-family uses, and a developer would know what this density would be before engaging in site planning work. If one wanted to make the density in architecturally integrated subdivisions correspond more closely to that in standard subdivisions, this could be accomplished by requiring that a fixed percentage (10 to 20 percent) of the tract size be subtracted (to accommodate road development) before dividing the remainder by the minimum square footage per dwelling unit.

Square feet per dwelling unit. The text of the foregoing section illustrates this approach to residential density control. Density expressed in dwelling units per acre constitutes another way of saying the same thing (i.e., 8,700 square feet per dwelling unit equals five units per acre). However, the author's preference is to use the approach illustrated above since it seems to involve fewer calculations when determining the density of most parcels of land.

One drawback of this technique is that it may not be as good a determinant of the number of people who reside on a tract of a given size (the true measure of density) as the other techniques described below since a developer may construct dwelling units of any size containing any number of bedrooms. In addition, this approach may provide a market incentive to build larger homes and two- and three-bedroom apartments rather than smaller units if one assumes that the developer's return is greater on the larger units. (This assumption may or may not be true, but the draftsman should not ignore the fact that his choice of density control techniques may have an impact on the type of units builders choose to construct.)

Square feet per bedroom. If the ordinance establishes increasing minimum square footage figures for dwelling units having one, two, and three or more bedrooms, this may control more closely the actual number of people who reside within a given area. However, it may also create a bias in the marketplace toward construction of one-bedroom units since a developer can maximize the number of permissible dwelling units on a given tract of land by building such units. Again, whether this regulatory approach would have this effect on a particular market should be investigated by the draftsman.

Floor/area ratio. Although a floor/area ratio (FAR) approach is used most often to control nonresidential density, some ordinances also use this technique to regulate residential density. A floor/area ratio is simply a fraction, expressed in decimal form, with the permissible square footage of building floor area as the numerator and the square footage of the lot as the denominator. Thus, with a FAR of .092, a developer could construct approximately 4,000 square feet of floor area per acre, or four dwelling units of 1,000 square feet each.

This technique also regulates actual density more closely than the square-footage-per-dwelling-unit approach. However, local planning boards and governing bodies may not grasp it as easily as other techniques. After all, in determining what the density of a particular area should be, "four dwelling units per acre" conjures up a mental picture not generated by "FAR of .092." In addition the FAR technique, unless modified, does not work well to regulate density in developments that include subdivisions where the developer has not predetermined the exact size of all dwelling units. In other words, with a given square footage of building area, a developer knows how many dwelling units are permissible only if he knows at the outset how large each dwelling unit will be. But if the development is intended to include some single-family residential lots, a developer cannot know how many lots to create unless he also determines in advance which style home will be located on each lot. Most developers prefer to give lot buyers a choice, but if the developer did this and the early buyers chose larger homes, the developer might use up his floor area allocation before all lots were developed. To avoid this, the ordinance could establish an assumed average size dwelling—say 1,200 square feet—and allocate this to each undeveloped lot within a proposed development.

This ordinance does not use floor/area ratios to regulate nonresidential density. It has been the author's experience that the combination of parking requirements, setback restrictions, and height limitations, together with the operation of market forces, satisfactorily control nonresidential density.

Section 183: Minimum Lot Widths

(a) No lot may be created that is so narrow or otherwise so irregularly shaped that it would be impracticable to construct on it a building that:

(1) Could be used for purposes that are permissible in that zoning district, and

(2) Could satisfy any applicable setback requirements for that district.

(b) Without limiting the generality of the foregoing standard, the following table indicates minimum lot widths that are recommended and are deemed presumptively to satisfy the standard set forth in Subsection (a). The lot width shall be measured along a straight line connecting the points at which a line that demarcates the required setback from the street intersects with lot boundary lines at opposite sides of the lot.

Zone	Lot Width (in feet)
R-40	100
R-20	100
R-15	85
R-11	80
R-7	70
R-3	50
B-1	None
B-2	50
B-3	70
B-4	100
B-5	100
M-1	100
M-2	100

(c) No lot created after the effective date of this chapter that is less than the recommended width shall be entitled to a variance from any building setback requirement.

Commentary:

Most ordinances establish inflexible minimum lot width standards. This often creates unnecessary hardships, particularly in residential developments, where the real concern should be density rather than lot width. The foregoing section establishes a general standard in Subsection (a) that can be used in the development review process. The table in Subsection (b) is provided as a guide to the developer, but the minimum lot widths set forth in this table are only presumptive.

**Section 184:
Building Setback Requirements**

(a) Subject to Sections 185 and 188 and the other provisions of this section, no portion of any building or any freestanding sign may be located on any lot closer to any lot line or to the street right-of-way line or centerline than is authorized in the table set forth in this section.

(1) If the street right-of-way line is readily determinable (by reference to a recorded map, set irons, or other means), the setback shall be measured from such right-of-way line. If the right-of-way line is not so determinable, the setback shall be measured from the street centerline.

Commentary:

It is important that the ordinance spell out the point from which front setbacks are to be measured. Street right-of-way lines are preferred, but in many areas it may be impossible to determine on the ground where the right-of-way is. Thus, the foregoing subdivision provides an alternative point of measurement, the street centerline.

(2) As used in this section, the term "lot boundary line" refers to lot boundaries other than those that abut streets.

(3) As used in this section, the term "building" includes any substantial structure which by nature of its size, scale, dimensions, bulk, or use tends to constitute a visual obstruction or generate activity similar to that usually associated with a building. Without limiting the generality of the foregoing, the following structures shall be deemed to fall within this description:

   a. Gas pumps and overhead canopies or roofs.

   b. Fences running along lot boundaries adjacent to public street rights-of-way if such fences exceed six feet in height and are substantially opaque.

(4) Notwithstanding any other provision of this chapter, a sign may be erected on or affixed to a structure that (i) has a principal function that is something other than the support of the sign (e.g., a fence), but (ii) does not constitute a building as defined in this chapter, only if such sign is located so as to comply with the setback requirement applicable to freestanding signs in the district where such sign is located.

Commentary:

This provision is necessary to prevent signs from being attached to certain structures located very near the street that are not regarded as buildings but that do have some function other than sign support (the typical fence would be the most common example). In the absence of this provision, such signs would be governed by neither the building nor sign setback requirements.

	Minimum Distance From: Street Right-of-Way Line		Street Centerline		Lot Boundary Line
Zone	Building	Freestanding Sign	Building	Freestanding Sign	Building and Freestanding Sign
R-40	40	20	70	50	20
R-20	35	17.5	65	47.5	15
R-15	30	15	60	45	15
R-11	25	12.5	55	52.5	12
R-7	20	10	50	40	10
R-3	20	10	50	40	8
B-1	—	—	30	30	—
B-2	15	7.5	45	37.5	10
B-3	15	7.5	45	37.5	15
B-4	40	20	70	50	15
B-5	60	30	90	60	20
M-1	30	15	60	45	20
M-2	40	20	70	50	25

Commentary:

Note that the foregoing table does not differentiate between side and rear setbacks. Some communities prefer to handle this differently, and those that do generally establish greater setbacks for the rear yard than the side yard.

(b) Whenever a lot in a nonresidential district has a common boundary line with a lot in a residential district, and the property line setback requirement applicable to the residential lot is greater than that applicable to the nonresidential lot, then the lot in the nonresidential district shall be required to observe the property line setback requirement applicable to the adjoining residential lot.

(c) Setback distances shall be measured from the property line or street right-of-way line to a point on the lot that is directly below the nearest extension of any part of the building that is substantially a part of the building itself and not a mere appendage to it (such as a flagpole, etc.).

Commentary:

The ordinance should describe how the setback lines are measured and what can encroach within a specified setback. This subsection illustrates one formulation. Note also that the setback requirements apply to buildings only, and not all structures, but see Subdivision 184(a)(3) for the special meaning given to the term "building" as used in this section.

(d) Whenever a private road that serves more than three lots or more than three dwelling units or that serves any nonresidential use tending to generate traffic equivalent to more than three dwelling units is located along a lot boundary, then:

(1) If the lot is not also bordered by a public street, buildings and freestanding signs shall be set back from the centerline of the private road just as if such road were a public street.

(2) If the lot is also bordered by a public street, then the setback distance on lots used for residential purposes (as set forth above in the column labeled "Minimum Distance from Lot Boundary Line") shall be measured from the inside boundary of the travelled portion of the private road.

Section 185: Accessory Building Setback Requirements

All accessory buildings in residential districts (i.e., those established by Section 135) must comply with the street right-of-way and side lot boundary setbacks set forth in Section 184 but (subject to the remaining provisions of this subsection) shall be required to observe only a four-foot setback from rear lot boundary lines.

(1) Where the high point of the roof or any appurtenance of an accessory building exceeds 12 feet in height, the accessory building shall be set back from rear lot boundary lines an additional two feet for every foot of height exceeding 12 feet.

(2) Maximum lot coverage of principal and accessory buildings shall not exceed 40 percent of the lot.

Section 186: Building Height Limitations

(a) For purposes of this section:

(1) The height of a building shall be the vertical distance measured from the mean elevation of the finished grade at the front of the building to the highest point of the building.

(2) A point of access to a roof shall be the top of any parapet wall or the lowest point of a roof's surface, whichever is greater. Roofs with slopes greater than 75 percent are regarded as walls.

(b) Subject to the remaining provisions of this section, building height limitations in the various zoning districts shall be as follows:

Zone	Height Limitation (in feet)
R-40, R-20, R-15,	35
R-11, R-7	35
R-3	60
B-1	85
B-2, B-3	35
B-2H, B-4, B-5	60
M-1, M-2	85

(c) Subject to Subsection (d), the following features are exempt from the district height limitations set forth in Subsection (b):

(1) Chimneys, church spires, elevator shafts, and similar structural appendages not intended as places of occupancy or storage,

(2) Flagpoles and similar devices,

(3) Heating and air conditioning equipment, solar collectors, and similar equipment, fixtures, and devices.

(d) The features listed in Subsection (c) are exempt from the height limitations set forth in Subsection (b) if they conform to the following requirements:

(1) Not more than one-third of the total roof area may be consumed by such features.

(2) The features described in Subdivision (c)(3) above must be set back from the edge of the roof a minimum distance of one foot for every foot by which such features extend above the roof surface of the principal building to which they are attached.

(3) The permit-issuing authority may authorize or require that parapet walls be constructed (up to a height not exceeding that of the features screened) to shield the features listed in Subdivisions (b)(1) and (3) from view.

(e) Notwithstanding Subsection (b), in any zoning district the vertical distance from the ground to a point of access to a roof surface of any nonresidential building or any multi-family residential building containing four or more dwelling units may not exceed 35 feet unless the fire chief certifies to the permit-issuing authority that such building is designed to provide adequate access for fire fighting personnel or the building inspector certifies that the building is otherwise designed or equipped to provide adequate protection against the dangers of fire.

Commentary:
> This subsection is probably necessary only in those communities that do not have available fire fighting equipment capable of reaching taller buildings.

(f) Towers and antennas are allowed in all zoning districts to the extent authorized in the Table of Permissible Uses, use classification 18.000.

Section 187: Cluster Subdivisions

(a) In any single-family residential subdivision in the zones indicated below, a developer may create lots that are smaller than those required by Section 181 if such developer complies with the provisions of this section and if the lots so created are not smaller than the minimums set forth in the following table:

Zone	Minimum Square Feet
R-7	5,250
R-11	8,250
R-15	11,250
R-20	15,000
R-40	15,000

(b) The intent of this section is to authorize the developer to decrease lot sizes and leave the land "saved" by so doing as usable open space, thereby lowering development costs and increasing the amenity of the project without increasing the density beyond what would be permissible if the land were subdivided into the size of lots required by Section 181.

(c) The amount of usable open space that must be set aside shall be determined by:

(1) Subtracting from the standard square footage requirement set forth in Section 181 the amount of square footage of each lot that is smaller than that standard;

(2) Adding together the results obtained in (1) for each lot.

(d) The provisions of this section may only be used if the usable open space set aside in a subdivision comprises at least 10,000 square feet of space that satisfies the definition of usable open space set forth in Section 198 and if such usable open space is otherwise in compliance with the provisions of Article XIII.

(e) The setback requirements of Sections 184 and 185 shall apply in cluster subdivisions.

Commentary:

> The cluster subdivision approach would be used primarily by the developer who intends to subdivide land and sell lots only, leaving to the purchaser complete discretion concerning the size and type of home and its location on the lot (subject, of course, to setback restrictions). If the developer intends to sell lots with houses already on them, he would probably use the provisions of Section 188, which confer upon the developer considerably greater design flexibility.
>
> Although the cluster subdivision is not intended to provide greater density than the standard subdivision, there is the possibility of a slight increase in density using the cluster approach because with smaller lots less land will be consumed in street rights-of-way.

Section 188: Architecturally Integrated Subdivisions

(a) In any architecturally integrated subdivision, the developer may create lots and construct buildings without regard to any minimum lot size, lot width, or setback restrictions except that:

(1) Lot boundary setback requirements shall apply where and to the extent that the subdivided tract abuts land that is not part of the subdivision, and

(2) Each lot must be of sufficient size and dimensions that it can support the structure proposed to be located on it, consistent with all other applicable requirements of this chapter.

(b) The number of dwelling units in an architecturally integrated subdivision may not exceed the maximum density authorized for the tract under Section 182.

(c) To the extent reasonably practicable, in residential subdivisions the amount of land "saved" by creating lots that are smaller than the standards set forth in Section 181 shall be set aside as usable open space.

(d) The purpose of this section is to provide flexibility, consistent with the public health and safety and without increasing overall density, to the developer who subdivides property and constructs buildings on the lots created in accordance with a unified and coherent plan of development.

Commentary:

> In the standard subdivision, minimum lot sizes are needed to control density, and setback requirements are necessary to ensure lot purchasers that their neighbors will not surprise them by constructing their homes right up to their lot lines. However, in an architecturally integrated subdivision, the approved plans show the location and minimum dimensions of all houses so there are no surprises. The development is constructed in accordance with an overall design scheme, and no one purchases a lot unless that design scheme is acceptable. In this way, the developer has total design flexibility subject only to the overall density limitation. See the commentary following Section 182 for a discussion of density in architecturally integrated residential developments.

Section 189: Density on Lots Where Portion Dedicated to City

(a) Subject to the other provisions of this section, if (i) any portion of a tract lies within an area designated on any officially adopted city plan as part of a proposed public park, greenway, or bikeway, and (ii) before the tract is developed, the owner of the tract, with the concurrence of the city, dedicates to the city that portion of the tract so designated, then, when the remainder of the tract is developed for residential purposes, the permissible density at which the remainder may be developed shall be calculated in accordance with the provisions of this section.

(b) If the proposed use of the remainder is a single-family detached residential subdivision, then the lots in such subdivision may be reduced in accordance with the provisions of Sections 187 and 188 except that the developer need not set aside usable open space to the extent that an equivalent amount of land has previously been dedicated to the city in accordance with Subsection (a).

(c) If the proposed use of the remainder is a two-family or multi-family project, then the permissible density at which the remainder may be developed shall be calculated by regarding the dedicated portion of the original lot as if it were still part of the lot proposed for development.

(d) If the portion of the tract that remains after dedication as provided in Subsection (a) is divided in such a way that the resultant parcels are intended for future subdivision or development, then each of the resultant parcels shall be entitled to its pro rata share of the "density bonus" provided for in Subsections (b) and (c).

Commentary:

> Land dedications most often occur at the time property is developed. However, the foregoing section provides an incentive to donate land before development of the remainder occurs by allowing the owner to include the dedicated land when calculating permissible density on the remainder.

Sections 190 through 195: Reserved

Article XIII Recreational Facilities and Open Space

Commentary:

In recent years, more local governments have recognized the need to require developers to provide recreational facilities and usable open space to serve residents of the development. These facilities not only provide a more desirable living environment for the residents of such developments, but also somewhat reduce the demand for comparable facilities developed or acquired at public expense.

Public recreational facilities owned by local governments vary widely in scale, from the minipark that may contain no more than a few benches to the regional park that may offer swimming pools, tennis courts, ball fields, lakes, and hiking trails. Some ordinances seek to require the developer to construct only those recreational facilities that are needed to serve the residents of his development. Where statutory authority is available, others may require a developer to contribute fees to a recreational fund so that the local government will have the resources to provide the larger scale recreational facilities necessitated by the cumulative impact of many developments.

The approach taken in this article is rather conservative because it requires the developer to install only those recreational facilities that the development in question needs. The ordinance does not offer the developer the alternative of paying fees in lieu of installing the improvements, nor does it require the payment of fees to contribute to a fund designed to finance community recreational facilities. Draftsmen may wish to explore these alternatives, but the legal authority to adopt either one should be carefully researched.

Section 196: Miniparks Required

(a) Subject to Subsection (c), all residential developments shall provide (through dedication or reservation; see Sections 199 and 200) recreational areas in the form of miniparks (as described in Section 197) in an amount equal to .0025 acres (108.9 square feet) per person expected to reside in that development (as determined in accordance with Subsection (b)). Such recreational areas shall be provided in addition to the open space areas required by Section 198.

Commentary:

See commentary following Subsection (b) of this section.

(b) For purposes of this section, one-bedroom dwelling units shall be deemed to house an average of 1.4 persons, two-bedroom units 2.2 persons, three-bedroom units 3.2 persons, and units with four or more bedrooms 4.0 persons. In residential subdivisions that are not approved as architecturally integrated subdivisions, each lot that is large enough for only a single dwelling unit shall be deemed to house an average of 3.2 persons. Each lot that is large enough to accommodate more than one dwelling unit shall be deemed to house 2.2 persons for each dwelling unit that can be accommodated.

Commentary:

Subsections (a) and (b) together provide one formula for determining the amount of recreational facilities required. The draftsman should check the specific figures carefully to see if they yield the desired result in the local situation.

(c) The council recognizes that miniparks must be of a certain minimum size to be usable and that such miniparks will not serve the intended purpose unless properly maintained. Therefore, residential developments that are small enough so that the amount of required minipark space does not exceed 2,000 square feet are exempt from the provisions of this section. However, as used in the foregoing sentence, the term development refers to the entire project developed on a single tract or contiguous multiple tracts under common ownership, regardless of whether the development is constructed in phases or stages. In addition, subdivided residential developments of less than 25 dwelling units shall also be exempt from the provisions of this section.

Commentary:

Subsection (c) deals with the reality that some developments—e.g., a quadraplex on an isolated lot—are too small to require the developer to construct a useful recreational facility. As indicated in the commentary that precedes this article, if statutory authority is available, the local government may wish to require such small-scale developers to contribute a fee in lieu of the recreational facilities, but this effort to achieve perfect equality may be more trouble than it is worth. The third sentence is designed to assure that the exemption is not abused.

The exemption of subdivided developments containing less than 25 dwelling units is included in recognition that someone must maintain commonly owned recreational facilities, and unless the local government wants to perform that chore, the someone must be a homeowners' association. The fewer the members in a homeowners' association the less likely it is that the association will have the resources to maintain common facilities properly and the more likely it is that the local government will be pressured to take over the maintenance of the facilities. The number 25 has no magic, but it seems an appropriate dividing line. (The same number is used in the context of developments allowed to maintain private roads; see Section 220.)

Section 197: Miniparks: Purpose and Standards

(a) The purpose of the minipark is to provide adequate active recreational facilities to serve the residents of the immediately surrounding neighborhood within the development. The following are illustrative of the types of facilities that shall be deemed to serve active recreational needs and therefore to count toward satisfaction of the minipark requirements of this article: tennis courts, racquetball courts, swimming pools, sauna and exercise rooms, meeting or activity rooms within clubhouses, basketball courts, swings, slides, and play apparatus.

(b) Each development shall satisfy its minipark requirement by installing the types of recreational facilities that are most likely to be suited to and used by the age bracket of persons likely to reside in that development. However, unless it appears that less than 5 percent of the residents of any development are likely to be children under 12, then at least 15 percent of the minipark must be satisfied by the construction of "tot lots" (i.e., areas equipped with imaginative play apparatus oriented to younger children as well as seating accommodations for parents).

Commentary:
> As a practical matter, the developer usually knows what market his development is designed to serve, and therefore the determination that this subsection requires is not hard to make. The "tot lot" requirement is included because experience demonstrates that while many developers would in any event install recreational facilities believed to make their developments more marketable, such as swimming pools or tennis courts, the "tot lot" type of facility is one that receives considerable use and is of substantial benefit but that would not otherwise be installed by most developers in the absence of an ordinance requirement.

(c) The total acreage of miniparks required by Section 196 shall be divided into miniparks of not less than 2,000 square feet nor more than 30,000 square feet.

(d) Miniparks shall be attractively landscaped and shall be provided with sufficient natural or man-made screening or buffer areas to minimize any negative impacts upon adjacent residences.

(e) Each minipark shall be centrally located and easily accessible so that it can be conveniently and safely reached and used by those persons in the surrounding neighborhood it is designed to serve.

(f) Each minipark shall be constructed on land that is relatively flat, dry, and capable of serving the purposes intended by this article.

Section 198: Usable Open Space

(a) Except as provided in Subsection (c), every residential development shall be developed so that at least 5 percent of the total area of the development remains permanently as usable open space.

Commentary:
> There is no magic in the figure 5 percent; it just seems to yield a reasonable result. Unless density levels are extremely high, unsubdivided developments and subdivided multi-family townhome developments will generally contain higher percentages of usable open space even without this requirement. Its principal utility comes in requiring the reservation of common open space areas in single-family subdivisions, where such reservations would not be likely to occur in the absence of such a provision.

(b) For purposes of this section, usable open space means an area that:

(1) Is not encumbered with any substantial structure,
(2) Is not devoted to use as a roadway, parking area, or sidewalk,
(3) Is left (as of the date development began) in its natural or undisturbed state if wooded, except for the cutting of trails for walking or jogging, or, if not wooded at the time of development, is landscaped for ball fields, picnic areas, or similar facilities, or is properly vegetated and landscaped with the objective of creating a wooded area or other area that is consistent with the objective set forth in Subdivision (4),

(4) Is capable of being used and enjoyed for purposes of informal and unstructured recreation and relaxation, and

(5) Is legally and practically accessible to the residents of the development out of which the required open space is taken, or to the public if dedication of the open space is required pursuant to Section 200.

(6) Consists of land no more than 25 percent of which lies within a floodplain or floodway as those terms are defined in Section 251.

(c) Subdivided residential developments of less than 25 dwelling units are exempt from the requirements of this section unless the city agrees that it will accept an offer of dedication of such open space, and in that case the offer of dedication shall be made.

Commentary:

See the commentary following Subsection 196(c) for an explanation of the exemption for subdivisions of less than 25 dwelling units. This exemption differs somewhat from that set forth in Subsection 196(c) which applies to miniparks in that it provides for the possibility that the local government might be willing to accept dedication of these smaller open space areas. The reason for the difference in treatment is the assumption that small open space areas would be considerably less costly to maintain than miniparks containing recreational facilities.

**Section 199:
Ownership and Maintenance of Recreational Areas and Required Open Space**

(a) Except as provided in Section 200, recreation facilities and usable open space required to be provided by the developer in accordance with this article shall not be dedicated to the public but shall remain under the ownership and control of the developer (or his successor) or a homeowners association or similar organization that satisfies the criteria established in Section 201.

(b) The person or entity identified in Subsection (a) as having the right of ownership and control over such recreational facilities and open space shall be responsible for the continuing upkeep and proper maintenance of the same.

Commentary:

The issue of who will own and maintain required recreational facilities and open space must be addressed in the ordinance. This section illustrates the position that most local governments would probably take due to limited resources.

**Section 200:
Dedication of Open Space**

(a) If any portion of any lot proposed for residential development lies within an area designated on the officially adopted recreation master plan as a neighborhood park or part of the greenway system or bikeway system, the area so designated (not exceeding 5 percent of the total lot area) shall be included as part of the area set aside to satisfy the requirement of Section 198. This area shall be dedicated to public use.

(b) If more than 5 percent of a lot proposed for residential development lies within an area designated as provided in Subsection (a), the city may attempt to acquire the additional land in the following manner:

(1) The developer may be encouraged to resort to the procedures authorized in Sections 187 or 188 and to dedicate the common open space thereby created; or

(2) The city may purchase or condemn the land.

Commentary:

This section seeks to provide a means of acquiring at no cost to the local government land that has been designated as particularly suitable for public use, while avoiding accusations that a developer has been unfairly singled out to make a disproportionate and uncompensated contribution to the public merely because he happens to own a choice piece of property. *All* developers are required to set aside the same minimum percentage of their property as usable open space, and the only additional burdens imposed on those whose land contains areas previously designated for public use are: (1) the 5 percent must be *dedicated* rather than merely reserved, and (2) the developer has less freedom in choosing which area to set aside than other developers.

Subsection (b) sets forth the ways in which the city may acquire more than 5 percent of the developer's property if necessary. Experience demonstrates that, so long as the developer can use the provisions of Sections 187 or 188 to maintain his overall density, the local government usually has little trouble in obtaining a voluntary dedication of whatever open space is desired, particularly if such open space is located within floodplains, steep slopes, or other undevelopable but environmentally attractive areas.

Section 201: Homeowners Associations

Homeowners associations or similar legal entities that, pursuant to Section 199, are responsible for the maintenance and control of common areas, including recreational facilities and open space, shall be established in such a manner that:

(1) Provision for the establishment of the association or similar entity is made before any lot in the development is sold or any building occupied;

(2) The association or similar legal entity has clear legal authority to maintain and exercise control over such common areas and facilities;

(3) The association or similar legal entity has the power to compel contributions from residents of the development to cover their proportionate shares of the costs associated with the maintenance and upkeep of such common areas and facilities.

Commentary:

Most city attorneys probably feel somewhat uncomfortable reviewing the documents establishing a homeowners' association, both because they do not like to sit in judgment over the work of another attorney and because of the well-recognized and essential distinction between requirements established by ordinance and those set forth in private covenants. Nevertheless, this review should be made simply to assure the local government that a viable homeowners' association has been established with sufficient authority to obtain the resources it needs to maintain the common facilities it is obligated to maintain.

Section 202: Flexibility in Administration Authorized

(a) The requirements set forth in this article concerning the amount, size, location, and nature of recreational facilities and open space to be provided in connection with residential developments are established by the council as standards that presumptively will result in the provision of that amount of recreational facilities and open space that is consistent with officially adopted city plans. The council recognizes, however, that due to the particular nature of a tract of land, or the nature of the facilities proposed for installation, or other factors, the underlying objectives of this article may be achieved even though the standards are not adhered to with mathematical precision. Therefore, the permit-issuing body is authorized to permit minor deviations from these standards whenever it determines that: (i) the objectives underlying these standards can be met without strict adherence to them; and (ii) because of peculiarities in the developer's tract of land or the facilities proposed it would be unreasonable to require strict adherence to these standards.

(b) Whenever the permit-issuing board authorizes some deviation from the standards set forth in this article pursuant to Subsection (a), the official record of action taken on the development application shall contain a statement of the reasons for allowing the deviation.

Sections 203 through 209: Reserved

Article XIV Streets and Sidewalks

Commentary:

Particularly in this article, the reader will observe that many standards are of necessity stated quite generally. These standards are hardly meaningless, however. They should provide enough guidance to withstand a challenge (in those jurisdictions where the doctrine of the nondelegability of legislative power is still viable) that unfettered discretion has been delegated to an administrative official. And more importantly, from the practical standpoint, they provide ordinance language that the planner reviewing site plans can rely on if necessary to convince a developer to modify his plans when changes are warranted.

One other technique that provides needed flexibility appears several times in this article and is worthy of comment. Several sections establish a specific requirement or standard (e.g., length of a cul-de-sac in Section 217) and then provide for possible exceptions with the language "unless no other alternative is practicable." The intent is to allow exceptions when compliance with the stated standard is not reasonably possible, without going through a cumbersome variance procedure. Note that the term used is "practicable" rather than "practical." The former term is meant to establish a more objective standard, dealing with what reasonably can be done, rather than what is "practical" from the developer's perspective.

**Section 210:
Street Classification**

(a) In all new subdivisions, streets that are dedicated to public use shall be classified as provided in Subsection (b).

(1) The classification shall be based upon the projected volume of traffic to be carried by the street, stated in terms of the number of trips per day;

(2) The number of dwelling units to be served by the street may be used as a useful indicator of the number of trips but is not conclusive;

(3) Whenever a subdivision street continues an existing street that formerly terminated outside the subdivision or it is expected that a subdivision street will be continued beyond the subdivision at some future time, the classification of the street will be based upon the street in its entirety, both within and outside of the subdivision.

(b) The classification of streets shall be as follows:

(1) *Minor*. A street whose sole function is to provide access to abutting properties. It serves or is designed to serve not more than

nine dwelling units and is expected to or does handle up to 75 trips per day.

(2) *Local.* A street whose sole function is to provide access to abutting properties. It serves or is designed to serve at least 10 but no more than 25 dwelling units and is expected to or does handle between 75 and 200 trips per day.

(3) *Cul-de-sac.* A street that terminates in a vehicular turnaround.

(4) *Subcollector.* A street whose principal function is to provide access to abutting properties but is also designed to be used or is used to connect minor and local streets with collector or arterial streets. Including residences indirectly served through connecting streets, it serves or is designed to serve at least 26 but not more than 100 dwelling units and is expected to or does handle between 200 and 800 trips per day.

(5) *Collector.* A street whose principal function is to carry traffic between minor, local, and subcollector streets and arterial streets but that may also provide direct access to abutting properties. It serves or is designed to serve, directly or indirectly, more than 100 dwelling units and is designed to be used or is used to carry more than 800 trips per day.

(6) *Arterial.* A major street in the city's street system that serves as an avenue for the circulation of traffic into, out, or around the city and carries high volumes of traffic.

(7) *Marginal Access Street.* A street that is parallel to and adjacent to an arterial street and that is designed to provide access to abutting properties so that these properties are somewhat sheltered from the effects of the through traffic on the arterial street and so that the flow of traffic on the arterial street is not impeded by direct driveway access from a large number of abutting properties.

Commentary:

The draftsman should bear in mind that streets should be classified only if and to the extent that the different classifications are subject to different standards.

Section 211:
Access to Lots

Every lot shall have access to it that is sufficient to afford a reasonable means of ingress and egress for emergency vehicles as well as for all those likely to need or desire access to the property in its intended use.

Commentary:

Many ordinances require that every lot front upon a public street. This requirement creates all sorts of unnecessary problems, and the foregoing is suggested as an alternative that provides greater flexibility while still leaving the city with sufficient authority to protect the public safety.

Section 212:
Access to Arterial Streets

Whenever a major subdivision that involves the creation of one or more new streets borders on or contains an existing or proposed arterial street, no direct driveway access may be provided from the lots within this subdivision onto this street.

Section 213:
Entrances to Streets

(a) All driveway entrances and other openings onto streets within the city's planning jurisdiction shall be constructed so that:

(1) Vehicles can enter and exit from the lot in question without posing any substantial danger to themselves, pedestrians, or vehicles travelling in abutting streets, and

(2) Interference with the free and convenient flow of traffic in abutting or surrounding streets is minimized.

(b) Specifications for driveway entrances are set forth in Appendix B to this chapter. If driveway entrances and other openings onto streets are constructed in accordance with the foregoing specifications and requirements, this shall be deemed prima facie evidence of compliance with the standard set forth in Subsection (a).

(c) For purposes of this section, the term prima facie evidence means that the permit-issuing authority may (but is not required to) conclude from this evidence alone that the proposed development complies with Subsection (a).

Commentary:

This section illustrates an approach that constitutes a reasonable accommodation between the competing demands of flexibility and certainty. Subsection (a) sets forth the general standard applicable to an extremely important element of project design. Subsection (b) references a set of specifications that gives the developer more concrete guidance. But Subsection (c) makes it clear that the ultimate standard remains as stated in Subsection (a), and the local government retains the freedom, reasonably and responsibly exercised, to apply this general standard to the particular development in question.

Section 214: Coordination with Surrounding Streets

(a) The street system of a subdivision shall be coordinated with existing, proposed, and anticipated streets outside the subdivision or outside the portion of a single tract that is being divided into lots (hereinafter, "surrounding streets") as provided in this section.

(b) Collector streets shall intersect with surrounding collector or arterial streets at safe and convenient locations.

(c) Subcollector, local, and minor residential streets shall connect with surrounding streets where necessary to permit the convenient movement of traffic between residential neighborhoods or to facilitate access to neighborhoods by emergency service vehicles or for other sufficient reasons, but connections shall not be permitted where the effect would be to encourage the use of such streets by substantial through traffic.

Commentary:

One of a planner's more difficult tasks is ensuring reasonable access to and through residential neighborhoods without encouraging through traffic. It seems that most residents today want to live on a dead-end street or cul-de-sac, while most public safety officials want to make certain that there is dual access to every neighborhood. The foregoing subsection attempts to provide the ordinance language necessary to implement a reasonable accommodation between these somewhat conflicting objectives.

(d) Whenever connections to anticipated or proposed surrounding streets are required by this section, the street right-of-way shall be extended and the street developed to the property line of the subdivided property (or to the edge of the remaining undeveloped portion of a single tract) at the point where the connection to the anticipated or proposed street is expected. In addition, the permit-issuing authority may require temporary turnarounds to be constructed at the end of such streets pending their extension when such turnarounds appear necessary to facilitate the flow of traffic or accommodate emergency vehicles. Notwithstanding the other provisions of this subsection, no temporary dead-end street in excess of 1,000 feet may be created unless no other practicable alternative is available.

**Section 215:
Relationship of Streets to Topography**

(a) Streets shall be related appropriately to the topography. In particular, streets shall be designed to facilitate the drainage and storm water runoff objectives set forth in Article XVI, and street grades shall conform as closely as practicable to the original topography.

(b) As indicated in Section 216, the maximum grade at any point on a street constructed without curb and gutter shall be 6 percent. On streets constructed with curb and gutter the grade shall not exceed 6 percent unless no other practicable alternative is available. However, in no case may streets be constructed with grades that, in the professional opinion of the public works director, create a substantial danger to the public safety.

Commentary:

> The maximum percentage grades for streets will obviously vary with the type of topography present in a particular locality.

**Section 216:
Street Width, Sidewalk, and Drainage Requirements in Subdivisions**

(a) Street rights-of-way are designed and developed to serve several functions: (i) to carry motor vehicle traffic, and in some cases, allow on-street parking; (ii) to provide a safe and convenient passageway for pedestrian traffic; and (iii) to serve as an important link in the town's drainage system. In order to fulfill these objectives, all public streets shall be constructed to meet either the standards set forth in Subsection (b) or Subsection (c).

(b) The following classifications of streets may be constructed with six-foot-wide shoulders and drainage swales on either side in lieu of curb and gutter, so long as the street grade does not exceed a grade of 6 percent. Such streets shall be constructed to meet the criteria indicated in the table that follows as well as specifications referenced in Section 219. No sidewalks shall be required.

Street Type	Minimum Right-of-Way Width (in feet)	Minimum Pavement Width (in feet)
Minor	45	18
Local	45	18
Subcollector	50	20

(c) Except as otherwise provided in Subsection (b), all streets shall be constructed with curb and gutter and shall conform to the other requirements of this subsection. Only standard 90 degree curb may be used, except that roll-type curb shall be permitted along minor and local streets within residential subdivisions. Street pavement width shall be measured from curb face to curb face where 90 degree curb is used, and from the center of the curb where roll-type curb is used.

Street Type	Minimum Right-of-Way Width (in feet)	Minimum Pavement Width (in feet)	Sidewalk Requirement
Minor	40	20	None
Local	40	24	One side
Subcollector	50	26	One side
Collector	50	34	One side

(d) The sidewalks required by this section shall be at least four feet in width and constructed according to the specifications set forth in Appendix C, except that the permit-issuing authority may permit the installation of walkways constructed with other suitable materials when it concludes that:

(1) Such walkways would serve the residents of the development as adequately as concrete sidewalks; and

(2) Such walkways would be more environmentally desirable or more in keeping with the overall design of the development.

(e) Whenever the permit-issuing authority finds that a means of pedestrian access is necessary from the subdivision to schools, parks, playgrounds, or other roads or facilities and that such access is not conveniently provided by sidewalks adjacent to the streets, the developer may be required to reserve an unobstructed easement of at least 10 feet in width to provide such access.

Commentary:

Streets are among the most expensive improvements a developer is required to install, and so the ordinance should reflect a policy that carefully weighs the costs imposed against the benefits received. This position is not suggested in the naive belief that all cost savings are necessarily passed on to the consumer (although in a truly competitive market this will be the case) but in recognition of the fact that whatever costs are incurred for streets beyond those that can be justified by public health and safety concerns will certainly be borne by the consumer.

Consistent with the above approach, the right-of-way and paving width requirements set forth in this section are more modest than those found in many ordinances. These are, however, virtually identical to the standards promulgated by the North Carolina Department of Transportation.

In addition to the costs involved, the foregoing section also reflects a concern for the problems that can be created by excess water runoff. Obviously, the more pavement area, the more runoff, which increases the danger of downstream flooding and the amount of pollutants carried in by streams. Similarly, while streets with curb and gutter may have advantages from the maintenance standpoint (the author has never encountered a public works director that did not favor curb and gutter requirements), they have the corresponding disadvantage, when compared to streets with drainage swales, of discharging substantially larger volumes of water into a channel. Gently sloping drainage swales (not ditches) can decrease both the volume and rate of run-off and help to filter out pollutants. However, some argue that streets constructed with gravel shoulders, rather than curb and gutter, tend to break up faster along the edges. Obviously, many issues need to be debated concerning these questions of street design, and there are no right or wrong answers, only difficult policy choices.

Finally, careful consideration should be given to requirements designed to ensure that streets are usable by pedestrians. When streets are constructed with shoulders and drainage swales, the pedestrian will have a satisfactory place to walk. In streets with curb and gutter, part of the trade-off made above for lesser pavement widths is the construction of sidewalks (except on minor streets where the traffic volumes are so minimal that pedestrians can safely use the streets).

Section 217:
General Layout of Streets

(a) Subcollector, local, and minor residential streets shall be curved whenever practicable to the extent necessary to avoid conformity of lot appearance.

(b) Cul-de-sacs and loop streets are encouraged so that through traffic on residential streets is minimized. Similarly, to the extent practicable, driveway access to collector streets shall be minimized to facilitate the free flow of traffic and avoid traffic hazards.

(c) All permanent dead-end streets (as opposed to temporary dead-end streets, see Subsection 214(d)) shall be developed as cul-de-sacs in accordance with the standards set forth in Subsection (d). Except where no other practicable alternative is available, such streets may not extend more than 550 feet (measured to the center of the turnaround).

(d) The right-of-way of a cul-de-sac shall have a radius of 50 feet. The radius of the paved portion of the turnaround (measured to the outer edge of the pavement) shall be 35 feet, and the pavement width shall be 12 feet without curb and gutter or 18 feet with curb and gutter. The unpaved center of the turnaround area shall be landscaped.

(e) Half streets (i.e., streets of less than the full required right-of-way and pavement width) shall not be permitted except where such streets, when combined with a similar street (developed previously or simultaneously) on property adjacent to the subdivision, creates or comprises a street that meets the right-of-way and pavement requirements of this chapter.

(f) Streets shall be laid out so that residential blocks do not exceed 1,000 feet, unless no other practicable alternative is available.

Section 218:
Street Intersections

(a) Streets shall intersect as nearly as possible at right angles, and no two streets may intersect at less than 60 degrees. Not more than two streets shall intersect at any one point, unless the public works director certifies to the permit-issuing authority that such an intersection can be constructed with no extraordinary danger to public safety.

(b) Whenever possible, proposed intersections along one side of a street shall coincide with existing or proposed intersections on the opposite side of such street. In any event, where a centerline offset (jog) occurs at an intersection, the distance between centerlines of the intersecting streets shall be not less than 150 feet.

(c) Except when no other alternative is practicable or legally possible, no two streets may intersect with any other street on the same side at a distance of less than 400 feet measured from centerline to centerline of the intersecting street. When the intersected street is an arterial, the distance between intersecting streets shall be at least 1,000 feet.

Section 219: Construction Standards and Specifications

Construction and design standards and specifications for streets, sidewalks, and curbs and gutters are contained in Appendix C, and all such facilities shall be completed in accordance with these standards.

Commentary:

It is better not to clutter the main text of the ordinance with detailed technical specifications that can be more usefully included in an appendix. Which requirements go where is largely a matter of choice. However, a guiding principle used in this ordinance is that requirements with which the developer must demonstrate compliance before receiving a permit (and therefore requirements with which lay boards may have to deal) are included in the text, while specifications that need only be reviewed by the technical staff after the permit is issued (but before construction begins) are placed in an appendix (see Subsection 49(c)).

Section 220: Public Streets and Private Roads in Subdivisions

Commentary:

The issue of when to allow the creation of lots on private roads constitutes one of the most intractable problems a draftsman may face. A simple solution is to allow no creation of lots served only by a private road. (Recall that a "private road" may be nothing more than an easement that crosses one tract to provide access to two or more other tracts. If only one lot is served, the access way is defined as a driveway rather than a private road.) But this approach may be regarded as unnecessarily harsh since it would prevent (using the classic illustration) property owners from conveying one or two lots from a larger tract to their children without meeting the public street standards. In addition, if apartment complexes and condominium developments are not required to have public streets (such developments are unsubdivided), does it make sense to require townhouse developments (which are, technically, subdivisions) to install public streets? On the other hand, local governments do not wish to allow the creation of streets not meeting public street standards under circumstances where there is a strong possibility that such streets would eventually have to be taken over and improved at public expense. The provisions that follow suggest one possible route through this precarious thicket.

(a) Except as otherwise provided in this section, all lots created after the effective date of this section shall abut a public street at least to the extent necessary to comply with the access requirement set forth in Section 211. For purposes of this subsection, the term "public street" includes a preexisting public street as well as a street created by the subdivider that meets the public street standards of this chapter and is dedicated for public use. Unless the recorded plat of a subdivision clearly shows a street to be private, the recording of such a plat shall constitute an offer of dedication of such street.

Commentary:

The last sentence of Subsection (a) is descriptive rather than operative; i.e., it describes the impact under case law or statute of the recording of a plat that shows a street. The draftsmen should check the law of the local jurisdiction on this point.

(b) Architecturally integrated residential subdivisions containing 25 or more dwelling units may be developed with private roads that do not meet the public street and sidewalk standards of this chapter so long as:

(1) The proposed development will have direct access onto a public street or, if the tract has access to a public street only via a private road, such private road is improved to public street standards;

(2) No road intended to be private is planned to be extended to serve property outside that development; and

(3) The standards applicable to unsubdivided developments set forth in Sections 221 and 222 are complied with.

Commentary:

For various reasons, public street construction standards are generally more exacting than the standards applicable to private roads. The different standards applicable to public streets (Section 216) and roads in unsubdivided developments (Section 221) suggested in this ordinance illustrate this approach. Many of the differences have more to do with the perception that higher initial standards yield long-term maintenance benefits than with a concern that the lower standards compromise the public safety. But given the fact that there are differences, there is a need to ensure that if private roads are to be allowed at all this permission is granted in circumstances where the likelihood that the public will have to take over the maintenance of such roads is minimized. The key factor is the existence of some legal entity having control over such roads and the ability to command the funds necessary to maintain them.

Rental developments generally present the least risk of a need for public takeover since the roads, drives, and parking areas are under the control of a single ownership entity that has the power, through rental payments, to generate the funds necessary to maintain these areas. If a maintenance problem arises, this generally is regarded as a matter that should be resolved between the owner and the tenants without need for the local government to provide the solution.

Next in line in terms of risk of need for a public takeover is a development using the condominium form of ownership. In a condominium, the common areas are owned by a unit owners' association that, by statute, generally has the right to assess unit owners for maintenance costs and this assessment becomes a lien against the unit owner's interest, with foreclosure (just like taxes) the ultimate enforcement weapon.

Townhouse developments and standard single-family subdivisions also frequently have homeowners' associations that own and maintain common areas, including private roads. However, these homeowners' associations may well be set up only by private covenants, rather than pursuant to statute as is likely to be the case for condominiums, and therefore the legal ability of these associations to enforce contributions from members may be somewhat in doubt (case law should be consulted). From a practical standpoint, the fewer the number of members in the association, the more likely it becomes that the association will collapse and be unable to fulfill its maintenance obligations. Subsection (b) chooses the number 25 as the appropriate dividing line between subdivisions that should and should not be allowed to have private roads not meeting public street standards.

(c) Architecturally integrated subdivisions containing any number of dwelling units may be developed with private roads that do meet the public street and sidewalk standards of this chapter but that are not intended for dedication to the public so long as:

(1) The proposed development will have direct access onto a public street or, if the tract has access to a public street only via a private road, such private road is improved to public street standards,

(2) No road intended to be private is planned or expected to be extended to serve property outside the development, and

(3) The subdivider demonstrates to the reasonable satisfaction of the council that the private roads will be properly maintained.

Commentary: The usual reason a developer will want to install private roads is that the costs of constructing such roads are lower than those associated with public streets. Occasionally, however, a developer may wish to market a development that can exclude the public from its streets even though those streets are constructed to public street standards. Under such circumstances, the concerns expressed in the previous subsection about possible public takeover do not arise, and so there is no limitation imposed on the minimum number of dwelling units in a development that wishes to take this approach.

(d) A subdivision in which the access requirement of Section 211 is satisfied by a private road that meets neither the public street standards nor the standards set forth in Section 221 may be developed so long as, since the effective date of this chapter, not more than three lots have been created out of that same tract.

(1) The intent of this subsection is primarily to allow the creation of not more than three lots developed for single-family residential purposes. Therefore, the permit-issuing authority may not approve any subdivision served by a private road authorized by this subsection in which one or more of the lots thereby created is intended for (i) two-family or multi-family residential use or (ii) any other residential or nonresidential use that would tend to generate more traffic than that customarily generated by three single-family residences.

(2) To ensure that the intent of this subsection is not subverted, the permit-issuing authority may, among other possible options, require that the approved plans show the types and locations of buildings on each lot or that the lots in a residential subdivision served by a private road be smaller than the permissible size of lots on which two-family or multi-family developments could be located or that restrictive covenants limiting the use of the subdivided property in accordance with this section be recorded before final plat approval.

Commentary: This subsection allows, in very limited circumstances, the creation of lots served only by unimproved driveways or easements that must meet only the basic access standard set forth in Section 211.

(e) No final plat that shows lots served by private roads may be recorded unless the final plat contains the following notations:

(1) "Further subdivision of any lot shown on this plat as served by a private road may be prohibited by the _____ Land Use Ordinance."

(2) "The policy of the City of _____ is that, if the city improves streets (i) that were never constructed to the standards required in the Land Use Ordinance for dedicated streets, and (ii) on which 75 percent of the dwelling units were constructed after the effective date of this chapter, then 100 percent of the costs of such improvements shall be assessed to abutting landowners."

Commentary: Subdivision (2) constitutes notification to a lot purchaser in a subdivision served by private roads of what the city's policy (adopted separately) is with respect to assessments for improvement of such streets. Obviously, the draftsman must consult local policies on this matter before including such a statement in the land-use ordinance.

(f) The recorded plat of any subdivision that includes a private road shall clearly state that such road is a private road. Further, the initial purchaser of a newly created lot served by a private road shall be furnished by the seller with a disclosure statement outlining the maintenance responsibilities for the road.

**Section 221:
Road and Sidewalk Requirements in Unsubdivided Developments**

(a) Within unsubdivided developments, all private roads and access ways shall be designed and constructed to facilitate the safe and convenient movement of motor vehicle and pedestrian traffic. Width of roads, use of curb and gutter, and paving specifications shall be determined by the provisions of this chapter dealing with parking (Article XVIII) and drainage (Article XVI). To the extent not otherwise covered in the foregoing articles, and to the extent that the requirements set forth in this article for subdivision streets may be relevant to the roads in unsubdivided developments, the requirements of this article may be applied to satisfy the standard set forth in the first sentence of this subsection.

(b) Whenever a road in an unsubdivided development connects two or more subcollector, collector, or arterial streets in such a manner that any substantial volume of through traffic is likely to make use of this road, such road shall be constructed in accordance with the standards applicable to subdivision streets and shall be dedicated. In other cases when roads in unsubdivided developments within the city are constructed in accordance with the specifications for subdivision streets, the city may accept an offer of dedication of such streets.

(c) In all unsubdivided residential development, sidewalks shall be provided linking dwelling units with other dwelling units, the public street, and on-site activity centers such as parking areas, laundry facilities, and recreational areas and facilities. Notwithstanding the foregoing, sidewalks shall not be required where pedestrians have access to a road that serves not more than nine dwelling units.

(d) Whenever the permit-issuing authority finds that a means of pedestrian access is necessary from an unsubdivided development to schools, parks, playgrounds, or other roads or facilities and that such access is not conveniently provided by sidewalks adjacent to the roads, the developer may be required to reserve an unobstructed easement of at least 10 feet to provide such access.

(e) The sidewalks required by this section shall be at least four feet wide and constructed according to the specifications set forth in Appendix C, except that the permit-issuing authority may permit the installation of walkways constructed with other suitable materials when it concludes that:

(1) Such walkways would serve the residents of the development as adequately as concrete sidewalks; and
(2) Such walkways could be more environmentally desirable or more in keeping with the overall design of the development.

**Section 222:
Attention to Handicapped in Street and Sidewalk Construction**

(a) Whenever curb and gutter construction is used on public streets, wheelchair ramps for the handicapped shall be provided at intersections and other major points of pedestrian flow. Wheelchair ramps and depressed curbs shall be constructed in accordance with published standards of the [appropriate state agency].

(b) In unsubdivided developments, sidewalk construction for the handicapped shall conform to the requirements of Section (_____) of the [appropriate state or local building code].

**Section 223:
Street Names and House Numbers**

(a) Street names shall be assigned by the developer subject to the approval of the permit-issuing authority. Proposed streets that are obviously in alignment with existing streets shall be given the same name. Newly created streets shall be given names that neither duplicate nor are phonetically similar to existing streets within the city's planning jurisdiction, regardless of the use of different suffixes (such as those set forth in Subsection (b)).

(b) Street names shall include a suffix such as the following:

(1) *Circle*. A short street that returns to itself.
(2) *Court or Place*. A cul-de-sac or dead-end street.
(3) *Loop*. A street that begins at the intersection with one street and circles back to end at another intersection with the same street.
(4) *Street*. All public streets not designated by another suffix.

(c) Building numbers shall be assigned by the city.

**Section 224:
Bridges**

All bridges shall be constructed in accordance with the standards and specifications of the [state or local] Department of Transportation, except that bridges on roads not intended for public dedication may be approved if designed by a licensed architect or engineer.

**Section 225:
Utilities**

Utilities installed in public rights-of-way or along private roads shall conform to the requirements set forth in Article XV, Utilities.

**Sections 226 through 235:
Reserved**

Article XV Utilities

Section 236:
Utility Ownership and Easement Rights

In any case in which a developer installs or causes the installation of water, sewer, electrical power, telephone, or cable television facilities and intends that such facilities shall be owned, operated, or maintained by a public utility or any entity other than the developer, the developer shall transfer to such utility or entity the necessary ownership or easement rights to enable the utility or entity to operate and maintain such facilities.

Section 237:
Lots Served by Governmentally Owned Water or Sewer Lines

(a) Whenever it is legally possible and practicable in terms of topography to connect a lot with a city water or sewer line by running a connecting line not more than 200 feet from the lot to such line, then no use requiring water or sewage disposal service may be made of such lot unless connection is made to such line.

(b) Connection to such water or sewer line is not legally possible if, in order to make connection with such line by a connecting line that does not exceed 200 feet in length, it is necessary to run the connecting line over property not owned by the owner of the property to be served by the connection, and, after diligent effort, the easement necessary to run the connecting line cannot reasonably be obtained.

(c) For purposes of this article, a lot is "served" by a city-owned water or sewer line if connection is required by this section.

Commentary:
> Most cities have ordinances that establish their policies relating to the provision of utility services. Most such ordinances require that properties that can reasonably be served by utility lines be connected to the public service. Such provisions apply not only to new land uses but to preexisting buildings and uses as well. To that extent, the foregoing provision may be superfluous, unless the draftsman prefers to include it as a reminder to developers and the ordinance administrator. However, if no other ordinance establishes this requirement, the land-use ordinance can be used to at least require connection for new development.

Section 238:
Sewage Disposal Facilities Required

Every principal use and every lot within a subdivision shall be served by a sewage disposal system that is adequate to accommodate the reasonable needs of such use or subdivision lot and that complies with all applicable health regulations.

Commentary:
> See commentary following Section 239.

**Section 239:
Determining Compliance With
Section 238**

(a) Primary responsibility for determining whether a proposed development will comply with the standard set forth in Section 238 often lies with an agency other than the city, and the developer must comply with the detailed standards and specifications of such other agency. The relevant agencies are listed in Subsection (b). Whenever any such agency requires detailed construction or design drawings before giving its official approval to the proposed sewage disposal system, the authority issuing a permit under this chapter may rely upon a preliminary review by such agency of the basic design elements of the proposed sewage disposal system to determine compliance with Section 238. However, construction of such system may not be commenced until the detailed plans and specifications have been reviewed and any appropriate permits issued by such agency.

(b) In the following table, the column on the left describes the type of development and the column on the right indicates the agency that must certify to the city whether the proposed sewage disposal system complies with the standard set forth in Section 238.

If	**Then**
(1) The use is located on a lot that is served by the city sewer system or a previously approved, privately owned package treatment plant, and the use can be served by a simple connection to the system (as in the case of a single-family residence) rather than the construction of an internal collection system (as in the case of a shopping center or apartment complex):	No further certification is necessary.
(2) The use (other than a subdivision) is located on a lot that is served by the city sewer system but service to the use necessitates construction of an internal collection system (as in the case of a shopping center or apartment complex); and	
a. The internal collection system is to be transferred to and maintained by the city:	The public works director must certify to the city that the proposed internal collection system meets the city's specifications and will be accepted by the city. (A "Permit to Construct" must be obtained from the Division of Environmental Management.)

b. The internal collection system is to be privately maintained:	The public works director must certify that the proposed collection system is adequate.
(3) The use (other than a subdivision) is not served by the city system but is to be served by a privately operated sewage treatment system (that has not previously been approved) with 3,000 gallons or less design capacity, the effluent from which does not discharge to surface waters:	The County Health Department (CHD) must certify to the city that the proposed system complies with all applicable state and local health regulations. If the proposed use is a single dwelling other than a mobile home, the developer must obtain an improvements permit from the CHD. If the proposed use is a single-family mobile home, the developer must present to the town a certificate of completion from the CHD.
(4) The use (other than a subdivision) is to be served by a privately operated sewage treatment system (not previously approved) that has a design capacity of more than 3,000 gallons or that discharges effluent into surface waters:	The Division of Environmental Management (DEM) must certify to the city that the proposed system complies with all applicable state regulations. (A "Permit to Construct" and a "Permit to Discharge" must be obtained from DEM.)
(5) The proposed use is a subdivision; and	
a. Lots within the subdivision are to be served by simple connection to existing city lines or lines of a previously approved private system:	No further certification is necessary.
b. Lots within the subdivision are to be served by the city system but the developer will be responsible for installing the necessary additions to the city system:	The public works director must certify to the city that the proposed system meets the city's specifications and will be accepted by the city. (A "Permit to Construct" must be obtained from the Division of Environmental Management of the N.C. Department of Natural Resources and Community Development.)

129 Utilities

	c. Lots within the subdivision are to be served by a sewage treatment system that has not been approved, that has a design capacity of 3,000 gallons or less, and that does not discharge into surface waters:	The County Health Department must certify that the proposed system complies with all applicable state and local health regulations. If each lot within the subdivision is to be served by a separate on-site disposal system, the CHD must certify that each lot shown on a major subdivision preliminary plat can probably be served, and each lot on a major or minor subdivision final plat can be served by an on-site disposal system.
	d. Lots within the subdivision are to be served by a privately operated sewage treatment system (not previously approved) that has a design capacity in excess of 3,000 gallons or that discharges effluent into surface waters:	The Division of Environmental Management must certify that the proposed system complies with all applicable state regulations. (A "Permit to Construct" and a "Permit to Discharge" must be obtained from DEM.)

Commentary: Section 238 establishes the general standard that every development must meet and Section 239 describes how the determination will be made whether different types of development satisfy this standard. Section 239 thus constitutes a type of roadmap for the developer and checklist for the administrator. Clearly, the draftsman must carefully check state and local regulations to complete a section such as this.

Section 240:
Water Supply System Required

Every principal use and every lot within a subdivision shall be served by a water supply system that is adequate to accommodate the reasonable needs of such use or subdivision lot and that complies with all applicable health regulations.

Commentary: See commentary following Section 239.

Section 241:
Determining Compliance with Section 240

(a) Primary responsibility for determining whether a proposed development will comply with the standard set forth in Section 240 often lies with an agency other than the city, and the developer must comply with the detailed standards and specifications of such other agency. The relevant agencies are listed in Subsection (b). Whenever any such agency requires detailed construction or design drawings before giving its official approval to the proposed water supply system, the authority issuing a permit under this chapter may rely upon a preliminary review by such agency of the basic design elements of the proposed water supply system to determine compliance with Section 240. However, construction of such system may not be commenced until the detailed plans and specifications have been reviewed and any appropriate permits issued by such agency.

(b) In the following table, the column on the left describes the type of development and the column on the right indicates the agency that must certify to the city whether the proposed water supply system complies with the standard set forth in Section 240.

If	**Then**
(1) The use is located on a lot that is served by the city water system or a previously approved, privately owned public water supply system and the use can be served by a simple connection to the system (as in the case of a single-family residence) rather than the construction of an internal distribution system (as in the case of a shopping center or apartment complex):	No further certification is necessary.
(2) The use (other than a subdivision) is located on a lot that is served by the city water system but service to the use necessitates construction of an internal distribution system (as in the case of a shopping center or apartment complex); and	
a. The internal distribution system is to be transferred to and maintained by the city:	The public works director must certify to the city that the proposed internal distribution system meets city specifications and will be accepted by the city. (A "Permit to Construct" must be obtained from the Division of Health Services.)
b. The internal distribution system is to be privately maintained:	The public works director must certify that the proposed collection system is adequate.
(3) The use (other than a subdivision) is located on a lot not served by the city system or a previously approved, privately owned public water supply system; and	

a. The use is to be served by a privately owned public water supply system that has not previously been approved:

The Division of Health Services (DHS) must certify that the proposed system complies with all applicable state and federal regulations. (A "Permit to Construct" must be obtained from DHS.) The Division of Environmental Management (DEM) must also approve the plans if the water source is a well and the system has a design capacity of 100,000 gallons per day or is located in certain areas designated by DEM. The public works director must also approve the distribution lines for possible future addition to the city system.

b. The use is to be served by some other source (such as an individual well):

The County Health Department must certify that the proposed system meets all applicable state and local regulations.

(4) The proposed use is a subdivision; and

a. Lots within the subdivision are to be served by simple connection to existing city lines or lines of a previously approved public water supply system:

No further certification is necessary.

b. Lots within the subdivision are to be served by the city system but the developer will be responsible for installing the necessary additions to such system:

The public works director must certify to the city that the proposed system meets city specifications and will be accepted by the city. (A "Permit to Construct" must be obtained from the Division of Health Services.)

c. Lots within the subdivision are to be served by a privately owned public water supply system that has not previously been approved:

The Division of Health Services (DHS) must certify that the proposed system complies with all applicable state and federal regulations. (A "Permit to Construct" must be obtained from DHS.) The Division of Environmental

	Management (DEM) must also approve the plans if the water source is a well and the system has a design capacity of 100,000 gallons per day or is located within certain areas designated by DEM. The public works director must also approve the distribution lines for possible future addition to the city system.
d. Lots within the subdivision are to be served by individual wells:	The County Health Department must certify to the city that each lot intended to be served by a well can be served in accordance with applicable health regulations.

Commentary: See commentary following Section 239.

Section 242:
Lighting Requirements

(a) Subject to Subsection (b), all public streets, sidewalks, and other common areas or facilities in subdivisions created after the effective date of this chapter shall be sufficiently illuminated to ensure the security of property and the safety of persons using such streets, sidewalks, and other common areas or facilities.

(b) To the extent that fulfillment of the requirement established in Subsection (a) would normally require street lights installed along public streets, this requirement shall be applicable only to subdivisions located within the corporate limits of the city.

(c) All roads, driveways, sidewalks, parking lots, and other common areas and facilities in unsubdivided developments shall be sufficiently illuminated to ensure the security of property and the safety of persons using such roads, driveways, sidewalks, parking lots, and other common areas and facilities.

(d) All entrances and exits in substantial buildings used for nonresidential purposes and in two-family or multi-family residential developments containing more than four dwelling units shall be adequately lighted to ensure the safety of persons and the security of the buildings.

Commentary:
> It would be well to supplement or replace the "adequate lighting" standard in the foregoing section with a more specific performance standard if one could be developed. In the absence of such a standard, the local government may obtain advice and assistance in reviewing proposed plans from the local power company.

Section 243:
Excessive Illumination

Lighting within any lot that unnecessarily illuminates any other lot and substantially interferes with the use or enjoyment of such other lot is prohibited. Lighting unnecessarily illuminates another lot if it clearly exceeds the standard set forth in Section 242 or if the standard set forth in Section 242 could reasonably be achieved in a manner that would not substantially interfere with the use or enjoyment of neighboring properties.

Section 244: Electric Power

Every principal use and every lot within a subdivision shall have available to it a source of electric power adequate to accommodate the reasonable needs of such use and every lot within such subdivision. Compliance with this requirement shall be determined as follows:

(1) If the use is not a subdivision and is located on a lot that is served by an existing power line and the use can be served by a simple connection to such power line (as opposed to a more complex distribution system, such as would be required in an apartment complex or shopping center), then no further certification is needed.

(2) If the use is a subdivision or is not located on a lot served by an existing power line or a substantial internal distribution system will be necessary, then the electric utility service provider must review the proposed plans and certify to the city that it can provide service that is adequate to meet the needs of the proposed use and every lot within the proposed subdivision.

Section 245: Telephone Service

Every principal use and every lot within a subdivision must have available to it a telephone service cable adequate to accommodate the reasonable needs of such use and every lot within such subdivision. Compliance with this requirement shall be determined as follows:

(1) If the use is not a subdivision and is located on a lot that is served by an existing telephone line and the use can be served by a simple connection to such power line (as opposed to a more complex distribution system, such as would be required in an apartment complex or shopping center), then no further certification is necessary.

(2) If the use is a subdivision or is not located on a lot served by an existing telephone line or a substantial internal distribution system will be necessary, then the telephone utility company must review the proposed plans and certify to the city that it can provide service that is adequate to meet the needs of the proposed use and every lot within the proposed subdivision.

Section 246: Underground Utilities

(a) All electric power lines (not to include transformers or enclosures containing electrical equipment including, but not limited to, switches, meters, or capacitors which may be pad mounted), telephone, gas distribution, and cable television lines in subdivisions constructed after the effective date of this chapter shall be placed underground in accordance with the specifications and policies of the respective utility service providers and located in accordance with Appendix C, Standard Drawing No. 6 or 7.

(b) Whenever an unsubdivided development is hereafter constructed on a lot that is undeveloped on the effective date of this chapter, then all electric power, telephone, gas distribution, and cable television lines installed to serve the development that are located on the development site outside of a previously existing public street right-of-way shall be placed underground in accordance with the specifications and policies of the respective utility companies.

Section 247:
Utilities To Be Consistent With Internal and External Development

(a) Whenever it can reasonably be anticipated that utility facilities constructed in one development will be extended to serve other adjacent or nearby developments, such utility facilities (e.g., water or sewer lines) shall be located and constructed so that extensions can be made conveniently and without undue burden or expense or unnecessary duplication of service.

(b) All utility facilities shall be constructed in such a manner as to minimize interference with pedestrian or vehicular traffic and to facilitate maintenance without undue damage to improvements or facilities located within the development.

Section 248:
As-Built Drawings Required

Whenever a developer installs or causes to be installed any utility line in any public right-of-way, the developer shall, as soon as practicable after installation is complete, and before acceptance of any water or sewer line, furnish the city with a copy of a drawing that shows the exact location of such utility lines. Such drawings must be verified as accurate by the utility service provider. Compliance with this requirement shall be a condition of the continued validity of the permit authorizing such development.

Section 249:
Fire Hydrants

(a) Every development (subdivided or unsubdivided) that is served by a public water system shall include a system of fire hydrants sufficient to provide adequate fire protection for the buildings located or intended to be located within such development.

(b) The presumption established by this ordinance is that to satisfy the standard set forth in Subsection (a), fire hydrants must be located so that all parts of every building within the development may be served by a hydrant by laying not more than 500 feet of hose connected to such hydrant. However, the fire chief may authorize or require a deviation from this standard if in his professional opinion another arrangement more satisfactorily complies with the standard set forth in Subsection (a).

(c) The fire chief shall determine the precise location of all fire hydrants, subject to the other provisions of this section. In general, fire hydrants shall be placed six feet behind the curb line of publicly dedicated streets that have curb and gutter.

(d) The fire chief shall determine the design standards of all hydrants based on fire flow needs. Unless otherwise specified by the fire chief, all hydrants shall have two 2½-inch hose connections and one 4½-inch hose connection. The 2½-inch hose connections shall be located at least 21½ inches from the ground level. All hydrant threads shall be national standard threads.

(e) Water lines that serve hydrants shall be at least six-inch lines, and, unless no other practicable alternative is available, no such lines shall be dead-end lines.

Section 250:
Sites for and Screening of Dumpsters

(a) Every development that, under the city's solid waste collection policies, is or will be required to provide one or more dumpsters for solid waste collection shall provide sites for such dumpsters that are:

(1) Located so as to facilitate collection and minimize any negative impact on persons occupying the development site, neighboring properties, or public rights-of-way, and

(2) Constructed according to specifications established by the public works director to allow for collection without damage to the development site or the collection vehicle.

(b) All such dumpsters shall be screened if and to the extent that, in the absence of screening, they would be clearly visible to:

(1) Persons located within any dwelling unit on residential property other than that where the dumpster is located.

(2) Occupants, customers, or other invitees located within any building on nonresidential property other than that where the dumpster is located, unless such other property is used primarily for purposes permitted exclusively in an M-1 or M-2 zoning district.

(3) Persons travelling on any public street, sidewalk, or other public way.

(c) When dumpster screening is required under this section, such screening shall be constructed, installed, and located to prevent or remedy the conditions requiring the screening.

Article XVI Floodways, Floodplains, Drainage, and Erosion

Part I. Floodways and Floodplains

Commentary:

The draftsman should incorporate into the ordinance the necessary provisions that will enable the local government to participate in the National Flood Insurance Program (see 42 U.S.C. 4001-4128 and implementing regulations, 44 C.F.R. Part 60). Under this program, the city must adopt increasingly comprehensive and strict regulations, depending on the nature of the flood hazards present in the community and the extent of flood-related information that has been furnished by the Federal Emergency Management Agency (FEMA), a branch of the U.S. Department of Housing and Urban Development. The provisions contained in this part illustrate how the requirements for participation in the final phase of the program may be integrated into the land-use ordinance. Substantively, the provisions are based to some degree on the model ordinance promulgated by FEMA, but integration of those substantive requirements into this ordinance renders many of the provisions of the model ordinance superfluous. The draftsman should carefully review the applicable federal regulations to determine which requirements need to be included under the circumstances present in the local community.

Section 251: Definitions

Unless otherwise specifically provided, or unless clearly required by the context, the words and phrases defined in this section shall have the meaning indicated when used in this article.

(1) *Base Flood.* The flood having a one percent chance of being equalled or exceeded in any given year. Also known as the 100-year flood.

(2) *Floodplain.* Any land area susceptible to being inundated by water from the base flood. As used in this chapter, the term refers to that area designated as subject to flooding from the base flood (100-year flood) on the "Flood Boundary and Floodway Map" prepared by the U.S. Department of Housing and Urban Development and dated _____, a copy of which is on file in the planning department. This area shall comprise the floodplain overlay zone and shall be designated as such on the official zoning map.

(3) *Floodway.* The channel of a river or other watercourse and the adjacent land areas that must be reserved in order to discharge the base flood without cumulatively increasing the water surface

elevation more than one foot. As used in this chapter, the term refers to that area designated as a floodway on the "Flood Boundary and Floodway Map" prepared by the U.S. Department of Housing and Urban Development and dated _____, a copy of which is on file in the planning department. This area shall comprise the floodway overlay zone and shall be designated as such on the official zoning map.

(4) *Habitable Floor.* Any floor usable for living purposes, which includes working, sleeping, eating, cooking, or recreation, or any combination thereof. A floor used only for storage is not a habitable floor.

(5) *Public Water Supply System.* Any water supply system furnishing potable water to 10 or more dwelling units or businesses or any combination thereof.

**Section 252:
Artificial Obstructions Within Floodways Prohibited**

(a) No artificial obstruction may be located within any floodway, except as provided in Section 253.

(b) For purposes of this section, an artificial obstruction is any obstruction, other than a natural obstruction, that is capable of reducing the flood-carrying capacity of a stream or may accumulate debris and thereby reduce the flood-carrying capacity of a stream. A natural obstruction includes any rock, tree, gravel, or analogous natural matter that is an obstruction and has been located within the floodway by a nonhuman cause.

**Section 253:
Permissible Uses Within Floodways**

Notwithstanding Article X of this chapter (Table of Permissible Uses), no permit to make use of land within a floodway may be issued unless the proposed use is listed as permissible *both* in the Table of Permissible Uses and in the following list:

(1) General farming, pasture, outdoor plant nurseries, horticulture, forestry, wildlife sanctuary, game farm, and other similar agricultural, wildlife, and related uses.

(2) Ground-level loading areas, parking areas, rotary aircraft ports, and other similar ground-level area uses.

(3) Lawns, gardens, play areas, and other similar uses.

(4) Golf courses, tennis courts, driving ranges, archery ranges, picnic grounds, parks, hiking or horseback-riding trails, open space, and other similar private and public recreational uses.

Commentary:

As indicated in Section 139, the floodplain and floodway districts are established as overlay districts.

**Section 254:
Construction Within Floodways and Floodplains Restricted**

(a) No zoning, special-use, or conditional-use permit may be issued for any development within a floodplain until the permit-issuing authority has reviewed the plans for any such development to assure that:

(1) The proposed development is consistent with the need to minimize flood damage, and

(2) All public utilities and facilities such as sewer, gas, electrical, and water systems are located and constructed to minimize or eliminate flood damage, and

(3) Adequate drainage is provided to minimize or reduce exposure to flood hazards, and

(4) All necessary permits have been received from those agencies from which approval is required by federal or state law.

(b) No building may be constructed and no substantial improvement of an existing building may take place within any floodway. With respect to mobile home parks that are nonconforming because they are located within a floodway, mobile homes may be relocated in such parks only if they comply with the provisions of Subsection (g).

(c) No new residential building may be constructed and no substantial improvement of a residential building may take place within any floodplain unless the lowest floor (including basement) of the building or improvement is elevated to or above the base flood level.

(1) Residential accessory structures shall be allowed within floodplains provided they are firmly anchored to prevent flotation.

(2) Anchoring of any accessory buildings may be done by bolting the building to a concrete slab or by over-the-top ties. When bolting to a concrete slab, one-half inch bolts six feet on center with a minimum of two per side shall be required. If over-the-top ties are used, a minimum of two ties with a force adequate to secure the building is required.

(d) No new residential building may be constructed and no substantial improvements of a nonresidential building may take place within any floodplain unless the lowest floor (including basement) of the building or improvement is elevated or floodproofed to or above the base flood level. Where floodproofing is used in lieu of elevation, a registered professional engineer or architect shall certify that any new construction or substantial improvement has been designed to withstand the flood depths, pressure, velocities, impact, and uplift forces associated with the base flood at the location of the building and that the walls below the base flood level are substantially impermeable to the passage of water.

(e) For purposes of this section, "substantial improvement" means for a building constructed prior to the effective date of this chapter, any repair, reconstruction, or improvement of a building the cost of which equals or exceeds 50 percent of the market value of the structure either (i) before the improvement or repair is started or (ii) if the structure has been damaged and is being restored, before the damage occurred. "Substantial improvement" occurs when the first alteration on any wall, ceiling, floor, or other structural part of the building commences, whether or not that alteration affects the external dimensions of the building. The term does not, however, include either (i) any project for improvement of a structure to comply with existing state or local health, sanitary, or safety code specifications that are solely necessary to insure safe living conditions, or (ii) any alteration of a building listed on the National Register of Historic Places or a State Inventory of Historic Places.

(f) No zoning, special-use, or conditional-use permit may be issued for any development within a floodplain until the permit-issuing authority has reviewed the plans to assure that any new construction or substantial improvements shall be:

139 Floodways, Floodplains, Drainage & Erosion

    (1) Designed (or modified) and adequately anchored to prevent flotation collapse, or lateral movement of the structure.

    (2) Constructed with materials and utility equipment resistant to flood damage.

    (3) Constructed by methods and practices that minimize flood damage.

(g) Notwithstanding any other provision of this chapter, no mobile home may be located or relocated within that portion of the floodplain outside of the floodway, unless the following criteria are met:

    (1) Ground anchors for tie downs are provided.

    (2) The following tie-down requirements are met:

        (i) Over-the-top ties are required at each of the four corners of the mobile home, with one additional tie per side at an intermediate location, for mobile homes less than 50 feet long. Two additional ties per side are required for mobile homes more than 50 feet long.

        (ii) Frame ties are required in conjunction with each over-the-top tie.

        (iii) All components of the anchoring must be capable of carrying a force of 4,800 pounds.

    (3) Lots or pads are elevated on compacted fill or by any other method approved by the administrator so that the lowest habitable floor of the mobile home is at or above the base flood level.

    (4) Adequate surface drainage and easy access for mobile home hauler is provided.

    (5) Load-bearing foundation supports such as piers or pilings must be placed on stable soil or concrete footings no more than 10 feet apart, and if the support height is greater than 72 inches, the support must contain steel reinforcement.

(h) Whenever any portion of a floodplain is filled in with fill dirt, slopes shall be adequately stabilized to withstand the erosive force of the base flood.

Commentary:

> The foregoing section includes many of the substantive provisions required by federal regulation. While inclusion of these provisions (plus those found in the remainder of this article and elsewhere in the ordinance) should qualify the local government for participation in the flood insurance program, the generality of some of them may create practical enforcement difficulties. For example, unless the local government's staff includes a person with the necessary expertise, it may be difficult to determine whether a proposed development complies with Subdivisions (a)(1) and (a)(2) above. A partial answer to this problem is suggested in Subsection (d); that is, the ordinance may require the developer to provide a certificate from a qualified professional that the standard will be met.

Section 255:
Special Provisions for Subdivisions

(a) An applicant for a conditional-use permit authorizing a major subdivision and an applicant for minor subdivision final plat approval shall be informed by the planning department of the use and construction restrictions contained in Sections 252, 253, and 254 if any portion of the land to be subdivided lies within a floodway or floodplain.

(b) Final plat approval for any subdivision containing land that lies within a floodway or floodplain may not be given unless the plat shows the boundary of the floodway or floodplain and contains in clearly discernible print the following statement: "Use of land within a floodway or floodplain is substantially restricted by Article XVI of the _____ City Code."

(c) Subject to the following sentence, a conditional-use permit for a major subdivision and final plat approval for any subdivision may not be given if:

(1) The land to be subdivided lies within a zone where residential uses are permissible and it reasonably appears that the subdivision is designed to create residential building lots, and

(2) Any portion of one or more of the proposed lots lies within a floodway or floodplain, and

(3) It reasonably appears that one or more lots described in Subdivisions (1) and (2) of this subsection could not practically be used as a residential building site because of the restrictions set forth in Sections 252, 253, and 254.

The foregoing provision shall not apply if the developer demonstrates to the reasonable satisfaction of the authority issuing the permit or approving the final plat that the proposed lots are not intended for sale as residential building lots.

Commentary:

The provisions of this section are not required by federal regulation but are suggested as a means of ensuring that potential lot purchasers are put on notice concerning the use limitations imposed by this article and offering some protection against the creation of lots that cannot practically be used under these restrictions.

Section 256:
Water Supply and Sanitary Sewer Systems in Floodways and Floodplains

Whenever any portion of a proposed development is located within a floodway or floodplain, the agency or agencies responsible for certifying to the city the adequacy of the water supply and sewage disposal systems for the development (as set forth in Sections 239 and 241 of this chapter) shall be informed by the developer that a specified area within the development lies within a floodway or floodplain. Thereafter, approval of the proposed system by that agency shall constitute a certification that:

(1) Such water supply system is designed to minimize or eliminate infiltration of flood waters into it.

(2) Such sanitary sewer system is designed to eliminate infiltration of flood waters into it and discharges from it into flood waters.

(3) Any on-site sewage disposal system is located to avoid impairment to it or contamination from it during flooding.

Section 257:
Additional Duties of Administrator Related to Flood Insurance and Flood Control

The administrator shall:

(1) For the purpose of the determination of applicable flood insurance risk premium rates within Zone A on the city's Flood Insurance Rate Map provided by the U.S. Department of Housing and Urban Development:

a. Obtain the elevation (in relation to mean sea level) of the lowest habitable floor (including basement) of all new or substantially improved structures; and

b. Obtain, for all structures that have been flood-proofed (whether or not such structures contain a basement) the elevation (in relation to mean sea level) to which the structure was floodproofed; and

c. Maintain a record of all such information.

(2) Notify, in riverine situations, adjacent communities and the [appropriate state agency] prior to any alteration or relocation of a watercourse, and submit copies of such notification to the Federal Insurance Administrator.

(3) Ensure that the flood-carrying capacity within the altered or relocated portion of any watercourse is maintained.

Section 258: Location of Boundaries of Floodplain and Floodway Districts

As used in this article, the terms floodplain and floodway refer in the first instance to certain areas whose boundaries are determined and can be located on the ground by reference to the specific fluvial characteristics set forth in the definitions of these terms. These terms also refer to overlay zoning districts whose boundaries are established on the map identified in Section 157, which boundaries are intended to correspond to the actual physical location of floodways and floodplains. (These overlay districts thus differ from other zoning districts whose boundaries are established solely according to planning or policy, rather than physical, criteria.) Therefore, the administrator is authorized to make necessary interpretations as to the exact location of the boundaries of floodways or floodplains if there appears to be a conflict between a mapped boundary and actual field conditions. Such interpretations, like other decisions of the administrator, may be appealed to the board of adjustment in accordance with the applicable provisions of this chapter.

Section 259: Setbacks from Streams Outside Designated Floodplains

In any area that is located outside a designated floodplain but where a stream is located, no building or fill may be located within a distance of the stream bank equal to five times the width of the stream at the top of the bank or 20 feet on each side, whichever is greater.

Commentary:

> This section, not required by federal regulation, is designed to assure protection from flood damage adjacent to streams that are not large enough to be included in the maps of flood hazard areas provided by FEMA. It illustrates one easily enforceable way to provide this protection in the absence of more detailed information.

Section 260: Reserved

Part II. Drainage, Erosion Control, Storm Water Management

Section 261: Natural Drainage System Utilized to Extent Feasible

(a) To the extent practicable, all development shall conform to the natural contours of the land and natural and preexisting man-made drainage ways shall remain undisturbed.

Commentary:

> This subsection is intended to provide the administrator with some ordinance language to lean on as he seeks to prevent the developer from disturbing natural drainage patterns any more than is necessary.

(b) To the extent practicable, lot boundaries shall be made to coincide with natural and preexisting man-made drainage ways within subdivisions to avoid the creation of lots that can be built upon only by altering such drainage ways.

Commentary:

> This provision provides some protection for the unwary buyer who might otherwise be sold a lot during the dry season, not realizing that a stream runs through the center of it when it rains.

**Section 262:
Developments Must Drain Properly**

(a) All developments shall be provided with a drainage system that is adequate to prevent the undue retention of surface water on the development site. Surface water shall not be regarded as unduly retained if:

(1) The retention results from a technique, practice or device deliberately installed as part of an approved sedimentation or storm water runoff control plan; or

(2) The retention is not substantially different in location or degree than that experienced by the development site in its predevelopment stage, unless such retention presents a danger to health or safety.

(b) No surface water may be channelled or directed into a sanitary sewer.

(c) Whenever practicable, the drainage system of a development shall coordinate with and connect to the drainage systems or drainage ways on surrounding properties or streets.

(d) Use of drainage swales rather than curb and gutter and storm sewers in subdivisions is provided for in Section 216. Private roads and access ways within unsubdivided developments shall utilize curb and gutter and storm drains to provide adequate drainage if the grade of such roads or access ways is too steep to provide drainage in another manner or if other sufficient reasons exist to require such construction.

(e) Construction specifications for drainage swales, curbs and gutters, and storm drains are contained in Appendix C.

Commentary:

> Apart from concerns about flooding, surface water presents problems (i) when it remains unduly on a development site, and (ii) when it drains off the site too fast, too much, or in the wrong place. This section deals with the former problem, and the next section with the latter. As a practical matter, enforcement of this section is not difficult because most developers are eager to take the necessary steps to insure that surface water drains off their own property adequately.

**Section 263:
Storm Water Management**

All developments shall be constructed and maintained so that adjacent properties are not unreasonably burdened with surface waters as a result of such developments. More specifically:

(1) No development may be constructed or maintained so that such development unreasonably impedes the natural flow of water

from higher adjacent properties across such development, thereby unreasonably causing substantial damage to such higher adjacent properties; and

(2) No development may be constructed or maintained so that surface waters from such development are unreasonably collected and channelled onto lower adjacent properties at such locations or at such volumes as to cause substantial damage to such lower adjacent properties.

Commentary:

This section consists of a summary statement of the case law in North Carolina concerning the respective rights and responsibilities of adjacent property owners with regard to storm water. The law in this area varies from jurisdiction to jurisdiction, so local law must be checked carefully before drafting a similar provision. The intent of such a provision is not to insure the developer against liability or guarantee the developer's neighbors that no storm water damage will result from the development, but merely to give the city the necessary tools to review the project with a view toward minimizing the likelihood that storm water runoff problems will occur when the development is completed.

An alternative way to deal with this topic is to establish specific performance standards and then require the developer to provide a certificate from a qualified professional that the development will meet those standards. For example, the ordinance might require that the volume or rate of postdevelopment runoff not exceed predevelopment runoff at all or by more than a certain percentage. This leaves the developer free to choose the means by which to meet the standard. Care must be taken, however, to establish a standard that is reasonable under all the applicable local circumstances.

Section 264: Sedimentation and Erosion Control

(a) No zoning, special-use, or conditional-use permit may be issued and final plat approval for subdivisions may not be given with respect to any development that would cause land disturbing activity subject to the jurisdiction of the [state or local] Sedimentation Control Commission, unless the commission has certified to the city, either that:

(1) An erosion control plan has been submitted to and approved by the commission; or

(2) The commission has examined the preliminary plans for the development and it reasonably appears that an erosion control plan can be approved upon submission by the developer of more detailed construction or design drawings. However, in this case, construction of the development may not begin (and no building permits may be issued) until the commission approves the erosion control plan.

(b) For purposes of this section, land disturbing activity means any use of the land by any person in residential, industrial, educational, institutional, or commercial development, and highway and road construction and maintenance that results in a change in the natural cover or topography and that may cause or contribute to sedimentation. Sedimentation occurs whenever solid particulate matter, mineral or organic, is transported by water, air, gravity, or ice from the site of its origin.

Commentary:

Section 263 is concerned with the volume, rate, and location of storm water runoff primarily after the development is completed. This section deals with what the storm water runoff may carry with it as it leaves the site, particularly during construction. North Carolina has enacted a Sedimentation Pollution Control Act that establishes certain standards for controlling sedimentation, sets up a State Sedimentation Control Commission, and authorizes local governments to adopt sedimentation control ordinances. The language above illustrates how the sedimentation problem can be dealt with when other agencies are chiefly responsible for enforcing the relevant requirements. In the absence of similar legislation, the city may wish to include substantive regulations dealing with sedimentation control in this article of the land-use ordinance.

A related concern is what pollutants may be carried off the site by storm water after the development is completed. This issue may be particularly important in areas within the watershed of a public water supply. To some degree, these concerns may be addressed by including in this article provisions establishing impervious surface limitations and requiring that undisturbed buffer areas of a specified width be left adjacent to streams.

Sections 265 through 269: Reserved

Article XVII Signs

Commentary:

Sign regulation has produced a substantial volume of litigation across the country, the most interesting and difficult of which has involved one of three issues: (1) Can sign regulations be justified on aesthetic grounds alone? (2) Can an ordinance legally require the termination of nonconforming signs without compensation? and (3) When do sign regulations run afoul of the First Amendment? These questions have been answered differently in different jurisdictions and so the draftsman must ascertain, to the degree that can be done, what the local jurisdiction will allow. The First Amendment questions are especially difficult to answer, and partly for this reason the text that follows takes a rather lenient approach with respect to the regulation of those signs that present the most sensitive First Amendment issues (see Sections 272 and 273). The other reason for this rather relaxed approach is that in the author's experience these noncommercial signs have not presented sufficient problems to warrant stricter regulation. This may not be the case everywhere, but the draftsman should venture cautiously in this area.

Section 270: Definitions

Unless otherwise specifically provided, or unless clearly required by the context, the words and phrases defined in this section shall have the meaning indicated when used in this article.

(1) *Sign*. Any device that (i) is sufficiently visible to persons not located on the lot where such device is located to accomplish either of the objectives set forth in subdivision ii of this definition, and (ii) is designed to attract the attention of such persons or to communicate information to them.

(2) *Billboard*. An off-premises sign owned by a person, corporation, or other entity that engages in the business of selling the advertising space on that sign.

(3) *Effective Date of this Article*. The effective date of this article as originally adopted, or the effective date of an amendment to it if the amendment makes a sign nonconforming.

(4) *Freestanding Sign*. A sign that is attached to, erected on, or supported by some structure (such as a pole, mast, frame, or other structure) that is not itself an integral part of or attached to a building or other structure whose principal function is something other than the support of a sign. A sign that stands without supporting elements, such as "sandwich sign," is also a free-standing sign. If the message is removed from a structure that was

originally designed and used as a freestanding sign, this structure shall still be considered a sign.

(5) *Internally Illuminated Signs.* Signs where the source of the illumination is inside the sign and light emanates through the message of the sign, rather than being reflected off the surface of the sign from an external source. Without limiting the generality of the foregoing, signs that consist of or contain tubes that (i) are filled with neon or some other gas that glows when an electric current passes through it and (ii) are intended to form or constitute all or part of the message of the sign, rather than merely providing illumination to other parts of the sign that contain the message, shall also be considered internally illuminated signs.

(6) *Off-Premises Signs.* A sign that draws attention to or communicates information about a business, service, commodity, accommodation, attraction, or other enterprise or activity that exists or is conducted, sold, offered, maintained, or provided at a location other than the premises on which the sign is located. A sign that draws attention to a cause or advocates or proclaims a political, religious, or other noncommercial message shall also be an off-premises sign unless such sign is excluded from regulation under Subdivision 272(9) or is subject to regulation under Subsection 273(a)(5).

(7) *On-Premises Sign.* A sign that draws attention to or communicates information about a business, service, commodity, accommodation, attraction, or other enterprise or activity that exists or is conducted, sold, offered, maintained, or provided on the premises where the sign is located.

(8) *Temporary Sign.* A sign that (i) is used in connection with a circumstance, situation, or event that is designed, intended, or expected to take place or to be completed within a reasonably short or definite period after the erection of such sign, or (ii) is intended to remain on the location where it is erected or placed for a period of not more than 15 days. If a sign display area is permanent but the message displayed is subject to periodic changes, that sign shall not be regarded as temporary.

Commentary:

Definitions are always important, but this is particularly true of sign definitions because of all of the possible types of signs. Note that the definition of the basic term sign is written very broadly, leaving to other sections the exemptions and limitations that make the ordinance workable.

**Section 271:
Permit Required for Signs**

(a) Except as otherwise provided in Sections 272 (Signs Excluded from Regulation) and 273 (Certain Temporary Signs: Permit Exceptions and Additional Regulations), no sign may be constructed, erected, moved, enlarged, illuminated or substantially altered except in accordance with the provisions of this section. Mere repainting or changing the message of a sign shall not, in and of itself, be considered a substantial alteration.

(b) If plans submitted for a zoning permit, special-use permit, or conditional-use permit include sign plans in sufficient detail that the permit-issuing authority can determine whether the proposed sign or signs comply with the provisions of this chapter, then issuance of the requested zoning, special-use, or conditional-use permit shall constitute approval of the proposed sign or signs.

Commentary: A single business on a single lot usually is in a position to submit sign plans along with other plans required for approval of that business. In such cases, the sign is approved along with other aspects of the development. However, when more than one business will be located on a lot (e.g., a shopping center), the developer generally does not know who all the tenants will be when seeking the development permit and therefore is required to apply at a later time for a sign permit (see next subsection).

(c) Signs not approved as provided in Subsection (b) or exempted under the provisions referenced in Subsection (a) may be constructed, erected, moved, enlarged, illuminated or substantially altered only in accordance with a sign permit issued by the administrator.

(1) Sign permit applications and sign permits shall be governed by the same provisions of this chapter applicable to zoning permits.

(2) In the case of a lot occupied or intended to be occupied by multiple business enterprises (e.g., a shopping center), sign permits shall be issued in the name of the lot owner or his agent rather than in the name of the individual business enterprise requesting a particular sign. The city may assist the owner by suggesting a formula whereby the maximum square footage of sign area allowed on the lot may be allocated equitably among all tenants, but the city shall be responsible for enforcing only the provisions of this chapter and not the provisions of any allocation formula, lease, or other private restriction.

Commentary: Administering the sign ordinance in the context of a shopping center or other development containing numerous businesses can present delicate problems. The reason is that the development as a whole is assigned a certain amount of sign area (see Section 276), but usually each business gets its own sign permit. Obviously, there must be some basis upon which to allocate sign area among the various businesses, and this responsibility should be with the developer. Subdivision (c)(2) helps to keep the responsibility where it belongs by issuing sign permits in the name of the developer, even though applications will likely be made by the individual businesses. At the same time, it encourages the city to assist the developer in devising an allocation formula that will ensure satisfactory sign area for all tenants.

Section 272:
Signs Excluded From Regulation

The following signs are exempt from regulation under this chapter except for those stated in Subsections 282(b) through (e).

(1) Signs not exceeding four square feet in area that are customarily associated with residential use and that are not of a commercial nature, such as (i) signs giving property identification names or numbers or names of occupants, (ii) signs on mailboxes or newspaper tubes, and (iii) signs posted on private property relating to private parking or warning the public against trespassing or danger from animals.

(2) Signs erected by or on behalf of or pursuant to the authorization of a governmental body, including legal notices, identification and informational signs, and traffic, directional, or regulatory signs.

(3) Official signs of a noncommercial nature erected by public utilities.

(4) Flags, pennants, or insignia of any governmental or nonprofit organization when not displayed in connection with a commercial promotion or as an advertising device.

(5) Integral decorative or architectural features of buildings or works of art, so long as such features or works do not contain letters, trademarks, moving parts, or lights.

(6) Signs directing and guiding traffic on private property that do not exceed four square feet each and that bear no advertising matter.

(7) Church bulletin boards, church identification signs, and church directional signs that do not exceed one per abutting street and 16 square feet in area and that are not internally illuminated.

(8) Signs painted on or otherwise permanently attached to currently licensed motor vehicles that are not primarily used as signs.

(9) Signs proclaiming religious, political, or other noncommercial messages (other than those regulated by Subdivision 273(5)) that do not exceed one per abutting street and 16 square feet in area and that are not internally illuminated.

Commentary:

Given the inclusive definition of sign in Section 270, the practicalities of administering the ordinance demand that the draftsman carefully consider what signs to exclude entirely from the remaining regulations (this section) and what signs to exempt from the requirement of getting a permit as well as certain other requirements (see Section 273). This section and the next illustrate just one way to handle these exclusions and partial exemptions.

Section 273:
Certain Temporary Signs:
Permit Exemptions and
Additional Regulations

(a) The following temporary signs are permitted without a zoning, special-use, conditional-use, or sign permit. However, such signs shall conform to the requirements set forth below as well as all other applicable requirements of this chapter except those contained in Sections 276 (Total Sign Surface Area) and 278 (Number of Freestanding Signs).

(1) Signs containing the message that the real estate on which the sign is located (including buildings) is for sale, lease, or rent, together with information identifying the owner or agent. Such signs may not exceed four square feet in area and shall be removed immediately after sale, lease, or rental. For lots of less than five acres, a single sign on each street frontage may be erected. For lots of five acres or more in area and having a street frontage in excess of 400 feet, a second sign not exceeding four square feet in area may be erected.

(2) Construction site identification signs. Such signs may identify the project, the owner or developer, architect, engineer, contractor

and subcontractors, funding sources, and may contain related information including but not limited to sale or leasing information. Not more than one such sign may be erected per site, and it may not exceed 32 square feet in area. Such signs shall not be erected prior to the issuance of a building permit and shall be removed within 10 days after the issuance of the final occupancy permit.

(3) Signs attached temporarily to the interior of a building window or glass door. Such signs, individually or collectively, may not cover more than 75 percent of the surface area of the transparent portion of the window or door to which they are attached. Such signs shall be removed within 30 days after placement.

(4) Displays, including lighting, erected in connection with the observance of holidays. Such signs shall be removed within 10 days following the holidays.

(5) Signs erected in connection with elections or political campaigns. Such signs shall be removed within three days following the election or conclusion of the campaign. No such sign may exceed 16 square feet in surface area.

(6) Signs indicating that a special event such as a grand opening, fair, carnival, circus, festival, or similar event is to take place on the lot where the sign is located. Such signs may be erected not sooner than two weeks before the event and must be removed not later than three days after the event.

(7) Temporary signs not covered in the foregoing categories, so long as such signs meet the following restrictions:

  (a) Not more than one such sign may be located on any lot.
  (b) No such sign may exceed four square feet in surface area.
  (c) Such sign may not be displayed for longer than three consecutive days nor more than 10 days out of any 365-day period.

(b) Other temporary signs not listed in Subsection (a) shall be regarded and treated in all respects as permanent signs, except that (as provided in Section 276) temporary signs shall not be included in calculating the total amount of permitted sign area.

Section 274: Determining the Number of Signs

(a) For the purpose of determining the number of signs, a sign shall be considered to be a single display surface or display device containing elements organized, related, and composed to form a unit. Where matter is displayed in a random manner without organized relationship of elements, each element shall be considered a single sign.

(b) A two-sided or multi-sided sign shall be regarded as one sign so long as:

(1) With respect to a V-type sign, the two sides are at no point separated by a distance that exceeds five feet; and

(2) With respect to double faced (back to back) signs, the distance between the backs of each face of the sign does not exceed three feet.

Section 275: Computation of Sign Area

(a) The surface area of a sign shall be computed by including the entire area within a single, continuous, rectilinear perimeter of not more than eight straight lines, or a circle or an ellipse, enclosing the extreme limits of the writing, representation, emblem, or other display, together with any material or color forming an integral part of the background of the display or used to differentiate the sign from the backdrop or structure against which it is placed, but not including any supporting framework or bracing that is clearly incidental to the display itself.

(b) If the sign consists of more than one section or module, all of the area, including that between sections or modules, shall be included in the computation of the sign area.

(c) With respect to two-sided, multi-sided, or three-dimensional signs, the sign surface area shall be computed by including the total of all sides designed to attract attention or communicate information that can be seen at any one time by a person from one vantage point. Without otherwise limiting the generality of the foregoing:

   (1) The sign surface area of a double faced, back to back sign shall be calculated by using the area of only one side of such sign, so long as the distance between the backs of such signs does not exceed three feet.

   (2) The sign surface area of a double faced sign constructed in the form of a "V" shall be calculated by using the area of only one side of such sign (the larger side if there is a size difference), so long as the angle of the "V" does not exceed 30 degrees and at no point does the distance between the backs of such sides exceed five feet.

Section 276: Total Sign Surface Area

(a) Unless otherwise provided in this article, the total surface area devoted to all signs on any lot shall not exceed the limitations set forth in this section, and all signs except temporary signs shall be included in this calculation.

(b) Unless otherwise provided in this article or in Article XI (Supplementary Use Regulations), the maximum sign surface area permitted on any lot in any residential district (see Section 135) is four square feet.

(c) Subject to the other provisions of this section, the maximum sign surface area permitted on any lot in a commercial district other than the B-5 district or manufacturing district shall be determined as follows:

   (1) There may be not more than 0.5 square feet of sign surface area per linear foot of lot street frontage up to 200 feet of frontage.

   (2) There may be up to 0.75 square feet of additional sign surface area per linear foot of lot street frontage in excess of 200 feet.

Commentary: Some ordinances calculate surface area in reference to building frontage rather than lot frontage. However, apart from the obvious fact that this approach will not work when there is no building on the lot, the spatial relationships that the ordinance is attempting to control are more directly regulated by using lot frontage as the basis for determining sign area.

(d) Subject to the other provisions of this section, the maximum sign surface area on any lot in the B-5 district shall be determined by multiplying the number of linear feet of street frontage of the lot by 1.0 feet. However, in no case may the total sign surface area exceed 500 square feet.

Commentary: This subsection allows additional sign area in the business district adjacent to major highways. Whether this is desirable is obviously a matter of policy. Because of the larger sign surface area allowed per square foot, this subsection also establishes a cap on the total allowable sign surface area. This is probably not necessary in other districts where the lower front-footage-to-sign-area ratio is applicable, especially since the next section does establish a cap on the sign surface area of freestanding signs.

(e) If a lot has frontage on more than one street, then the total sign surface area permitted on that lot shall be the sum of the sign surface area allotments related to each street on which the lot has frontage. However, the total sign surface area that is oriented toward a particular street may not exceed the portion of the lot's total sign surface area allocation that is derived from frontage on that street.

(f) Whenever a lot is situated such that it has no street frontage on any lot boundary and an applicant desires to install on such a lot a sign that is oriented toward a street, then the total sign surface area permitted on that lot shall be the sign surface area that would be allowed if the lot boundary closest to the street toward which such sign is to be oriented fronted on such street. The applicant shall be restricted to using only one street and the closest lot boundary to this street for determining the total permitted sign surface area. However, the applicant shall be given the opportunity to determine the one street used in the calculations.

(g) The sign surface area of any sign located on a wall of a structure may not exceed 50 percent of the total surface area of the wall on which the sign is located.

Section 277:
Freestanding Sign Surface Area

(a) For purposes of this section, a side of a freestanding sign is any plane or flat surface included in the calculation of the total sign surface area as provided in Section 275. For example, wall signs typically have one side. Freestanding signs typically have two sides (back to back), although four-sided and other multi-sided signs are also common.

(b) Subject to Subsection (c), a single side of a freestanding sign may not exceed 0.3 square feet in surface area for every linear foot of street frontage along the street toward which such sign is primarily oriented. However, in no case may a single side of a freestanding sign exceed 50 square feet in surface area if the lot on which the sign is located has less than 200 feet of frontage on the street toward which that sign is primarily oriented, 75 square feet on lots with 200 or more but less than 400 feet of frontage, and 100 square feet on lots with 400 or more feet of frontage.

Commentary: This subsection limits the amount of freestanding sign surface area to 60 percent of the total area permissible on the lot. Larger signs are permitted on larger lots in recognition that such signs will have more open land around and between them, reducing their visual impact.

(c) In the B-5 district, a single side of a freestanding sign may not exceed 0.75 square feet in surface area for every linear foot of street frontage along the street toward which such sign is primarily oriented. However, in no case may a single side of such signs exceed 250 square feet in surface area.

(**d**) With respect to freestanding signs that have no discernible sides, such as spheres or other shapes not composed of flat planes, no such freestanding sign may exceed the maximum total surface area allowed under Subsections (b) or (c) for a single side of a freestanding sign.

Section 278:
Number of Freestanding Signs

(**a**) Except as authorized by this section, no development may have more than one freestanding sign.

(**b**) If a development is located on a corner lot that has at least 100 feet of frontage on each of the two intersecting public streets, then the development may have not more than one freestanding sign along each side of the development bordered by such streets.

(**c**) If a development is located on a lot that is bordered by two public streets that do not intersect at the lot's boundaries (double front lot), then the development may have not more than one freestanding sign on each side of the development bordered by such streets.

Section 279:
Subdivision and Multi-Family Development Entrance Signs

At any entrance to a residential subdivision or multi-family development, there may be not more than two signs identifying such subdivision or development. A single side of any such sign may not exceed 16 square feet, nor may the total surface area of all such signs located at a single entrance exceed 32 square feet.

Section 280:
Location and Height Requirements

(**a**) Freestanding signs shall observe the setback requirements set forth in Section 184.

(**b**) No sign may extend above any parapet or be placed upon any roof surface, except that for purposes of this section, roof surfaces constructed at an angle of 75 degrees or more from horizontal shall be regarded as wall space. This subsection shall not apply to displays, including lighting, erected in connection with the observation of holidays on the roofs of residential structures.

(**c**) No sign attached to a building may project more than 12 inches from the building wall.

(**d**) No sign or supporting structure may be located in or over the traveled portion of any public right-of-way unless the sign is attached to a structural element of a building and an encroachment permit has been obtained from the city.

(**e**) No part of a freestanding sign may exceed a height, measured from ground level, of 25 feet in the B-5, M-1, and M-2 districts and 15 feet in all other districts.

Section 281:
Sign Illumination and Signs Containing Lights

(**a**) Unless otherwise prohibited by this chapter, signs may be illuminated if such illumination is in accordance with this section.

(**b**) No sign within 150 feet of a residential zone may be illuminated between the hours of midnight and 6 a.m., unless the impact of such lighting beyond the boundaries of the lot where it is located is entirely inconsequential.

(c) Lighting directed toward a sign shall be shielded so that it illuminates only the face of the sign and does not shine directly into a public right-of-way or residential premises.

(d) Except as herein provided, (i) internally illuminated signs are not permissible in the _____ zoning district, and (ii) where permissible, internally illuminated freestanding signs may not be illuminated during hours that the business or enterprise advertised by such sign is not open for business or in operation. This subsection shall not apply to the following types of signs:

   (1) Signs that constitute an integral part of a vending machine, telephone booth, device that indicates the time, date, or weather conditions, or similar device whose principal function is not to convey an advertising message.

   (2) Signs that do not exceed two square feet in area and that convey the message that a business enterprise is open or closed or that a place of lodging does or does not have a vacancy.

(e) Subject to Subsection (g), illuminated tubings or strings of lights that outline property lines, sales areas, roof lines, doors, windows, or similar areas are prohibited.

(f) Subject to Subsection (g), no sign may contain or be illuminated by flashing or intermittent lights or lights of changing degrees of intensity, except signs indicating the time, date or weather conditions.

(g) Subsections (e) and (f) do not apply to temporary signs erected in connection with the observance of holidays.

Section 282: Miscellaneous Restrictions and Prohibitions

(a) As provided in the Table of Permissible Uses (use classification 27.000), no off-premises signs (except those exempted from regulation or from permit requirements under Sections 272 or 273) may be located in any district other than a B-5, M-1, or M-2 district.

(b) No sign may be located so that it substantially interferes with the view necessary for motorists to proceed safely through intersections or to enter onto or exit from public streets or private roads.

(c) Signs that revolve or are animated or that utilize movement or apparent movement to attract the attention of the public are prohibited. Without limiting the foregoing, banners, streamers, animated display boards, pennants, and propellers are prohibited, but signs that only move occasionally because of wind are not prohibited if their movement (i) is not a primary design feature of the sign, and (ii) is not intended to attract attention to the sign. The restriction of this subsection shall not apply to signs specified in Subdivision 272(4) or to signs indicating the time, date, or weather conditions.

(d) No sign may be erected so that by its location, color, size, shape, nature, or message it would tend to obstruct the view of or be confused with official traffic signs or other signs erected by governmental agencies.

(e) Freestanding signs shall be securely fastened to the ground or to some other substantial supportive structure so that there is virtually no danger that either the sign or the supportive structure may be moved by the wind or other forces of nature and cause injury to persons or property.

Section 283: Maintenance of Signs

(a) All signs and all components thereof, including without limitation supports, braces, and anchors, shall be kept in a state of good repair. With respect to freestanding signs, components (supporting structures, backs, etc.) not bearing a message shall be constructed of materials that blend with the natural environment or shall be painted a neutral color to blend with the natural environment.

(b) If a sign other than a billboard advertises a business, service, commodity, accommodation, attraction, or other enterprise or activity that is no longer operating or being offered or conducted, that sign shall be considered abandoned and shall, within 30 days after such abandonment, be removed by the sign owner, owner of the property where the sign is located, or other party having control over such sign.

(c) If the message portion of a sign is removed, leaving only the supporting "shell" of a sign or the supporting braces, anchors, or similar components, the owner of the sign or the owner of the property where the sign is located or other person having control over such sign shall, within 30 days of the removal of the message portion of the sign, either replace the entire message portion of the sign or remove the remaining components of the sign. This subsection shall not be construed to alter the effect of Subsection 285(c), which prohibits the replacement of a nonconforming sign. Nor shall this subsection be construed to prevent the changing of the message of a sign.

(d) The area within 10 feet in all directions of any part of a freestanding sign shall be kept clear of all debris and all undergrowth more than five inches in height.

Section 284: Unlawful Cutting of Trees or Shrubs

No person may, for the purpose of increasing or enhancing the visibility of any sign, damage, trim, destroy, or remove any trees, shrubs, or other vegetation located:

(a) Within the right-of-way of any public street or road, unless the work is done pursuant to the express written authorization of [the city or other agency having jurisdiction over the streets].

(b) On property that is not under the ownership or control of the person doing or responsible for such work, unless the work is done pursuant to the express authorization of the person owning the property where such trees or shrubs are located;

(c) In any area where such trees or shrubs are required to remain under a permit issued under this ordinance.

Section 285: Nonconforming Signs

(a) Subject to the remaining restrictions of this section, nonconforming signs that were otherwise lawful on the effective date of this article may be continued until they are required to be removed under Section 286.

(b) No person may engage in any activity that causes an increase in the extent of nonconformity of a nonconforming sign. Without limiting the generality of the foregoing, no nonconforming sign may be enlarged or altered in such a manner as to aggravate the nonconforming condition. Nor may illumination be added to any nonconforming sign.

(c) A nonconforming sign may not be moved or replaced except to bring the sign into complete conformity with this chapter.

(d) If a nonconforming sign is destroyed by natural causes, it may not thereafter be repaired, reconstructed, or replaced except in conformity with all the provisions of this chapter, and the remnants of the former sign structure shall be cleared from the land. For purposes of this section, a nonconforming sign is "destroyed" if damaged to an extent that the cost of repairing the sign to its former stature or replacing it with an equivalent sign equals or exceeds the value (tax value if listed for tax purposes) of the sign so damaged.

(e) The message of a nonconforming sign may be changed so long as this does not create any new nonconformities (for example, by creating an off-premises sign under circumstances where such a sign would not be allowed).

(f) Subject to the other provisions of this section, nonconforming signs may be repaired and renovated so long as the cost of such work does not exceed within any 12-month period 50 percent of the value (tax value if listed for tax purposes) of such sign.

(g) If a nonconforming sign other than a billboard advertises a business, service, commodity, accommodation, attraction, or other enterprise or activity that is no longer operating or being offered or conducted, that sign shall be considered abandoned and shall be removed within 30 days after such abandonment by the sign owner, owner of the property where the sign is located, or other party having control over such sign.

(h) If a nonconforming billboard remains blank for a continuous period of 180 days, that billboard shall be deemed abandoned and shall, within 30 days after such abandonment, be altered to comply with this article or be removed by the sign owner, owner of the property where the sign is located, or other person having control over such sign. For purposes of this section, a sign is "blank" if:

   (1) It advertises a business, service, commodity, accommodation, attraction, or other enterprise or activity that is no longer operating or being offered or conducted; or

   (2) The advertising message it displays becomes illegible in whole or substantial part; or

   (3) The advertising copy paid for by a party other than the sign owner or promoting an interest other than the rental of the sign has been removed.

(i) As soon as reasonably possible after the effective date of this chapter, the administrator shall make every reasonable effort to identify all the nonconforming signs within the city's planning jurisdiction. He shall then contact the person responsible for each such sign (as well as the owner of the property where the nonconforming sign is located, if different from the former) and inform such person (i) that the sign is nonconforming, (ii) how it is nonconforming, (iii) what must be done to correct it and by what date, and (iv) the consequences of failure to make the necessary corrections. The administrator shall keep complete records of all correspondence, communications, and other actions taken with respect to such nonconforming signs.

Section 286:
Amortization of Nonconforming Signs

(a) Subject to the remaining subsections of this section, a nonconforming sign that exceeds the height, size, or spacing limitations by more than 10 percent or that is nonconforming in some other way shall, within three years after the effective date of this chapter, be altered to comply with the provisions of this article or be removed.

(b) If the nonconformity consists of too many freestanding signs on a single lot or an excess of total sign area on a single lot, the person responsible for the violation may determine which sign or signs need to be altered or removed to bring the development into conformity with the provisions of this article.

(c) The following types of nonconforming signs or signs that are nonconforming in any of the following ways shall be altered to comply with the provisions of this article or removed within 90 days after the effective date of this article:

(1) Portable signs and temporary signs.
(2) Signs that are in violation of Section 281 or Subsections 282(b), (c), or (d).

(d) Off-premises signs that are protected from enforced removal by the Outdoor Advertising Control Act shall not be subject to the provisions of Subsection (a) of this section unless and until just compensation is provided in accordance with the cited statute.

Commentary:

Requiring the elimination of nonconforming signs after an appropriate "amortization" period has become a commonplace practice and one that has generally received judicial approval. However, before drafting provisions such as the foregoing, the case law of the jurisdiction in question should be consulted.

Subsection (d) deals with the particular case of billboards on highways that are part of the National System of Interstate and Defense Highways or the Federal-Aid Primary Highway System. State legislation (such as the Outdoor Advertising Control Act in North Carolina) adopted to comply with the Federal Highway Beautification Act (23 U.S.C. Sec. 131) may preempt the local government's authority to require the removal without compensation of billboards along these highways.

Sections 287 through 289:
Reserved

Article XVIII Parking

Section 290: Definitions

Unless otherwise specifically provided or unless clearly required by the context, the words and phrases defined below shall have the meaning indicated when used in this section.

(1) *Circulation Area.* That portion of the vehicle accommodation area used for access to parking or loading areas or other facilities on the lot. Essentially, driveways and other maneuvering areas (other than parking aisles) comprise the circulation area.

(2) *Driveway.* That portion of the vehicle accommodation area that consists of a travel lane bounded on either side by an area that is not part of the vehicle accommodation area.

(3) *Gross Floor Area.* The total area of a building measured by taking the outside dimensions of the building at each floor level intended for occupancy or storage.

(4) *Loading and Unloading Area.* That portion of the vehicle accommodation area used to satisfy the requirements of Section 300.

(5) *Vehicle Accommodation Area.* That portion of a lot that is used by vehicles for access, circulation, parking, and loading and unloading. It comprises the total of circulation areas, loading and unloading areas, and parking areas (spaces and aisles).

(6) *Parking Area Aisles.* That portion of the vehicle accommodation area consisting of lanes providing access to parking spaces.

(7) *Parking Space.* A portion of the vehicle accommodation area set for the parking of one vehicle.

Section 291: Number of Parking Spaces Required

(a) All developments in all zoning districts other than the B-1 district shall provide a sufficient number of parking spaces to accommodate the number of vehicles that ordinarily are likely to be attracted to the development in question.

Commentary:

> This subsection substitutes a performance standard, albeit a very nonquantitative performance standard, for the table of parking requirements that constitutes the basic standard in most zoning ordinances. As indicated in the following, a table is included in this section but the figures derived from this table only establish a rebuttable presumption that the basic standard set forth in this subsection is satisfied.

Note that developments in the B-1 district are not required to provide parking. This exception is provided because the B-1 is the central business district and land in this district may be developed, or the city may wish to have it developed, so intensively that parking can only be accommodated in off-site parking garages. Of course, in smaller towns this situation may not prevail and the exception would not be warranted.

(b) The presumptions established by this article are that: (i) a development must comply with the parking standards set forth in Subsection (e) to satisfy the requirement stated in Subsection (a), and (ii) any development that does meet these standards is in compliance. However, the Table of Parking Requirements is only intended to establish a presumption and should be flexibly administered, as provided in Section 292.

(c) Uses in the Table of Parking Requirements (Subsection (e)), are indicated by a numerical reference keyed to the Table of Permissible Uses, Section 146. When determination of the number of parking spaces required by this table results in a requirement of a fractional space, any fraction of one-half or less may be disregarded, while a fraction in excess of one-half shall be counted as one parking space.

(d) The council recognizes that the Table of Parking Requirements set forth in Subsection (e) cannot and does not cover every possible situation that may arise. Therefore, in cases not specifically covered, the permit-issuing authority is authorized to determine the parking requirements using this table as a guide.

(e) Table of Parking Requirements

Use	Parking Requirement
1.110 1.120	2 spaces per dwelling unit plus one space per room rented out (see Accessory Uses, Section 150).
1.200	2 spaces for each dwelling unit, except that one-bedroom units require only one space.
1.300	With respect to multi-family units located in buildings where each dwelling unit has an entrance and living space on the ground floor, the requirement shall be 1½ spaces for each one-bedroom unit and 2 spaces for each unit with two or more bedrooms. Multi-family units limited to persons of low- or moderate-income or the elderly require only 1 space per unit. All other multi-family units require 1 space for each bedroom in each unit plus 1 additional space for every four units in the development.
1.400	3 spaces for every five beds except for uses exclusively serving children under 16, in which case 1 space for every three beds shall be required.
1.510	1 space for each bedroom.
1.520 1.530	1 space for each room to be rented plus additional space (in accordance with other sections of this table) for restaurant or other facilities.

Use	Parking Requirement
1.700	4 spaces for offices of physicians or dentists; 2 spaces for attorneys, 1 space for all others.
2.111	1 space per 200 square feet of gross floor area.
2.112	1 space per 150 square feet of gross floor area.
2.120 2.130	1 space per 400 square feet of gross floor area.
2.210	1 space per 200 square feet of gross floor area.
2.220 2.230	1 space per 400 square feet of gross floor area.
3.110	1 space per 200 square feet of gross floor area.
3.120	1 space per 400 square feet of gross floor area.
3.130	1 space per 150 square feet of gross floor area.
3.210	1 space per 200 square feet of gross floor area.
3.220	1 space per 400 square feet of gross floor area.
3.230	1 space per 200 square feet of area within main building plus reservoir land capacity equal to 5 spaces per window (10 spaces if window serves two stations).
4.110	1 space per 400 square feet of gross floor area.
4.120 4.200	1 space for every two employees on the maximum shift except that, if permissible in the commercial districts, such uses may provide 1 space per 200 square feet of gross floor area.
5.110	1.75 spaces per classroom in elementary schools, 5 spaces per classroom in high schools.
5.120	1 space per 100 square feet of gross floor area.
5.130	1 space per 150 square feet of gross floor area.
5.200	1 space for every four seats in the portion of the church building to be used for services plus spaces for any residential use as determined in accordance with the parking requirements set forth above for residential uses, plus 1 space for every 200 square feet of gross floor area designed to be used neither for services nor residential purposes.
5.300 5.400	1 space per 300 square feet of gross floor area.
6.110	1 space for every three persons that the facilities are designed to accommodate when fully utilized (if they can be measured in such a fashion—example, tennis courts or bowling alleys) plus 1 space per 200 square feet of gross floor area used in a manner not susceptible to such calculation.

Use	Parking Requirement
6.120 6.130	1 space for every four seats.
6.210 6.220	1 space per 200 square feet of area within enclosed buildings, plus 1 space for every three persons that the outdoor facilities are designed to accommodate when used to the maximum capacity.
6.230	Miniature golf course, skateboard park, water slide, and similar uses—1 space per 300 square feet of area plus 1 space per 200 square feet of building gross floor area; Driving range—1 space per tee plus 1 space per 200 square feet in building gross floor area; Par Three Course—2 spaces per golf hole plus 1 space per 200 square feet of building gross floor area.
6.240	1 space per horse that could be kept at the stable when occupied to maximum capacity.
6.250	1 space for every three seats.
6.260	1 space per speaker outlet.
7.100	2 spaces per bed or 1 space per 150 square feet of gross floor area, whichever is greater.
7.200	3 spaces for every five beds. Multi-family units developed or sponsored by a public or nonprofit agency for limited income families or the elderly require only 1 space per unit.
7.300 7.400	1 space for every two employees on maximum shift.
8.100	1 space per 100 square feet of gross floor area.
8.200 8.300	Same as 8.100 plus 1 space for every four outside seats.
8.400	Same as 8.200 plus reservoir lane capacity equal to 5 spaces per drive-in window.
9.100 9.200 9.300 9.400	1 space per 200 square feet of gross floor area.
9.500	1 space per 200 square feet of gross floor area of building devoted primarily to gas sales operation, plus sufficient parking area to accommodate vehicles at pumps without interfering with other parking spaces.
9.600	Conveyer type—1 space for every three employees on the maximum shift plus reservoir capacity equal to five times the capacity of the washing operation. Self-service type—2 spaces for drying and cleaning purposes per stall plus two reservoir spaces in front of each stall.

Use	Parking Requirement
10.210 10.220	1 space for every two employees on the maximum shift but not less than 1 space per 5,000 square feet of area devoted to storage (whether inside or outside).
11.000	1 space per 200 square feet of gross floor area.
12.000	1 space per 200 square feet of gross floor area.
13.000	1 space per 200 square feet of gross floor area.
14.000	1 space for every two employees on maximum shift.
15.100 15.200	1 space per 200 square feet of gross floor area.
15.300	1 space for every two employees on maximum shift.
15.400	1 space per 100 square feet of gross floor area.
16.000	1 space per 200 square feet of gross floor area.
19.000	1 space per 1,000 square feet of lot area used for storage, display, or sales.
20.000	1 space per 100 square feet of gross floor area.
21.200	1 space per 200 square feet of gross floor area.
22.000	1 space per employee plus 1 space per 200 square feet of gross floor area.
24.000	1 space per 200 square feet of gross floor area.
25.000	1 space per 200 square feet of gross floor area.

Commentary:

The author would like to be able to assert that each of the foregoing presumptive standards is grounded in thorough research and has been verified by experience. The reality is that with the exception of those few recurring uses where it has been possible to inform guesswork with experience, most of the presumptive standards are at best hopeful estimates. Few reliable sources of information are available to provide assistance in this area. Some types of enterprises, e.g., fast-food franchises, do have their own well-documented standards, but for these few types of businesses the table is unnecessary anyway since their own standards will assure sufficient parking. This lack of satisfactory information upon which to base many of the entries in this table is one of the principal reasons why it is used only as a presumptive standard.

**Section 292:
Flexibility in Administration Required**

(a) The council recognizes that, due to the particularities of any given development, the inflexible application of the parking standards set forth in Subsection 291(e) may result in a development either with inadequate parking space or parking space far in excess of its needs. The former situation may lead to traffic congestion or parking violations in adjacent streets as well as unauthorized parking in nearby private lots. The latter situation wastes money as well as space that could more desirably be used for valuable development or environmentally useful open space. Therefore, as suggested in Section 291, the permit-issuing authority may permit deviations from the presumptive requirements of Subsection 291(e) and may require more parking or allow less parking whenever it finds that such deviations are more likely to satisfy the standard set forth in Subsection 291(a).

(b) Without limiting the generality of the foregoing, the permit-issuing authority may allow deviations from the parking requirements set forth in Subsection 291(e) when it finds that:

(1) A residential development is irrevocably oriented toward the elderly;

(2) A business is primarily oriented to walk-in trade.

(c) Whenever the permit-issuing authority allows or requires a deviation from the presumptive parking requirements set forth in Subsection 291(e), it shall enter on the face of the permit the parking requirement that it imposes and the reasons for allowing or requiring the deviation.

Commentary:
> This provision helps to minimize arbitrariness in administration by requiring a written statement of why the deviation from the presumptive requirement is allowed or required. The written statement should also help to establish precedent for use in future cases.

(d) If the permit-issuing authority concludes, based upon information it receives in the consideration of a specific development proposal, that the presumption established by Subsection 291(e) for a particular use classification is erroneous, it shall initiate a request for an amendment to the Table of Parking Requirements in accordance with the procedures set forth in Article XX.

Commentary:
> There are two types of situations in which the presumptive standard may be demonstrated to be inaccurate. First, when a use classification is very general and includes many different types of business (e.g., classification 2.111, miscellaneous, high-volume retail), it may well be that a particular type of business could demonstrate that the standard is inaccurate given the unique circumstances that apply to that type of business. In such a case, an amendment to the table would not be warranted. Second, it may be that an applicant demonstrates to the satisfaction of the permit-issuing entity that the presumptive requirement is inaccurate with respect to all uses that fall within that classification. For example, when the First Kennel applies for a permit, it may become apparent that the presumptive table is simply wrong. In such a case, the presumption can be ignored but the ordinance needs to be amended.

Section 293: Parking Space Dimensions

(a) Subject to Subsections (b) and (c), each parking space shall contain a rectangular area at least 19 feet long and 9 feet wide. Lines demarcating parking spaces may be drawn at various angles in relation to curbs or aisles, so long as the parking spaces so created contain within them the rectangular area required by this section.

(b) In parking areas containing 10 or more parking spaces, up to 20 percent of the parking spaces need contain a rectangular area of only 7½ feet in width by 15 feet in length. If such spaces are provided, they shall be conspicuously designated as reserved for small or compact cars only.

(c) Wherever parking areas consist of spaces set aside for parallel parking, the dimensions of such parking spaces shall be not less than 22 feet by 9 feet.

Commentary:
> Because paving is expensive and may have some adverse environmental consequences (increased volume of storm water runoff, carrying more pollutants), the draftsman should consciously examine parking space, aisle, and driveway dimensions. The possibility of allowing compact spaces, suggested by Subsection (b) should also be investigated.

Section 294: Required Widths of Parking Area Aisles and Driveways

(a) Parking area aisle widths shall conform to the following table, which varies the width requirement according to the angle of parking.

Aisle Width	Parking Angle				
	0°	30°	45°	60°	90°
One-Way Traffic	13	11	13	18	24
Two-Way Traffic	19	20	21	23	24

(b) Driveways shall be not less than 10 feet in width for one-way traffic and 18 feet in width for two-way traffic, except that 10-feet-wide driveways are permissible for two-way traffic when (i) the driveway is not longer than 50 feet, (ii) it provides access to not more than 6 spaces, and (iii) sufficient turning space is provided so that vehicles need not back into a public street.

Section 295: General Design Requirements

(a) Unless no other practicable alternative is available, vehicle accommodation areas shall be designed so that, without resorting to extraordinary movements, vehicles may exit such areas without backing onto a public street. This requirement does not apply to parking areas consisting of driveways that serve one or two dwelling units, although backing onto arterial streets is discouraged.

(b) Vehicle accommodation areas of all developments shall be designed so that sanitation, emergency, and other public service vehicles can serve such developments without the necessity of backing unreasonable distances or making other dangerous or hazardous turning movements.

(c) Every vehicle accommodation area shall be designed so that vehicles cannot extend beyond the perimeter of such area onto adjacent properties or public rights-of-way. Such areas shall also be designed so that vehicles do not extend over sidewalks or tend to bump against or damage any wall, vegetation, or other obstruction.

(d) Circulation areas shall be designed so that vehicles can proceed safely without posing a danger to pedestrians or other vehicles and without interfering with parking areas.

Section 296: Vehicle Accommodation Area Surfaces

(a) Vehicle accommodation areas that (i) include lanes for drive-in windows or (ii) contain parking areas that are required to have more than 10 parking spaces and that are used regularly at least five days per week shall be graded and surfaced with asphalt, concrete or other material that will provide equivalent protection against potholes, erosion, and dust. Specifications for surfaces meeting the standard set forth in this subsection are contained in Appendix D.

Commentary:

> The arguments in favor of requiring paved parking lots are that such lots improve appearance and are beneficial from the standpoint of public safety. The arguments against are based on cost and the environmental consequences of impervious surface. Presumably, the larger the development, the more weight the public safety and appearance arguments take on and the less significant concerns about cost become (i.e., the larger developer can more easily afford the expense of paving). Where the line should be drawn between paving and no paving is a matter of judgment.

(b) Vehicle accommodation areas that are not provided with the type of surface specified in Subsection (a) shall be graded and surfaced with crushed stone, gravel, or other suitable material (as provided in the specifications set forth in Appendix D) to provide a surface that is stable and will help to reduce dust and erosion. The perimeter of such parking areas shall be defined by bricks, stones, railroad ties, or other similar devices. In addition, whenever such a vehicle accommodation area abuts a paved street, the driveway leading from such street to such area (or, if there is no driveway, the portion of the vehicle accommodation area that opens onto such streets), shall be paved as provided in Subsection (a) for a distance of 15 feet back from the edge of the paved street. This subsection shall not apply to single-family or two-family residences or other uses that are required to have only one or two parking spaces.

(c) Parking spaces in areas surfaced in accordance with Subsection (a) shall be appropriately demarcated with painted lines or other markings. Parking spaces in areas surfaced in accordance with Subsection (b) shall be demarcated whenever practicable.

(d) Vehicle accommodation areas shall be properly maintained in all respects. In particular, and without limiting the foregoing, vehicle accommodation area surfaces shall be kept in good condition (free from potholes, etc.) and parking space lines or markings shall be kept clearly visible and distinct.

Section 297: Joint Use of Required Parking Spaces

(a) One parking area may contain required spaces for several different uses, but except as otherwise provided in this section, the required space assigned to one use may not be credited to any other use.

(b) To the extent that developments that wish to make joint use of the same parking spaces operate at different times, the same spaces may be credited to both uses. For example, if a parking lot is used in connection with an office building on Monday through Friday but is generally 90 percent vacant on weekends, another development that operates only on weekends could be credited with 90 percent of the spaces on that lot. Or, if a church parking lot is generally occupied only to 50 percent of capacity on days other than Sunday, another development could make use of 50 percent of the church lot's spaces on those other days.

(c) If the joint use of the same parking spaces by two or more principal uses involves satellite parking spaces, then the provisions of Section 298 are also applicable.

Section 298: Satellite Parking

(a) If the number of off-street parking spaces required by this chapter cannot reasonably be provided on the same lot where the principal use associated with these parking spaces is located, then spaces may be provided on adjacent or nearby lots in accordance with the provisions of this section. These off-site spaces are referred to in this section as satellite parking spaces.

(b) All such satellite parking spaces (except spaces intended for employee use) must be located within 400 feet of a public entrance of a principal building housing the use associated with such parking, or within 400 feet of the lot on which the use associated with such parking is located if the use is not housed within any principal building. Satellite parking spaces intended for employee use may be located within any reasonable distance.

(c) The developer wishing to take advantage of the provisions of this section must present satisfactory written evidence that he has the permission of the owner or other person in charge of the satellite parking spaces to use such spaces. The developer must also sign an acknowledgement that the continuing validity of his permit depends upon his continuing ability to provide the requisite number of parking spaces.

(d) Persons who obtain satellite parking spaces in accordance with this section shall not be held accountable for ensuring that the satellite parking areas from which they obtain their spaces satisfy the design requirements of this article.

Section 299: Special Provisions For Lots With Existing Buildings

Notwithstanding any other provisions of this chapter, whenever (i) there exists a lot with one or more structures on it constructed before the effective date of this chapter, and (ii) a change in use that does not involve any enlargement of a structure is proposed for such lot, and (iii) the parking requirements of Section 291 that would be applicable as a result of the proposed change cannot be satisfied on such lot because there is not sufficient area available on the lot that can practically be used for parking, then the developer need only comply with the requirements of Section 291 to the extent that (i) parking space is practically available on the lot where the development is located, and (ii) satellite parking space is reasonably available as provided in Section 297. However, if satellite parking subsequently becomes reasonably available, then it shall be a continuing condition of the permit authorizing development on such lot that the developer obtain satellite parking when it does become available.

Commentary:

> Almost every town has one or more business areas where, before the passage of any zoning ordinance, buildings were constructed on small lots with relatively little room left for parking. In some cases, the number of available parking spaces may satisfy the requirements of a subsequently passed zoning ordinance with respect to the type of use in operation when the ordinance was passed but would not meet ordinance standards for other potential uses of the building. For example, a building originally used as a retail store may have had sufficient parking spaces

under the ordinance but would not meet ordinance standards if the use were changed to a restaurant. Under these circumstances, there are two options: either prohibit the change in use or adopt a provision such as the foregoing to allow the change under the limited circumstances specified above. This calls for a policy decision, determining which is the lesser of potential evils—parking problems on adjacent streets and properties or a vacant building. This section opts for the parking problems. See also Subsection 124(f), which provides that when the original parking situation is nonconforming under the circumstances outlined above, a change to another use whose parking requirements continue to leave the parking situation nonconforming shall not be prohibited.

Section 300:
Loading and Unloading Areas

(a) Subject to Subsection (e), whenever the normal operation of any development requires that goods, merchandise, or equipment be routinely delivered to or shipped from that development, a sufficient off-street loading and unloading area must be provided in accordance with this section to accommodate the delivery or shipment operations in a safe and convenient manner.

(b) The loading and unloading area must be of sufficient size to accommodate the numbers and types of vehicles that are likely to use this area, given the nature of the development in question. The following table indicates the number and size of spaces that, presumptively, satisfy the standard set forth in this subsection. However, the permit-issuing authority may require more or less loading and unloading area if reasonably necessary to satisfy the foregoing standard.

Gross Leasable Area of Building	Number of spaces*
1,000 - 19,999	1
20,000 - 79,999	2
80,000 - 127,999	3
128,000 - 191,000	4
192,000 - 255,999	5
256,000 - 319,999	6
320,000 - 391,999	7

Plus one (1) space for each additional 72,000 square feet or fraction thereof.

*Minimum dimensions of 12 feet × 55 feet and overhead clearance of 14 feet from street grade required.

(c) Loading and unloading areas shall be so located and designed that the vehicles intended to use them can (i) maneuver safely and conveniently to and from a public right-of-way, and (ii) complete the loading and unloading operations without obstructing or interfering with any public right-of-way or any parking space or parking lot aisle.

(d) No area allocated to loading and unloading facilities may be used to satisfy the area requirements for off-street parking, nor shall any portion of any off-street parking area be used to satisfy the area requirements for loading and unloading facilities.

(e) Whenever (i) there exists a lot with one or more structures on it constructed before the effective date of this chapter, and (ii) a change in use that does not involve any enlargement of a structure is proposed for such lot, and (iii) the loading area requirements of this section cannot be satisfied because there is not sufficient area available on the lot that can practicably be used for loading and unloading, then the developer need only comply with this section to the extent reasonably possible.

Sections 301 through 303: Reserved

Article XIX Screening and Trees

Commentary:

The provisions in this article are extremely important for ensuring the quality of development that most communities seek. The difference between a development that most people consider attractive and one generally regarded as unattractive very frequently relates directly to the number of trees that remain on the development site and the sense of visual separation created by screening between the development and the street and surrounding lots.

Clearly, aesthetic concerns are the basis for the requirements of this article. But it is possible to justify these regulations on other grounds as well (see Sections 304 and 314). In addition, standards concerning retention or planting of shade trees and screening can be stated rather specifically in the ordinance, substantially reducing the possibility that developers would be subjected to the unrestricted aesthetic judgments of those who administer the ordinance. These factors differentiate these provisions from regulations that might seek to impose other sorts of landscaping requirements.

This is not to suggest that general landscaping is by any means less important to the aesthetics of a project than screening and shade trees, only that it is more difficult to establish ordinance requirements governing this topic that are not legally suspect. However, landscaping plans can still be requested and reviewed by an appearance commission, which can make suggestions to the developer for improvements. Experience has proven that this process can be extremely useful in ensuring attractively landscaped projects, even if the commission's recommendations are not legally enforceable.

Part I. Screening

**Section 304:
Council Findings Concerning the Need for Screening Requirements**

The council finds that:

(1) Screening between two lots lessens the transmission from one lot to another of noise, dust, and glare.

(2) Screening can lessen the visual pollution that may otherwise occur within an urbanized area. Even minimal screening can provide an impression of separation of spaces, and more extensive screening can shield entirely one use from the visual assault of an adjacent use.

(3) Screening can establish a greater sense of privacy from visual or physical intrusion, the degree of privacy varying with the intensity of the screening.

(4) The provisions of this part are necessary to safeguard the public health, safety and welfare.

Commentary: As a general matter, findings are not recommended for inclusion in the text of the ordinance. However, an exception is made here and in Section 314 because regulations establishing screening and tree retention requirements are still somewhat unusual, and in the event these requirements are challenged, findings such as these may help a court that is inclined to uphold these regulations justify its decision.

Section 305: General Screening Standard

Every development shall provide sufficient screening so that:

(1) Neighboring properties are shielded from any adverse external effects of that development;

(2) The development is shielded from the negative impacts of adjacent uses such as streets or railroads.

Commentary: This article uses the same general performance standard plus presumptive specific table approach found in Article XVIII, Parking. See commentary following Subsection 291(a).

Section 306: Compliance With Screening Standard

(a) The table set forth in Section 308, in conjunction with the explanations in Section 307 concerning the types of screens, establishes screening requirements that presumptively satisfy the general standards established in Section 305. However, this table is only intended to establish a presumption and should be flexibly administered in accordance with Section 309.

Commentary: The table that appears in Section 308 may cause a bit of eye strain, but it provides a convenient method of establishing screening requirements for all possible combinations of adjoining uses. Of course, the table requires a fair amount of effort to construct, since each box represents a policy decision, but once constructed it is easy to use.

The benefitted and burdened distinctions represent a judgment as to which of two adjoining uses has the greater negative impacts. The use that has the greater impact is the burdened use because it has the burden of installing the screening necessary to shield the benefitted use from these negative impacts.

(b) The numerical designations contained in the Table of Screening Requirements (Section 308) are keyed to the Table of Permissible Uses (Section 146), and the letter designations refer to types of screening as described in Section 307. This table indicates the type of screening that is presumptively required between two uses. Where such screening is required, only one of the two adjoining uses is responsible for installing the screening. The use assigned this responsibility is referred to as the burdened use in Section 308, and the other use is the benefitted use.

(1) To determine which of two adjoining uses is required to install the screening, find the use classification number of one of the adjoining uses in the burdened use column and follow that column across the page to its intersection with the use classification number in the benefitted use column that corresponds to the other adjoining use. If the intersecting square contains a letter, then the use whose classification number is in the burdened column is responsible for installing that level of screening. If the intersecting square does not contain a letter, then begin the process again, starting this time in the burdened column with the other adjoining use.

(2) To merely determine the type of screening a proposed new development must install, begin under the burdened column with the use classification number of the proposed use and follow that line across the page to its intersection with the use classification number of each use that adjoins the property to be developed. For each intersecting square that contains a letter, the developer must install the level of screening indicated.

(c) If, when the analysis described in Subdivision (b)(1) is performed, the burdened use is an existing use but the required screening is not in place, then this lack of screening shall constitute a nonconforming situation, subject to all the provisions of Article VIII of this chapter.

(d) Notwithstanding any other provision of this article, a two-family or multi-family development shall be required, at the time of construction, to install any screening that is required between it and adjacent existing uses according to the table set forth in Section 308, regardless of whether, in relation to such other uses, the two-family or multi-family development is the benefitted or burdened use.

Commentary:

Normally, if a benefitted use locates next to a preexisting burdened use, the benefitted use has the option of whether to install screening to protect itself from the impacts of its neighbor. Presumably, the benefitted property owner will weigh the costs and benefits of installing such screening and make a decision accordingly. However, Subsection (d) makes an exception in the case of the owners of residential property that is likely to be rented. This reflects a policy determination that tenants of such property should have the benefit of screening from more obtrusive adjacent uses, and in the absence of such a provision, many owners of such property would not choose to provide this protection.

**Section 307:
Descriptions of Screens**

The following three basic types of screens are hereby established and are used as the basis for the Table of Screening Requirements set forth in Section 308.

(1) *Opaque Screen, Type A*. A screen that is opaque from the ground to a height of at least six feet, with intermittent visual obstructions from the opaque portion to a height of at least 20 feet. An opaque screen is intended to exclude all visual contact between uses and to create a strong impression of spacial separation. The

opaque screen may be composed of a wall, fence, landscaped earth berm, planted vegetation, or existing vegetation. Compliance of planted vegetative screens or natural vegetation will be judged on the basis of the average mature height and density of foliage of the subject species, or field observation of existing vegetation. The opaque portion of the screen must be opaque in all seasons of the year. At maturity, the portion of intermittent visual obstructions should not contain any completely unobstructed openings more than 10 feet wide. The portion of intermittent visual obstructions may contain deciduous plants. Suggested planting patterns that will achieve this standard are included in Appendix E.

(2) *Semi-Opaque Screen, Type B.* A screen that is opaque from the ground to a height of three feet, with intermittent visual obstruction from above the opaque portion to a height of at least 20 feet. The semi-opaque screen is intended to partially block visual contact between uses and to create a strong impression of the separation of spaces. The semi-opaque screen may be composed of a wall, fence, landscaped earth berm, planted vegetation, or existing vegetation. Compliance of planted vegetative screens or natural vegetation will be judged on the basis of the average mature height and density of foliage of the subject species, or field observation of existing vegetation. At maturity, the portion of intermittent visual obstructions should not contain any completely unobstructed openings more than 10 feet wide. The zone of intermittent visual obstruction may contain deciduous plants. Suggested planting patterns which will achieve this standard are included in Appendix E.

(3) *Broken Screen, Type C.* A screen composed of intermittent visual obstructions from the ground to a height of at least 20 feet. The broken screen is intended to create the impression of a separation of spaces without necessarily eliminating visual contact between the spaces. It may be composed of a wall, fence, landscaped earth berm, planted vegetation, or existing vegetation. Compliance of planted vegetative screens or natural vegetation will be judged on the basis of the average mature height and density of foliage of the subject species, or field observation of existing vegetation. The screen may contain deciduous plants. Suggested planting patterns which will achieve this standard are included in Appendix E.

Commentary:

The numbers of levels of screening and their composition are matters of local choice. Note also that the above provisions state that the screening capabilities of plants and trees, in terms of meeting the requirements of the three levels, are determined by the capabilities of such plants and trees of *maturity*. This means that it may be quite a few years between the completion of a development and the time the screening actually achieves the required effect. If this is deemed undesirable, a provision would be added requiring plantings to be of sufficient maturity so that the desired screening effect is achieved within a specified number of years.

Section 308: Table of Screening Requirements

BURDENED USE		BENEFITTED USE 1.000 1.111, 1.112, 1.121	1.113, 1.114, 1.122	1.200	1.300	1.410, 420, 430	1.440	1.510, 520	1.530	2.000 2.100	2.200	3.000 3.100	3.200	4.000 4.100	4.200	5.000 5.100	5.200	5.300	5.400	6.000 6.100	6.200, 210, 220	6.230	6.240	6.250
1.000	1.111, 1.112, 1.121																							
	1.113, 1.114, 1.122	B																						
	1.200	C																						
	1.300	B																						
	1.410, 420, 430	C	C																					
	1.440	B	B																					
	1.510, 520	B	B																					
	1.530	A	A	A	B	A	B	C			B	C				A	A	A	C	B				
2.000	2.100	A	A	A	B	A	B	B		C	C					A	A	A	C	B				
	2.200	A	A	A	A	A	B	A	C	B	B	C				A	A	A	C	B				
3.000	3.100	A	A	A	B	A	A	B	C							A	A	B	B	B				
	3.200	A	A	A	A	A	A	B								A	A	A	B	B				
4.000	4.100	A	A	A	A	A	A	A	B	A	A	A				A	A	A	A	B	B	B	B	
	4.200	A	A	A	A	A	A	A	A	A	A	A	A			A	A	A	A	A	A	B	B	A
5.000	5.100	A	A	A	A	A	A	A																
	5.200	A	A	A	A	A	A																	
	5.300	A	A	A	A	A	A																	
	5.400	A	A	A	A	A	A									B	B	B						
6.000	6.100	A	A	A	B	A	A	C			C					A	A	A	C					
	6.200, 210, 220	A	A	A	B	A	A	B																
	6.230	A	A	A	A	A	A	B	B	B	C	B	C			A	A	A	B	C				
	6.240	A	A	A	B	A	A	B		B	C	B	C			B	B	B	C					
	6.250	A	A	A	A	A	A	A	A	A	A	A	A	B	A	A	A	A	A	A	A	A	A	A
	6.260	A	A	A	A	A	A									B								
7.000		A	A	A	A	A	B	B								A	A	A	C					
8.000		A	A	A	A	A	A	A		B	C	B	C			A	A	A	C					
9.000		A	A	A	A	A	A	A	B	B	C	B	C			A	A	A	C					
10.000		A	A	A	A	A	A	A		B	C	B	C			B	B	B		B				
11.000		A	A	A	A	A	A	A	A	A	A	A	B	A	A	A	A	A	A	A	A	A		C
12.000		A	A	A	A	A	A	A		A	B	A	B			A	A	A	B	B				
13.000		A	A	A	A	A	A	B		B	C	B	C			B	B	B	C	C				
14.000	14.100, 200	B	B	B	B	B	B	B																
	14.300, 400	A	A	A	A	A	A	A		A	A	A	A		B	A	A	A	A	A	A	A	A	B
15.000	15.100	A	A	A	A	A	A	B		B	C	B	C			A	A	A	A	A				
	15.200	A	A	A	A	A	A	A		B	C	B	B	B		A	A	A	A	A				
	15.300	A	A	A	A	A	A	A		A	A	A	A	B		A	A	A	A	A		A		B
	15.400	A	A	A	A	A	A	B		B	B	B	B			A	A	A	B	B				
16.000		A	A	A	B	A	A	B		B	C	B	C			A	A	A	B	B				
17.000		A	A	A	A	A	A	A		A	A	A	A	B	C	A	A	A	A	A		A	A	
18.000	18.100	A	A	A	B	A	A	B		B	C	B	C			A	A	A	B	B		B	B	
	18.200	A	A	A	A	A	A	A		A	A	A	A			A	A	A	A	A		A	A	
19.000		A	A	A	A	A	A	A	C	B	C	B	C			A	A	A	B	B		C		
20.000		A	A	A	A	A	A	A									A	B	B					
21.000	21.100	A	A	A	B	A	B	C																
	21.200	A	A	A	A	A	A	B		A	A	A	C			A	A	A	A	A			C	C
22.000		A	A	A	A	B	B	C	C															
24.000		A	A	A	A	A	A	A			A	B	A	B	C	A	A	A	A	A		A	C	B
25.000		A	A	A	B	A	A	B					C			A	A	A						
26.000																								
27.000		A	A	A	A	A	A																	
Streets																								
Railroads		B	B	B	B	B	B	B	B	B	B	B	B			B	B	B	B	B		B	B	B

172 A Unified Development Ordinance

173 Screening and Trees

**Section 309:
Flexibility in Administration Required**

(a) The council recognizes that because of the wide variety of types of developments and the relationships between them, it is neither possible nor prudent to establish inflexible screening requirements. Therefore, as provided in Section 306, the permit-issuing authority may permit deviations from the presumptive requirements of Section 308 and may either require more intensive or allow less intensive screening whenever it finds such deviations are more likely to satisfy the standard set forth in Section 305 without imposing unnecessary costs on the developer.

(b) Without limiting the generality of Subsection (a), the permit-issuing authority may modify the presumptive requirements for:

(1) Commercial developments located adjacent to residential uses in business zoning districts,

(2) Commercial uses located adjacent to other commercial uses within the same zoning district,

(3) Uses located within planned unit developments (for screening requirements within planned residential developments, see Section 158).

(c) Whenever the permit-issuing authority allows or requires a deviation from the presumptive requirements set forth in Section 308, it shall enter on the face of the permit the screening requirement that it imposes to meet the standard set forth in Section 305 and the reasons for allowing or requiring the deviation.

(d) If the permit-issuing authority concludes, based upon information it receives in the consideration of a specific development proposal, that a presumption established by Section 308 is erroneous, it shall initiate a request for an amendment to the Table of Screening Requirements in accordance with the procedures set forth in Article XX.

Commentary:

See the commentary following Subsections 292(c) and (d), which deals with similar provisions relating to parking.

**Section 310:
Combination Uses**

(a) In determining the screening requirements that apply between a combination use and another use, the permit-issuing authority shall proceed as if the principal uses that comprise the combination use were not combined and reach its determination accordingly, relying on the table set forth in Section 308 interpreted in the light of Section 309.

(b) When two or more principal uses are combined to create a combination use, screening shall not be required between the component principal uses unless they are clearly separated physically and screening is determined to be necessary to satisfy the standard set forth in Section 305.

**Section 311:
Subdivisions**

When undeveloped land is subdivided and undeveloped lots only are sold, the subdivider shall not be required to install any screening. Screening shall be required, if at all, only when the lots are developed, and the responsibility for installing such screening shall be determined in accordance with the other requirements of Part I of this article.

**Sections 312 and 313:
Reserved**

Part II. Shading

Section 314:
Council Findings and Declaration of Policy on Shade Trees

(a) The council finds that:

(1) Trees are proven producers of oxygen, a necessary element for human survival,

(2) Trees appreciably reduce the ever increasing environmentally dangerous carbon dioxide content of the air and play a vital role in purifying the air we breathe,

(3) Trees transpire considerable amounts of water each day and thereby purify the air much like the air-washer devices used on commercial air conditioning systems,

(4) Trees have an important role in neutralizing waste water passing through the ground from the surface to ground water tables and lower aquifers,

(5) Trees, through their root systems, stabilize the ground water tables and play an important and effective part in soil conservation, erosion control, and flood control,

(6) Trees are an invaluable physical, aesthetic, and psychological counterpoint to the urban setting, making urban life more comfortable by providing shade and cooling the air and land, reducing noise levels and glare, and breaking the monotony of human developments on the land, particularly parking areas, and

(7) For the reasons indicated in Subdivision (6), trees have an important impact on the desirability of land and therefore on property values.

(b) Based upon the findings set forth in Subsection (a), the council declares that it is not only desirable but essential to the health, safety, and welfare of all persons living or working within the city's planning jurisdiction to protect certain existing trees and, under the circumstances set forth in this article, to require the planting of new trees in certain types of developments.

Commentary:

See commentary following Section 304.

Section 315:
Required Trees Along Dedicated Streets

Along both sides of all newly created streets that are constructed in accordance with the public street standards set forth in Article XIV, the developer shall either plant or retain sufficient trees so that between the paved portion of the street and a line running parallel to and 50 feet from the centerline of the street, there is for every 30 feet of street frontage at least an average of one deciduous tree that has or will have when fully mature a trunk at least 12 inches in diameter. When trees are planted by the developer pursuant to this section, the developer shall choose trees that meet the standards set forth in Appendix E.

Section 316:
Retention and Protection of Large Trees

(a) Every development shall retain all existing trees 18 inches in diameter or more unless the retention of such trees would unreasonably burden the development.

Commentary:

This subsection is intended to provide the necessary leverage to enable the administrator to require that significant trees be retained if reasonably possible. The flexibility inherent in this provision provides room for argument, but no other approach is practical.

(b) No excavation or other subsurface disturbance may be undertaken within the drip line of any tree 18 inches in diameter or more, and no impervious surface (including, but not limited to, paving or buildings) may be located within 12½ feet (measured from the center of the trunk) of any tree 18 inches in diameter or more unless compliance with this subsection would unreasonably burden the development. For purposes of this subsection, a drip line is defined as a perimeter formed by the points farthest away from the trunk of a tree where precipitation falling from the branches of that tree lands on the ground.

Commentary:
> Experience has demonstrated that it will be of little use to leave a tree standing if the area within its drip line is disturbed—especially if it is paved—since the tree will almost certainly die. As a practical matter of enforcement, it may be necessary to require the developer to establish some barrier around the protected area during construction, and the ordinance language suggested above might well be modified to require this.

(c) The retention or protection of trees 18 inches in diameter or more as provided in Subsections (a) and (b) unreasonably burdens a development if, to accomplish such retention or protection, the desired location of improvements on a lot or the proposed activities on a lot would have to be substantially altered and such alteration would work an unreasonable hardship upon the developer.

(d) If space that would otherwise be devoted to parking cannot be so used because of the requirements of Subsections (a) or (b), and, as a result, the parking requirements set forth in Article XVIII cannot be satisfied, the number of required spaces may be reduced by the number of spaces "lost" because of the provisions of Subsections (a) and (b), up to a maximum of 15 percent of the required spaces.

**Section 317:
Shade Trees in Parking Areas**

(a) Vehicle accommodation areas that are required to be paved by Section 295 must be shaded by deciduous trees (either retained or planted by the developer) that have or will have when fully mature a trunk at least 12 inches in diameter. When trees are planted by the developer to satisfy the requirements of this subsection, the developer shall choose trees that meet the standards set forth in Appendix E.

(b) Each tree of the type described in Subsection (a) shall be presumed to shade a circular area having a radius of 15 feet with the trunk of the tree as the center, and there must be sufficient trees so that, using this standard, 20 percent of the vehicle accommodation area will be shaded.

(c) No paving may be placed within 12½ feet (measured from the center of the trunk) of any tree retained to comply with Subsection (a), and new trees planted to comply with Subsection (a) shall be located so that they are surrounded by at least 200 square feet of unpaved area.

Commentary:
> See commentary following Subsection 316(b). Newly planted trees do not necessarily require that the area within their eventual drip lines remain

Screening and Trees

unpaved, so long as they are not completely surrounded with impervious surface.

(d) Vehicle accommodation areas shall be laid out and detailed to prevent vehicles from striking trees. Vehicles will be presumed to have a body overhang of three feet, six inches.

Sections 318 and 319: Reserved

Article XX Amendments

Section 320:
Amendments in General

(a) Amendments to the text of this chapter or to the zoning map may be made in accordance with the provisions of this article.

(b) The term major map amendment shall refer to an amendment that addresses the zoning district classification of five or more tracts of land in separate ownership or any parcel of land (regardless of the number of lots or owners) in excess of 50 acres. All other amendments to the zoning district map shall be referred to as minor map amendments.

Commentary:

> Changes in both the ordinance text and the zoning map constitute ordinance amendments. However, map changes, especially those defined above as minor map amendments, are really different in nature than the usual ordinance amendment since the governing body is required to focus on a particular tract or tracts of land and make judgments about what law should be applicable to a few property owners rather than the general public. In some jurisdictions, the minor map amendment process is regarded as administrative or quasi-judicial, rather than legislative, and must be attended with the same procedural safeguards (competent evidence, written findings, etc.) applicable to other administrative hearings. However, in most jurisdictions, the minor map amendment process is still regarded as legislative, and the provisions of this article reflect that point of view. There are, however, some differences in the types of notice required to adjacent property owners, depending on whether the map amendment is major or minor (see Section 323).

Section 321:
Initiation of Amendments

(a) Whenever a request to amend this chapter is initiated by the city council, the planning board, the board of adjustment, or the city administration, the city attorney in consultation with the planning staff shall draft an appropriate ordinance and present that ordinance to the council so that a date for a public hearing may be set.

(b) Any other person may also petition the council to amend this chapter. The petition shall be filed with the administrator and shall include, among the information deemed relevant by the administrator:

   (1) The name, address, and phone number of the applicant,
   (2) A description of the land affected by the amendment if a change in zoning district classification is proposed,
   (3) Stamped envelopes containing the names and addresses of all those to whom notice of the public hearing must be sent as provided in Section 323,

(4) A description of the proposed map change or a summary of the specific objective of any proposed change in the text of this chapter.

(c) Upon receipt of a petition as provided in Subsection (b), the administrator shall either:

(1) Treat the proposed amendment as one initiated by the city administration and proceed in accordance with Subsection (a) if he believes that the proposed amendment has significant merit and would benefit the general public, or

(2) Forward the petition to the council with or without written comment for a determination of whether an ordinance should be drafted and a public hearing set in accordance with Subsection (d).

(d) Upon receipt of a proposed ordinance as provided in Subsection (a), the council may establish a date for a public hearing on it. Upon receipt of a petition for an ordinance amendment as provided in Subsection (b), the council may summarily deny the petition or set a date for a public hearing on the requested amendment and order the attorney, in consultation with the administrator, to draft an appropriate ordinance.

Commentary:

> Some ordinances address the potential problem of repeated amendment requests by the same property owner by stating that, if an initial request has been denied, a new request covering the same property may not be submitted within a specified period of time (usually one or two years). This section deals with this problem by allowing subsequent requests to be submitted but not requiring the council to set public hearings on them. The council may summarily deny nonmeritorious requests.

Section 322:
Planning Board Consideration of Proposed Amendments

(a) If the council sets a date for a public hearing on a proposed amendment, it shall also refer the proposed amendment to the planning board for its consideration.

(b) The planning board shall endeavor to review the proposed amendment in such a timely fashion that any recommendations it may have can be presented to the council at the public hearing on the amendment. However, if the planning board is not prepared to make recommendations at the public hearing, it may request the council to delay final action on the amendment until such time as the planning board can present its recommendations.

(c) The council need not await the recommendations of the planning board before taking action on a proposed amendment, nor is the council bound by any recommendations of the planning board that are before it at the time it takes action on a proposed amendment.

Commentary:

> See the commentary following Subsection 57(a) for the rationale as to why the planning board should consider a proposed amendment and make its recommendation before the public hearing.

Section 323:
Hearing Required; Notice

(a) No ordinance that amends any of the provisions of this chapter may be adopted until a public hearing has been held on such ordinance.

Commentary:

> The provisions of this and the following subsection are established by state law in North Carolina. The draftsman should consult the law in his jurisdiction.

(b) The administrator shall publish a notice of the public hearing on any ordinance that amends the provisions of this chapter once a week for two successive weeks in a newspaper having general circulation in the area. The notice shall be published for the first time not less than 10 days nor more than 25 days before the date fixed for the hearing. In computing this period, the date of publication shall not be counted but the date of the hearing shall be.

(c) With respect to minor map amendments, the administrator shall mail written notice of the public hearing to the record owners for tax purposes of all properties whose zoning classification is changed by the proposed amendment as well as the owners of all properties any portion of which is within 150 feet of the property rezoned by the amendment.

Commentary:

> Note that this subsection only requires written notice to property owners affected by *minor* map amendments. The distinction is based on the practicalities of notifying potentially very large numbers of property owners in the case of major map revisions.

(d) The planning staff shall also post notices of the public hearing in the vicinity of the property rezoned by the proposed amendment and take any other action deemed by the planning staff to be useful or appropriate to give notice of the public hearing on any proposed amendment.

(e) The notice required or authorized by this section shall:

(1) State the date, time, and place of the public hearing,

(2) Summarize the nature and character of the proposed change,

(3) If the proposed amendment involves a change in zoning district classification, reasonably identify the property whose classification would be affected by the amendment,

(4) State that the full text of the amendment can be obtained from the city clerk, and

(5) State that substantial changes in the proposed amendment may be made following the public hearing.

(f) The planning staff shall make every reasonable effort to comply with the notice provisions set forth in this section. However, it is the council's intention that no failure to comply with any of the notice provisions (except those set forth in Subsection (b)) shall render any amendment invalid.

Commentary:

> Many case decisions state that a local government must strictly adhere to the procedures specified in the ordinance or else an amendment will be declared invalid. This section represents an attempt, which may or may not be successful, to avoid this result if the staff makes a reasonable and good faith effort to comply with the notice provisions.

Section 324:
Council Action on Amendments

(a) At the conclusion of the public hearing on a proposed amendment, the council may proceed to vote on the proposed ordinance, refer it to a committee for further study, or take any other action consistent with its usual rules of procedure.

(b) The council is not required to take final action on a proposed amendment within any specific period of time, but it should proceed as expeditiously as practicable on petitions for amendments since inordinate delays can result in the petitioner incurring unnecessary costs.

(c) Voting on amendments to this chapter shall proceed in the same manner as other ordinances, subject to Section 326.

Section 325:
Ultimate Issue Before Council on Amendments

In deciding whether to adopt a proposed amendment to this chapter, the central issue before the council is whether the proposed amendment advances the public health, safety, or welfare. All other issues are irrelevant, and all information related to other issues at the public hearing may be declared irrelevant by the mayor and excluded. In particular, when considering proposed minor map amendments:

(1) The council shall not consider any representations made by the petitioner that if the change is granted the rezoned property will be used for only one of the possible range of uses permitted in the requested classification. Rather, the council shall consider whether the entire range of permitted uses in the requested classification is more appropriate than the range of uses in the existing classification.

Commentary:

This language is included primarily as a response to some rather peculiar North Carolina cases that have held that if the council relies on the representations of a developer as to the particular project he will build if a rezoning is obtained, this constitutes unlawful "contract zoning" even if no contract was intended by either party or would otherwise be inferred or implied. However, if the phrase "shall not consider" is changed to "shall not regard as controlling," this provision might be useful in all jurisdictions to admonish the council to consider rezoning requests in the light of what could legally occur in the new zoning district rather than just what the rezoning applicant has in mind when making the request.

(2) The council shall not regard as controlling any advantages or disadvantages to the individual requesting the change, but shall consider the impact of the proposed change on the public at large.

Commentary:

This provision urges the council to avoid the pitfall that lies at the heart of the "spot zoning" problem. Spot zoning, meaning the zoning of a small tract in a different manner than surrounding property, is objectionable only when such zoning is not in the public interest; i.e., when the decision to zone in that way is made primarily to benefit particular property owners rather than the public at large. To be constitutional, zoning must be designed principally to further the public interest, not private preferences.

Section 326:
Protests to Zoning District Changes

(a) If a petition opposing a change in the zoning classification of any property is filed in accordance with the provisions of this section, then the proposed amendment may be adopted only by a favorable vote of three-fourths of the council membership.

(b) To trigger the three-fourths vote requirement, the petition must:

(1) Be signed by the owners of 20 percent or more either of (i) the lots included in a proposed change, or (ii) the lots within 100 feet of

either side or the rear of the tract to be rezoned, or (iii) the lots directly opposite the tract to be rezoned and extending 100 feet from the street frontage of such opposite lots.

(2) Be in the form of a written petition actually bearing the signatures of the requisite number of property owners and stating that the signers do protest the proposed change or amendment.

(3) Be received by the city clerk in sufficient time to allow the city at least two normal working days before the date established for a public hearing on the proposed amendment to determine the sufficiency and accuracy of the petition.

(4) Be on a form provided by the city clerk and contain all the information requested on this form.

Commentary: This section illustrates ordinance language that implements or is consistent with statutory requirements in a number of states. The author does not recommend including such provisions if it is possible to avoid them.

Appendix A Information Required with Applications

A–1:
In General

(a) As provided in Section 49, it is presumed that all of the information listed in this appendix must be submitted with an application for a zoning, sign, special-use, or conditional-use permit to enable the permit-issuing authority to determine whether the development, if completed as proposed, will comply with all the requirements of this chapter. As set forth in Section 92, applications for variances are subject to the same provisions. However, the permit-issuing authority may require more information or accept as sufficient less information according to the circumstances of the particular case. A developer who believes information presumptively required by this appendix is unnecessary shall contact the planning staff for an interpretation.

Commentary:

> This appendix converts quite easily into a form that can be used both to let a particular developer know exactly what information he must submit and to act as a checklist when the application comes in to see if all required items have been included. To do this, two blank spaces should be placed to the left of each item of information presumptively required under Sections A–2 through A–8. When the administrator meets with the developer before an application is submitted, he can address each item and indicate with a check mark whether that information is required (it may be easier to check the items not needed). The administrator keeps a copy and the developer leaves knowing precisely what he must submit. When the application is received, the other column of blanks becomes a checklist for the administrator to ensure that all required information has been furnished.

(b) As also provided in Section 49, the administrator shall develop application processes, including standard forms, to simplify and expedite applications for simple developments that do not require the full range of information called for in this appendix. In particular, developers seeking only permission to construct single-family or two-family residences or to construct new or modify existing signs should contact the administrator for standard forms.

A–2:
Written Application

Every applicant for a variance or a zoning, sign, special-use or conditional-use permit shall complete a written application containing at least the following information:

(1) The name, address, and phone number of the applicant.

(2) If the applicant is not the owner of the property in question, (i) the name, address, and phone number of the owner, and (ii) the legal relationship of the applicant to the owner that entitles the applicant to make application.

(3) The date of the application.

(4) Identification of the particular permit sought.

(5) A succinct statement of the nature of the development proposed under the permit or the nature of the variance.

(6) Identification of the property in question by street address and tax map reference.

(7) The zoning district within which the property lies.

(8) The number of square feet in the lot where the development is to take place.

(9) The gross floor area of all existing or proposed buildings located on the lot where the development is to take place.

(10) If the proposed development is a two-family or multi-family residential development or an architecturally integrated subdivision, the number of one-, two-, three-, or four-bedroom dwelling units proposed for construction.

A–3:
Development Site Plans

Subject to Section A–1 of this appendix, every application for a variance or a zoning, sign, special-use or conditional-use permit shall contain plans that locate the development site and graphically demonstrate existing and proposed natural, man-made, and legal features on and near the site in question, all in conformity with Sections A–4 through A–6 of this appendix.

A–4:
Graphic Materials Required for Plans

(a) The plans shall include a location map that shows the location of the project in the broad context of the city or planning jurisdiction. This location map may be drawn on the development site plans or it may be furnished separately using reduced copies of maps of the city's planning jurisdiction available at the planning and inspections department.

(b) Development site plans shall be drawn to scale, using such a scale that all features required to be shown on the plans are readily discernible. Very large developments may require that plans show the development in sections to accomplish this objective without resort to plans that are so large as to be cumbersome, or the objective may be accomplished by using different plans or plans drawn to different scales to illustrate different features. In all cases, the permit-issuing authority shall make the final determination whether the plans submitted are drawn to the appropriate scale, but the applicant for a conditional- or special-use permit may rely in the first instance on the recommendations of the administration.

(c) Development site plans should show on the first page the following information:

(1) Name of applicant.

(2) Name of development (if any).

(3) North arrow.

(4) Legend.

(5) Scale.

(d) All of the features required to be shown on plans by Sections A–5 and A–6 may be included on one set of plans, so long as the features are distinctly discernible.

A–5:
Existing Natural, Man-Made, and Legal Features

(a) Development site plans shall show all existing natural, man-made, and legal features on the lot where the development is to take place, including but not limited to those listed below. In addition, the plans shall also show those features, indicated in the following by an asterisk, that are located within 50 feet in any direction of the lot where the development is to take place, and shall specify (by reference to the Table of Permissible Uses or otherwise) the use made of adjoining properties.

(b) Existing natural features:

(1) Tree line of wooded areas.

(2) Individual trees 18 inches in diameter or more, identified by common or scientific name.

(3) Orchards or other agricultural groves by common or scientific name.

*(4) Streams, ponds, drainage ditches, swamps, boundaries of floodways and floodplains.

(5) (If the proposed development is a subdivision of more than 50 lots or if more than five acres of land are to be developed), base flood elevation data (See Article XVI, Part I).

*(6) Contour lines (shown as dotted lines) with no larger than two-foot contour intervals. (As indicated in Subsection A–6(b)(17), proposed contour lines shall be shown as solid lines.)

(c) Existing man-made features:

*(1) Vehicle accommodation areas (including parking areas, loading areas and circulation areas, see Section 290), all designated by surface material and showing the layout of existing parking spaces and direction of travel lanes, aisles, or driveways.

(2) Streets, private roads, sidewalks, and other walkways, all designated by surface material.

(3) Curbs and gutters, curb inlets and curb cuts, and drainage grates.

(4) Other storm water or drainage facilities, including manholes, pipes, and drainage ditches.

(5) Underground utility lines, including water, sewer, electric power, telephone, gas, cable television.

(6) Aboveground utility lines and other utility facilities.

*(7) Fire hydrants.

*(8) Buildings, structures and signs (including dimensions of each).

(9) Location of exterior light fixtures.

*(10) Location of dumpsters.

(d) Existing legal features:

    (1) The zoning of the property, including zoning district lines where applicable.

    (2) Property lines (with dimensions identified).

    (3) Street right-of-way lines.

    (4) Utility or other easement lines.

A–6:
Proposed Changes in Existing Features or New Features

(a) Development site plans shall show proposed changes in (i) existing natural features (see A–5(b)), (ii) existing man-made features (see A–5(c)), and (iii) existing legal features (see A–5(d)).

(b) Development site plans shall also show proposed new legal features (especially new property lines, street right-of-way lines, and utility and other easements), as well as proposed man-made features, including, but not limited to, the following:

    (1) The number of square feet in every lot created by a new subdivision.

    (2) Lot dimensions, including lot widths measured in accordance with Section 183.

    (3) The location and dimensions of all buildings and freestanding signs on the lot, as well as the distances all buildings and freestanding signs are set back from property lines, streets or street right-of-way lines (see Section 184).

    (4) Principal side(s) building elevations for typical units of new buildings or exterior remodelings of existing buildings, showing building heights (see Section 185) and proposed wall sign or window sign area.

    (5) The location and dimensions of all recreational areas provided in accordance with Article XIII, with each area designated as to type of use.

    (6) Areas intended to remain as usable open space. The plans shall clearly indicate whether such open space areas are intended to be offered for dedication to public use or to remain privately owned.

    (7) Streets, labeled by classification (see Section 210) and street name showing whether curb and gutter or shoulders and swales are to be provided and indicating street paving widths. Private roads in subdivisions shall also be shown and clearly labeled as such.

    (8) Curbs and gutters, curb inlets and curb cuts, drainage grates.

    (9) Other storm water or drainage facilities, including manholes, pipes, drainage ditches, retention ponds, etc.

    (10) Sidewalks and walkways, showing widths and surface material.

    (11) Bridges.

    (12) Outdoor illumination with lighting fixtures sufficiently identified to demonstrate compliance with Section 242.

(13) Underground utility lines, including water, sewer, electric power, telephone, gas, cable television. Water and sewer pipe line signs shall be labeled.

(14) Aboveground utility lines and other facilities.

(15) Fire hydrants.

(16) Dumpsters.

(17) New contour lines resulting from earth movement (shown as solid lines) with no larger than two-foot contour intervals (existing lines should be shown as dotted lines).

(18) Scale drawings of all signs requiring permits pursuant to Article XVII, together with an indication of the location and dimensions of all such signs.

(19) Vehicle accommodation areas (including parking areas, loading areas, and circulation areas, see Section 290), all designated by surface material and showing the dimensions and layout of proposed parking spaces and the dimensions and direction of travel of lanes, aisles, and driveways.

(20) Proposed plantings or construction of other devices to comply with the screening requirements of Article XIX, Part I, as well as proposed plantings of trees to comply with the shading requirements of Article XIX, Part II. Plans shall label shrubbery by common or scientific name, show the distance between plants and indicate the height at the time of planting and expected mature height and width. Plans shall label trees by common or scientific name, show the circles of the mature crowns (major trees shall be drawn at diameter = 30 feet; dwarf or decorative trees shall be drawn at their actual mature crown), and indicate the height at the time of planting.

A–7: Documents and Written Information in Addition to Plans

In addition to the written application and the plans, whenever the nature of the proposed development makes information or documents such as the following relevant, such documents or information shall be provided. The following is a representative list of the types of information or documents that may be requested:

(1) Documentation confirming that the applicant has a legally sufficient interest in the property proposed for development to use it in the manner requested, or is the duly appointed agent of such a person.

(2) Certifications from the appropriate agencies that proposed utility systems are or will be adequate to handle the proposed development, as set forth in Article XV, and that all necessary easements have been provided.

(3) Detailed description of play apparatus or other recreational facilities to be provided in miniparks.

(4) Legal documentation establishing homeowners associations or other legal entities responsible for control over required common areas and facilities.

(5) Bonds, letters of credit, or other surety devices.

(6) Stamped envelopes containing the names and addresses of all those to whom notice of a public hearing must be sent to comply with Section 52 or Section 102.

(7) Complete documentation justifying any requested deviation from specific requirements established by this chapter as presumptively satisfying design standards.

(8) Written evidence of permission to use satellite parking spaces under the control of a person other than the developer when such spaces are allowed pursuant to Section 298.

(9) Written evidence of good faith efforts to acquire satellite parking under the circumstances set forth in Section 299.

(10) Verification that 4.000 classification uses will meet the performance standards set forth in Article XI. Such verification shall be made by a licensed engineer or other qualified expert unless it is utterly apparent from the nature of the proposed development that such expert verification is unnecessary.

(11) Time schedules for the completion of phases in staged development, as required by Section 61.

(12) The environmental impact of a development, including its effect on historically significant or ecologically fragile or important areas and its impact on pedestrian or traffic safety or congestion.

A–8:
Number of Copies of Plans and Documents

With respect to all plans and other documents required by this appendix, the developer shall submit the number of copies (not to exceed 10) that the administrator deems necessary to expedite the review process and to provide necessary permanent records.

Appendix B Specifications on Driveway Entrances

All driveway entrances and other openings onto city-maintained streets shall, at a minimum, conform to the requirements set forth in [reference the city's driveway entrance regulations or those of the county or state. If such regulations do not exist, then they should be prepared by the draftsman in consultation with appropriate professionals and included here].

Appendix C   Specifications for Street Design and Construction

Commentary:

The draftsman should obviously work closely with appropriate engineering or public works personnel in drafting the specifications covered in this appendix.

C–1:
Design Speed, Sight Distance, Centerline Radius

	Minor	Local	Sub-Collector	Collector
Design Speed	25 mph	25 mph	30 mph	35 mph
Minimum Sight Distance on Vertical Curve	150 feet	150 feet	200 feet	200 feet
Minimum Centerline Radius	150 feet	150 feet	200 feet	250 feet

C–2:
Cut and Fill Slopes

Cut and fill slopes on any street right-of-way may not exceed 2:1.

C–3:
Sight Distances at Intersections

(a) At no-stop intersections, the intersection shall be constructed so that a person standing at a location on the centerline of any street 90 feet from the intersection of the street centerlines has an unobstructed view to a point located on the centerline of the intersecting street 90 feet (in either direction) from the intersection of the street centerlines. See Standard Drawing No. 1.

(b) Subject to Subsection (c), at stop intersections, the intersection shall be constructed so that a person standing 10 feet back of the intersection of right-of-way lines on the stop street has an unobstructed view to a point on the right-of-way line of the intersecting through street located 70 feet from the intersection of the right-of-way lines. See Standard Drawing No. 2.

(c) At stop intersections where a residential street intersects with a state-maintained primary road, the intersection shall be constructed so that a person standing 30 feet back of the intersection of right-of-way lines on the stop street has an unobstructed view to a point on the centerline of the through street located 150 feet from the intersection of the street right-of-way lines. See Standard Drawing No. 3.

C–4:
Radius at Street Intersections

At street intersections, the intersections of the paved surfaces shall be rounded with a minimum radius as shown in Standard Drawings No. 4 and No. 5. Where streets intersect at less than right angles, a greater radius may be required.

C–5:
Clearing and Grubbing

Clearing and grubbing shall be performed within the limits shown on the plans. All timber, brush, roots, stumps, trees, or other vegetation cut during the clearing operations shall become the contractor's responsibility to dispose of, and shall be either removed from the project by him, or satisfactorily disposed of on-site.

C–6:
Grading and Compaction

Streets shall be graded in accordance with the lines and grade set by the engineer. Before placing curb and gutter or base on the graded subgrade, the subgrade shall be compacted to 100 percent AASHO T99 for a depth of six inches and then shall be proof rolled in the presence of the engineer. Places that are found to be loose, or soft, or composed of unsuitable materials, whether in the subgrade or below it, must be dug out and refilled with suitable material. All embankments or fills shall be made in one-foot horizontal lifts of suitable material. The fill shall be rolled with a sheepsfoot roller after each lift, followed by a wheel roller, each weighing not less than eight tons.

C–7:
Street Base

Base course for streets shall generally be eight inches thick, unless otherwise directed by the public works director, and shall be crushed stone conforming to D.O.T. Type ABC stone. The stone base course shall be placed in four-inch layers, watered as necessary, and compacted to 100 percent AASHO T99. The contractor shall be responsible for keeping the stone base free of contamination from clay or other foreign materials. Handling and placement of stone base shall all be in accordance with D.O.T. specifications.

C–8:
Street Surfaces

The asphalt surface course shall meet D.O.T. specifications for Type I-2 asphalt. The asphalt shall be placed in one two-inch layer, and shall be handled and placed in accordance with D.O.T. specifications.

C–9:
Pavement Section Variations

Sections C–6, C–7, and C–8 set the standards that shall apply under normal soils conditions. However, where soils are unusually good or unusually unstable, the public works director may allow or require the developer to have soil tests run and a pavement design made by a qualified soils engineer. Under these circumstances, the public works director may allow pavement sections constructed to lesser standards than those set forth above (for good soils) or require pavement sections constructed to greater standards than those set forth above (for unstable soils).

C–10:
Street Cross Sections

Streets shall be constructed and utilities located in accordance with Standard Drawing No. 6 or No. 7.

C–11:
Curb and Gutter

(a) The concrete curb and gutter shall be constructed according to the lines and grades established by the engineer. The concrete shall meet the state highway requirements. The curb and gutter shall be 30 inches wide, and shall have a vertical curb face. The forms shall be of metal, free of marks or kinks, and shall be rigidly held in position. The engineer shall approve the positioning of the forms before concrete is poured. The concrete shall be placed in the forms in a manner to prevent segregation, and tamped or vibrated sufficiently to prevent honeycombs. The concrete shall be finished smooth and even by means of rollers or floats. Expansion joints shall be provided every 30 feet, and false joints every 10 feet.

(b) Curb and gutter shall be constructed in accordance with Standard Drawing No. 8.

C–12:
Sidewalks

Sidewalk construction shall be similar to street construction, with subgrade compacted to 100 percent AAASHO T99. Concrete sidewalks shall be four inches thick (increasing to six inches thick at driveway entrances), and shall be at least four feet wide. Expansion joints shall be provided every 30 feet; false joints at 10 feet.

C–13:
Wheel Chair Ramps

Where required, wheel chair ramps shall be constructed in accordance with Standard Drawing No. 9.

C–14:
Storm Water Runoff Control

(a) The minimum design frequency for storm runoff shall be 10 years for storm sewer collection and 25 years for cross drainage (i.e., drainage facilities crossing a street).

(b) All storm drainage pipe shall be reinforced concrete and no pipe may be smaller than 15 inches in diameter.

(c) Culvert outlet protection and swale erosion protection shall be designed based on a 10-year storm.

(d) All storm drainage structures and pipes shall be designed and constructed in accordance with Department of Transportation specifications and Standard Drawings No. 10 through No. 14. However, in case of a conflict, the standard drawings shall prevail.

C–15:
Sedimentation Control

Road shoulders, swales, back-of-curbs, and cut and fill banks shall be completely dressed up by the contractor and seeded as soon as possible.

Standard Drawing No. 1
Recommended Street Connection
Sight Distance for No-Stop Condition

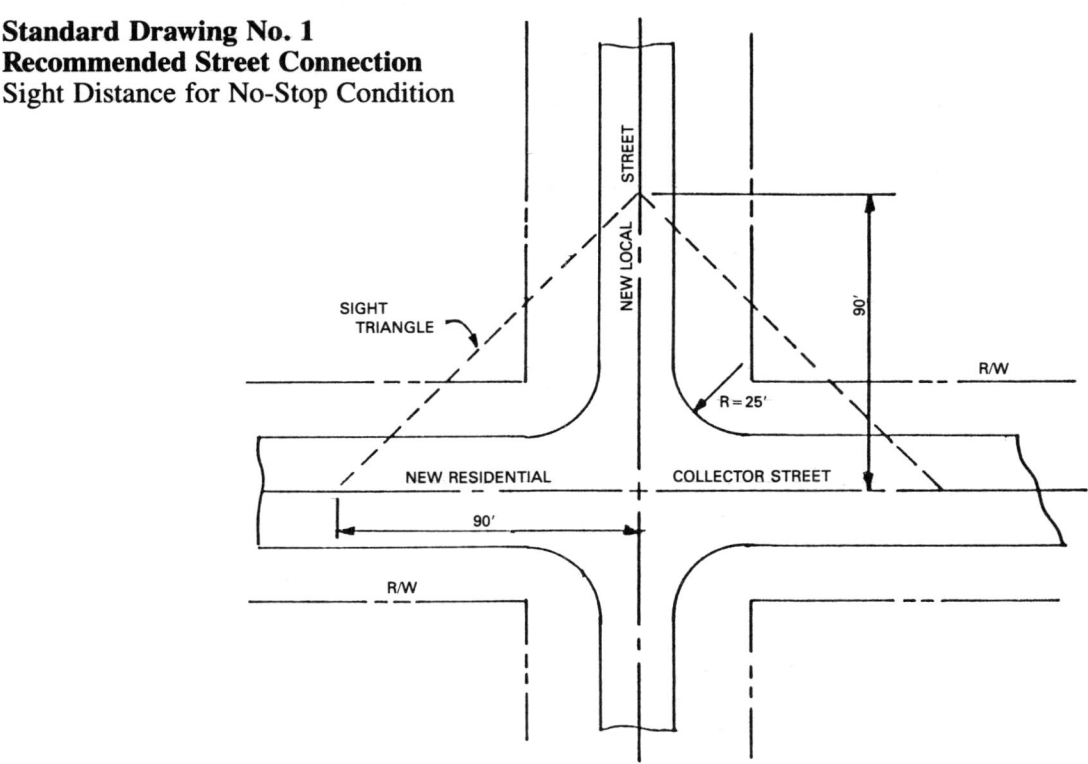

Standard Drawing No. 2
Recommended Street Connection
Sight Distance for Stop Condition

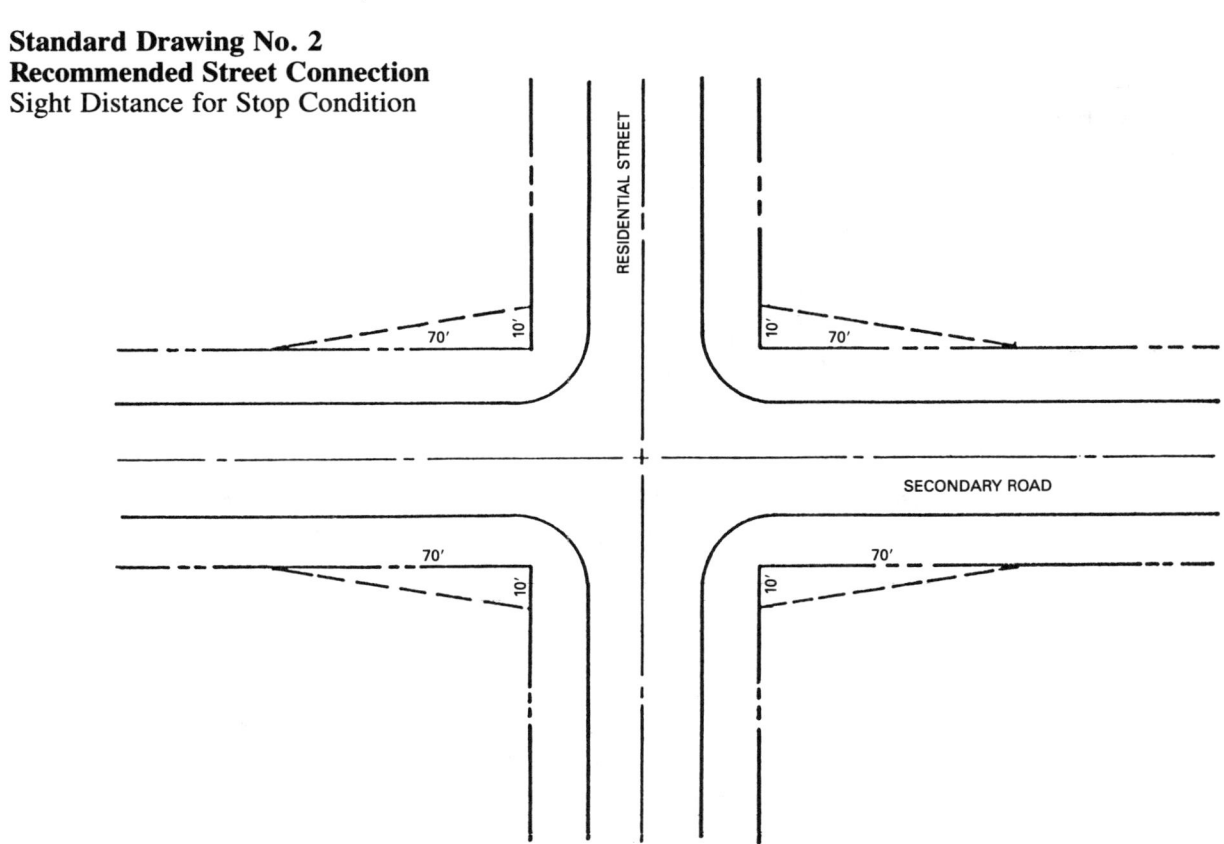

Standard Drawing No. 3
Recommended Street Connection
Sight Distance for Stop Condition

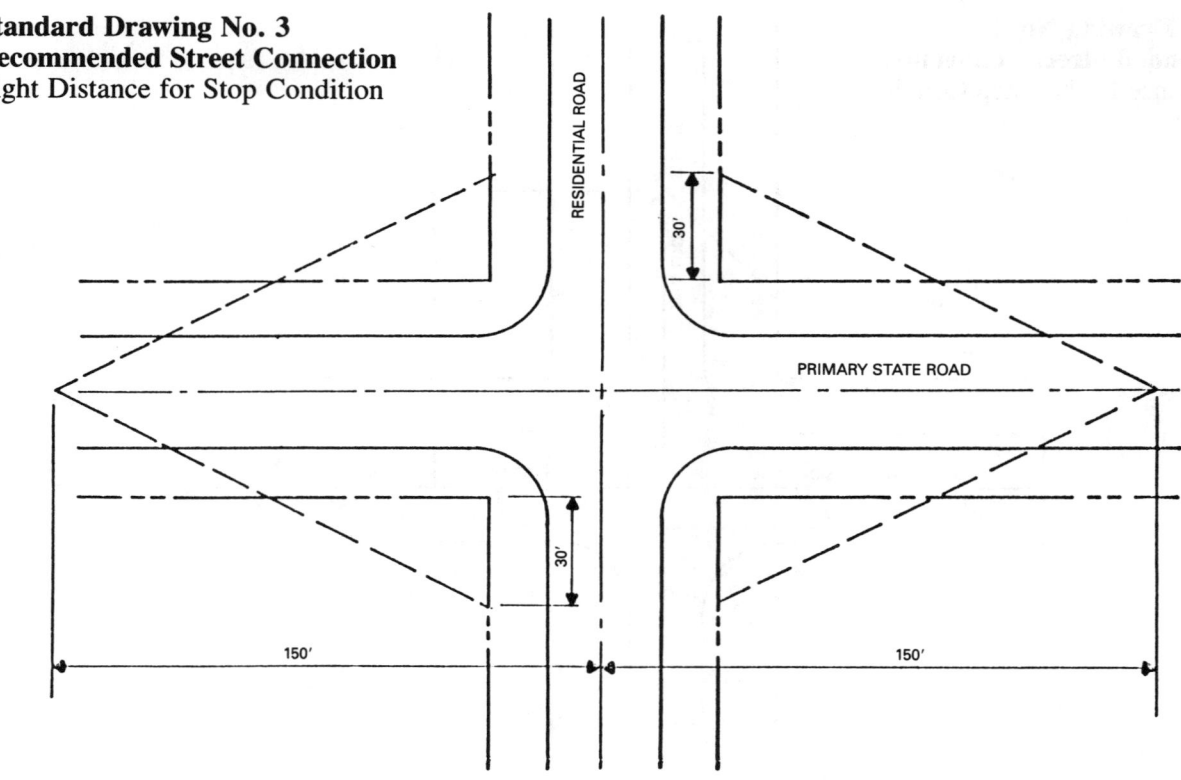

Standard Drawing No. 4
Recommended Street Connection
Curb & Gutter

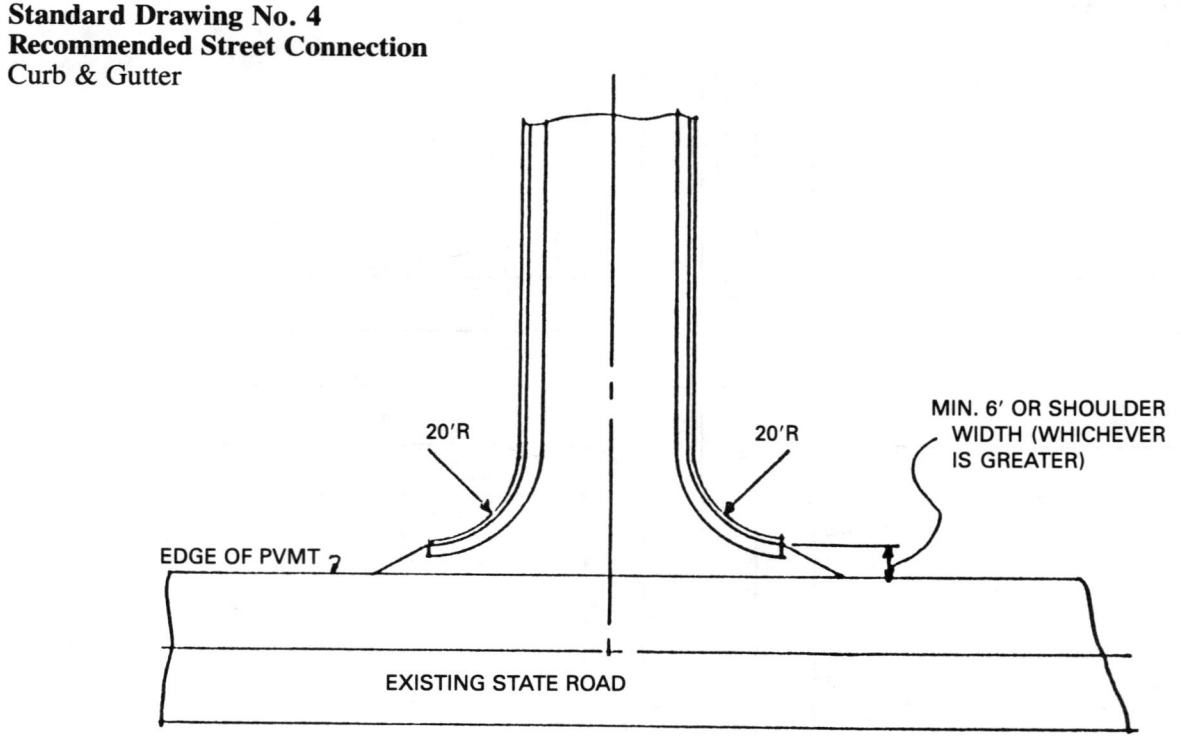

195 Appendix C

Standard Drawing No. 5
Recommended Street Connection
No Curb & Gutter

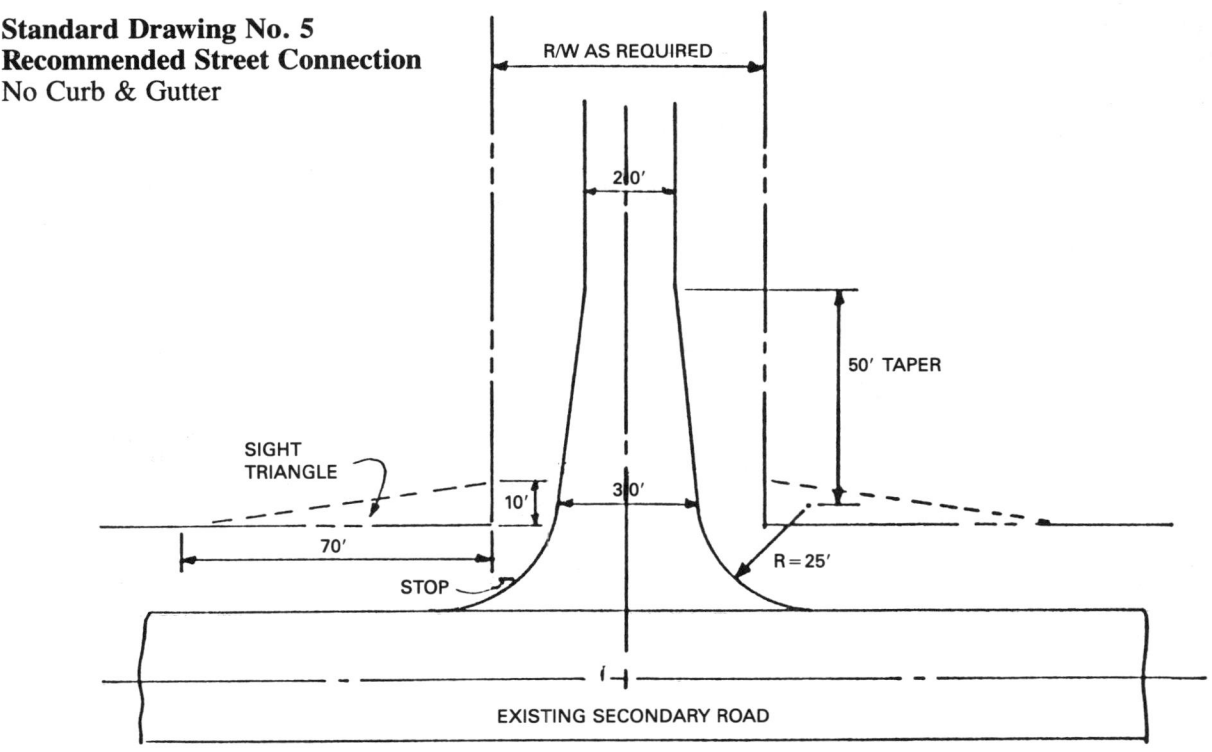

Standard Drawing No. 6
Residential Street
No Curb & Gutter

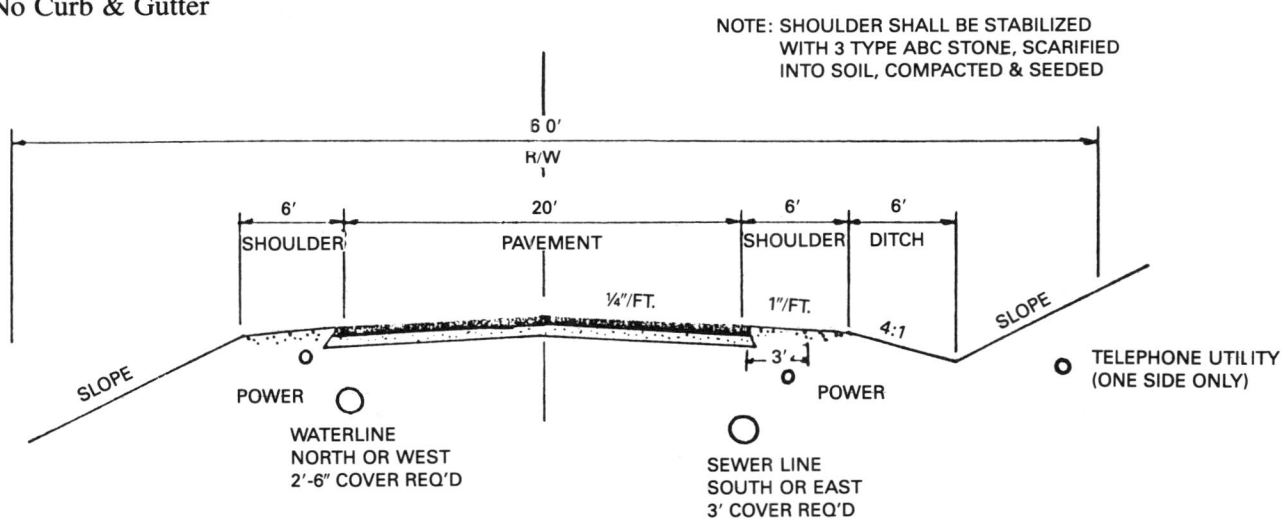

TERRAIN	MAX. SLOPE
LEVEL	2:1
ROLLING	2:1
HILLY	1½:1

Standard Drawing No. 7
Residential Street
Curb & Gutter

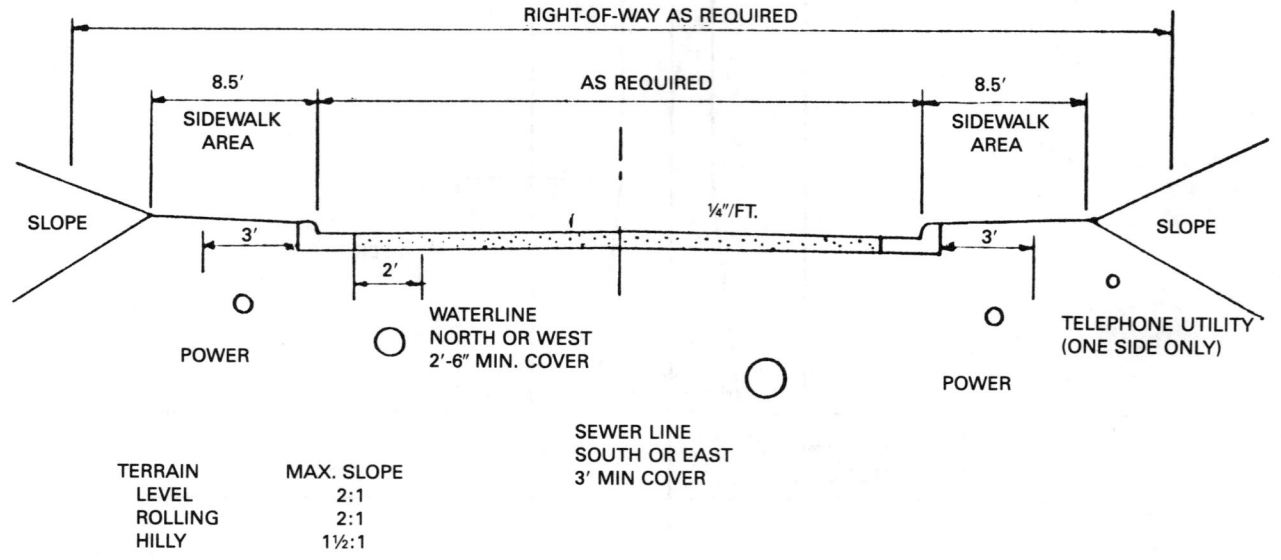

TERRAIN	MAX. SLOPE
LEVEL	2:1
ROLLING	2:1
HILLY	1½:1

Standard Drawing No. 8
Standard Curb & Gutter

Concrete Driveway & Gutter

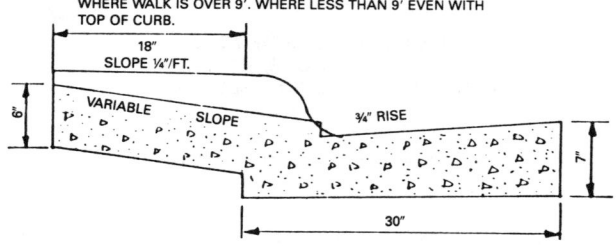

Plan of Driveway Entrance

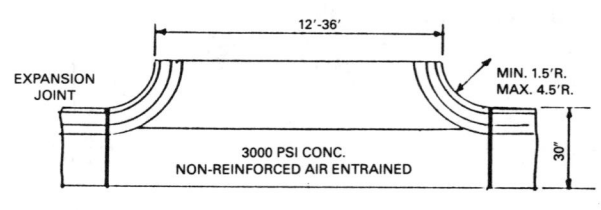

Curb & Gutter

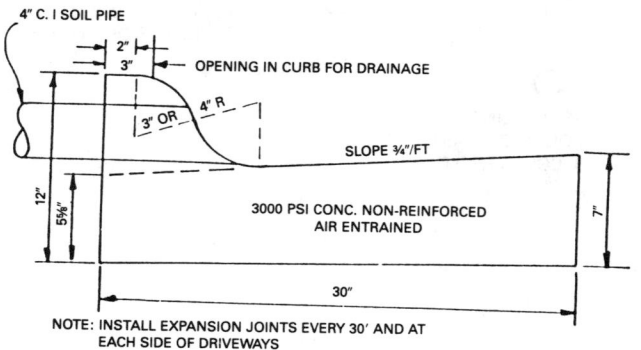

Traffic Island Curb

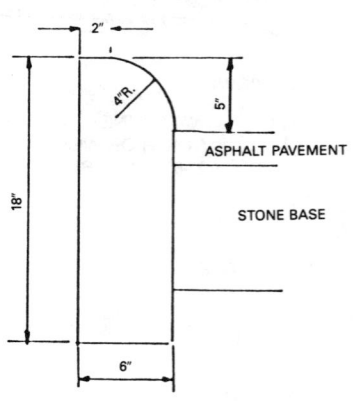

Standard Drawing No. 9
Standard Wheel Chair Ramp

Plan

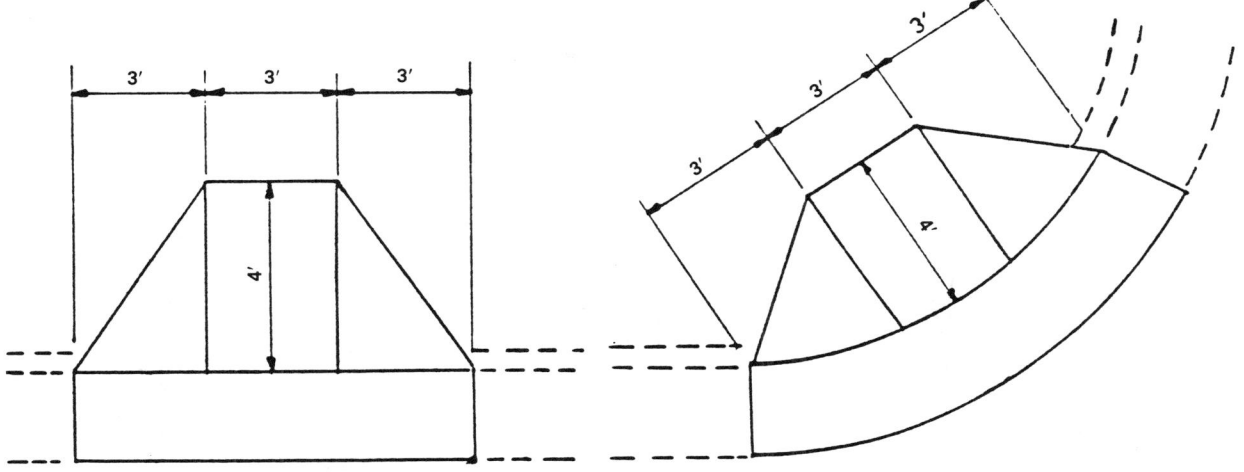

Front Elevation

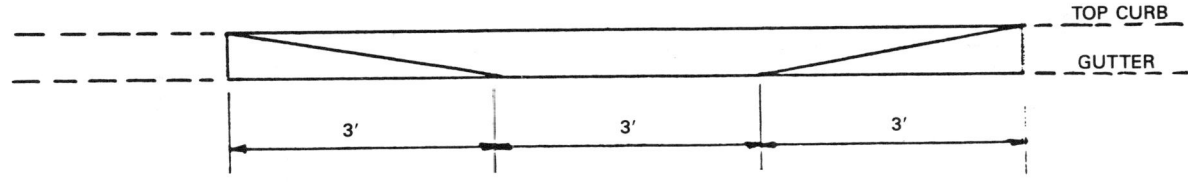

Section Thru Ramp

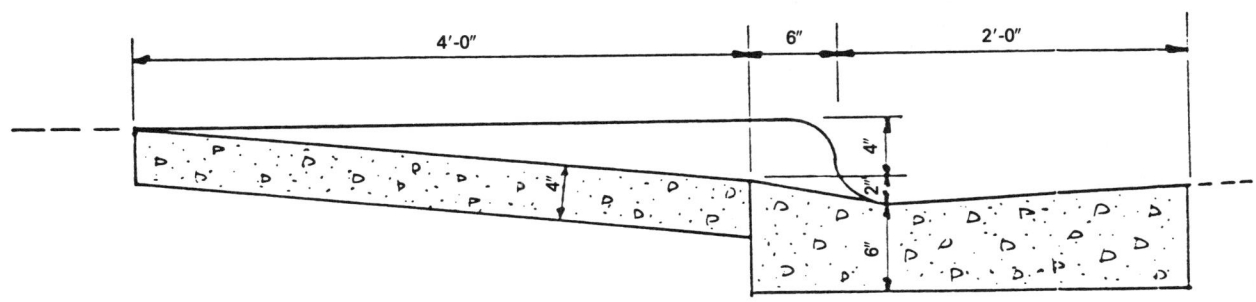

Standard Drawing No. 10
Standard Catch Basin

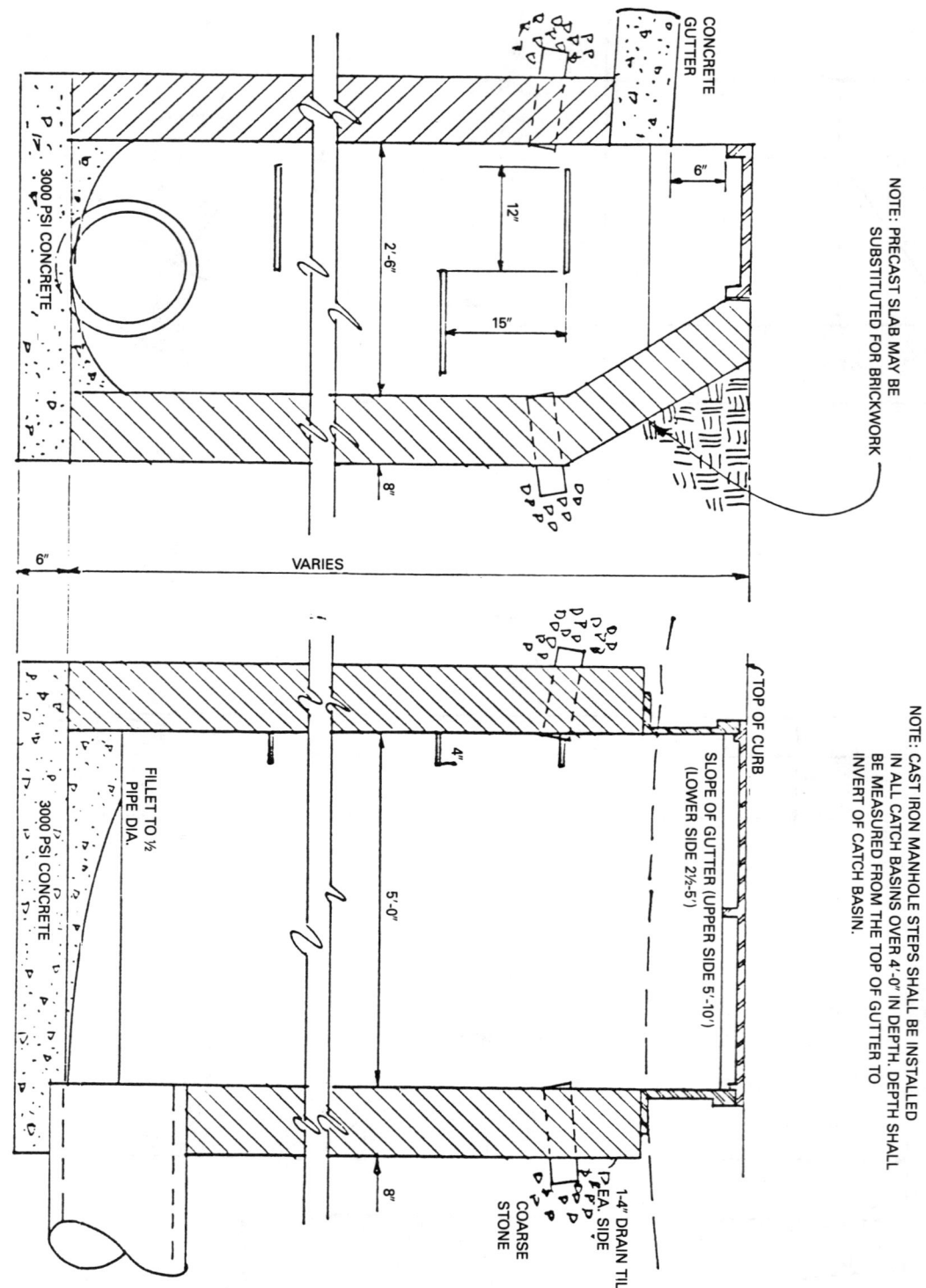

**Standard Drawing No. 11
Storm Water Manhole**

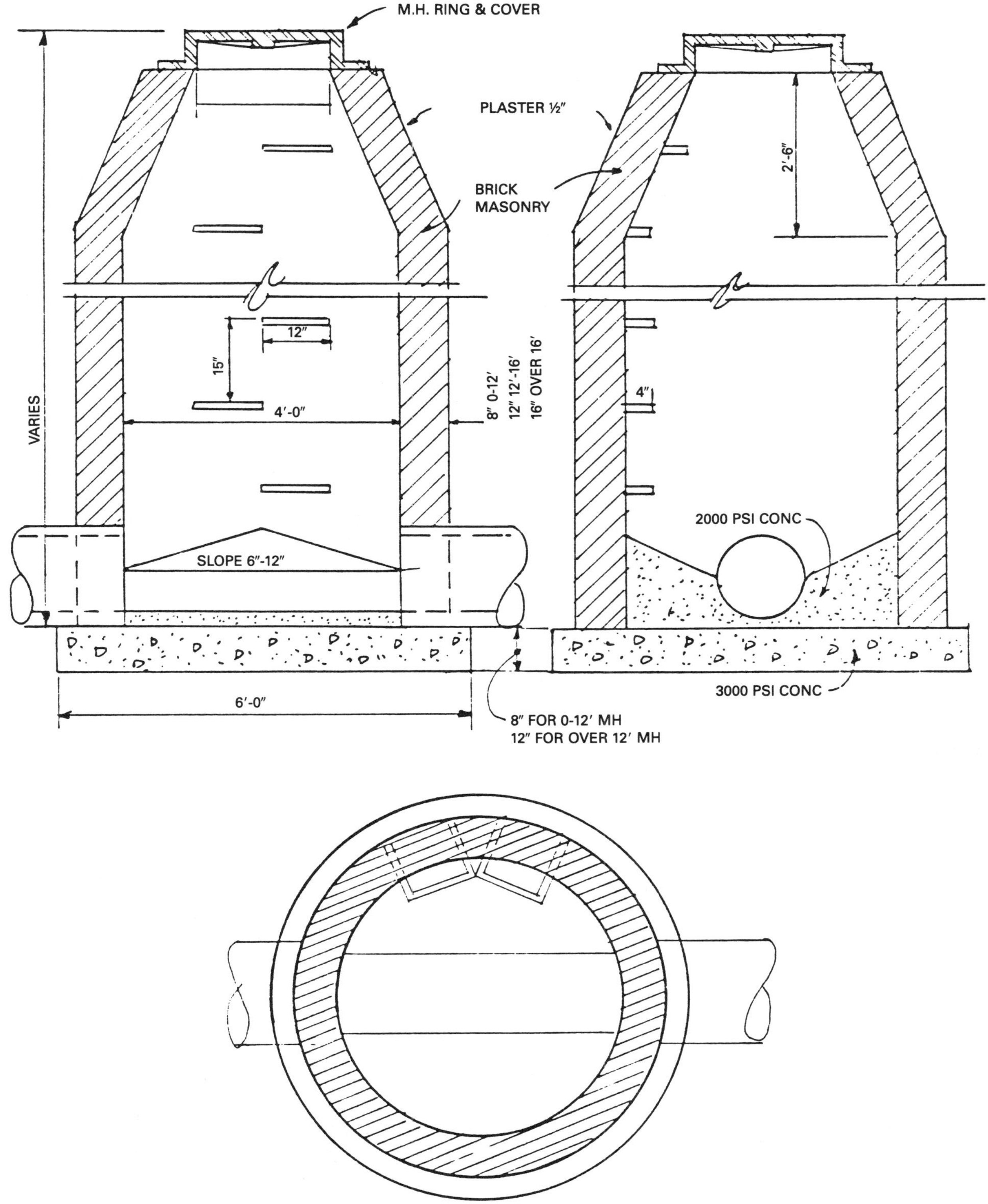

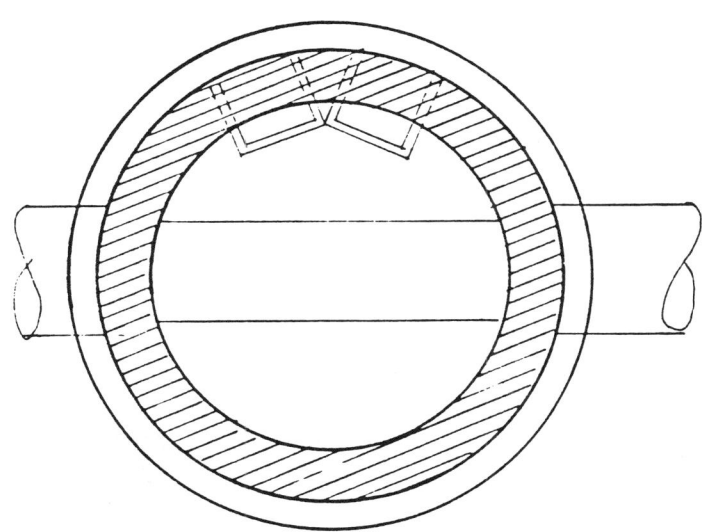

**Standard Drawing No. 12
Yard Inlet Cover**

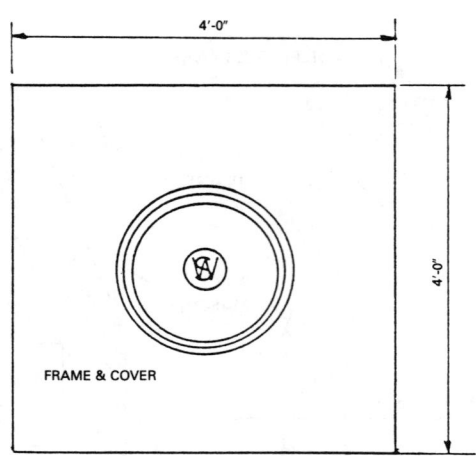

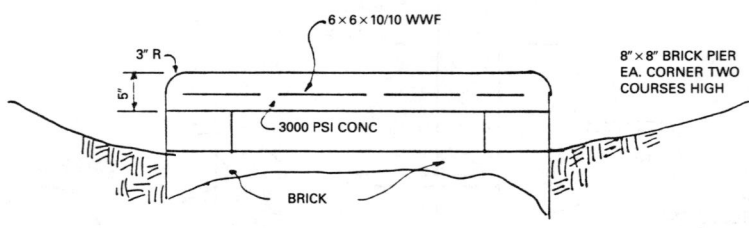

**Standard Drawing No. 13
Yard Inlet**

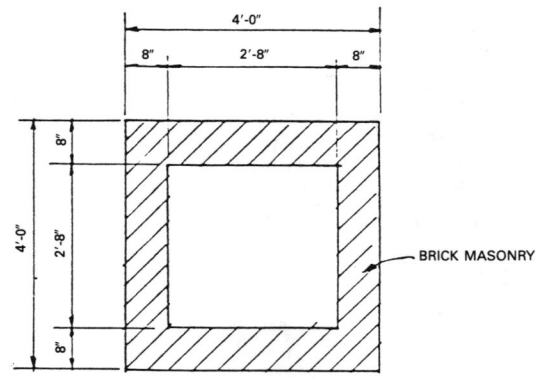
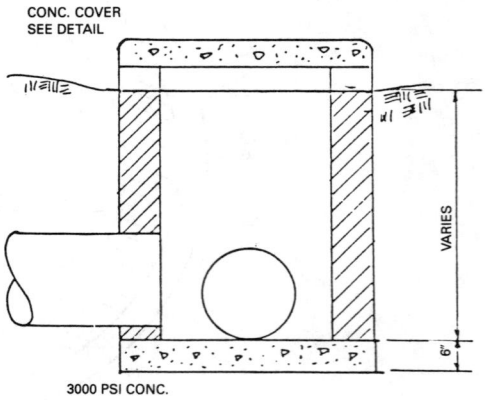

Standard Drawing No. 14
Sedimentation Control

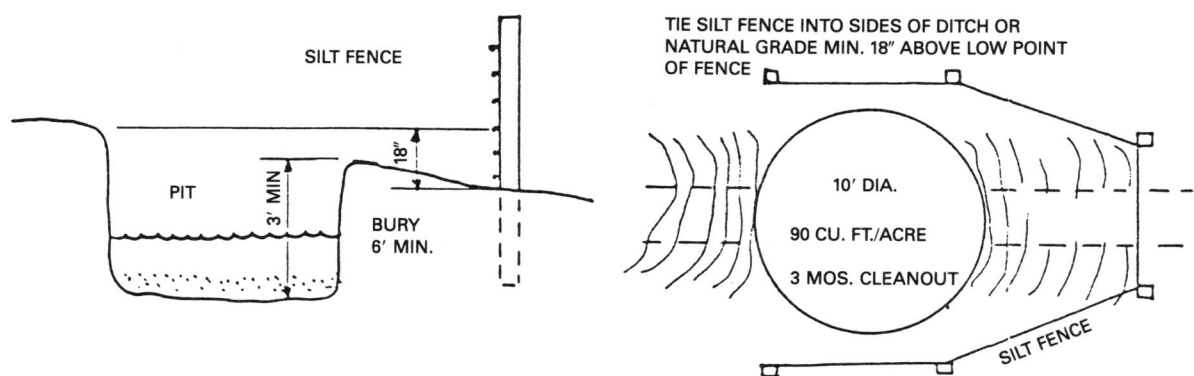

FENCE AND SEDIMENT PIT FOR POINTS OF CONCENTRATED DRAINAGE

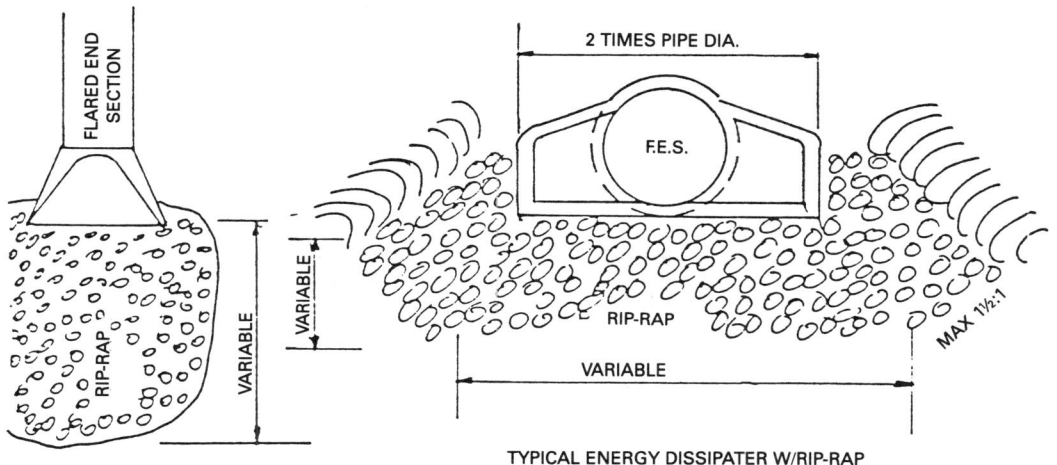

TYPICAL ENERGY DISSIPATER W/RIP-RAP

NOTE:
FLARED END PIPES GREATER THAN 36" WILL REQUIRE CONC SLAB AND/OR RIP-RAP TO PROTECT BOTH ENDS OF PIPE

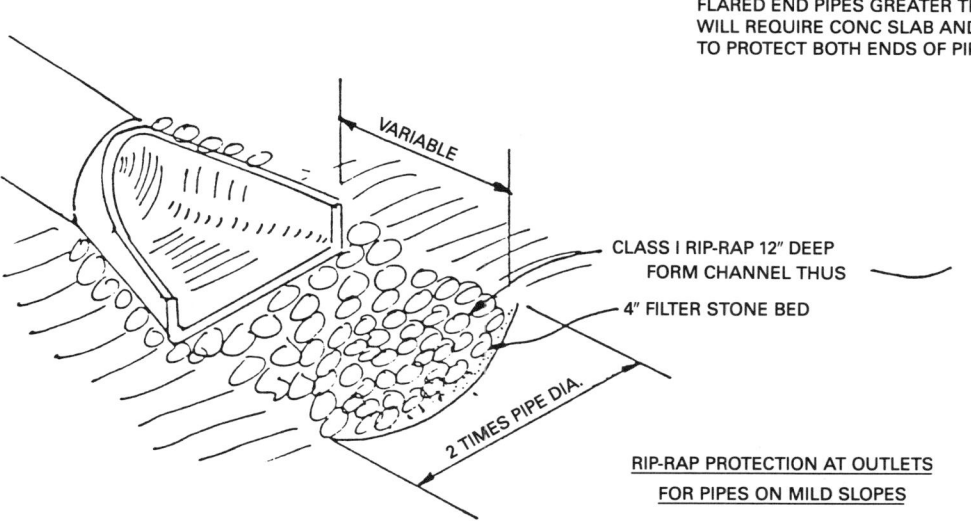

RIP-RAP PROTECTION AT OUTLETS FOR PIPES ON MILD SLOPES

Appendix D Vehicle Accommodation Area Surfaces

D–1:
Paved Surfaces

Vehicle accommodation areas paved with asphalt shall be constructed in the same manner as street surfaces (Appendix C, Sections C–6 through C–9). If concrete is used as the paving material, vehicle accommodation areas shall be similarly constructed except that six inches of concrete shall be used instead of two inches of asphalt. The public works director may allow other paving meterials to be used so long as the equivalent level of stability is achieved.

D–2:
Unpaved Surfaces

Vehicle accommodation areas without paving shall be constructed in the same manner as paved areas except that crushed stone of the following types may be used in lieu of asphalt, concrete, or other paving material:

Size 13 Crushed Stone

Appendix E Guide for Landscaping

Commentary:

This appendix contains no mandatory requirements but does provide information that may help the developer satisfy the requirements of Article XIX, Screening and Trees. Sections E–11 through E–16 are abbreviated, containing only two illustrative descriptions of the trees and shrubs listed in Section E–10.

E–1:
Guide for Protecting Existing Trees

Section 316 provides for the retention and protection of large trees when land is developed. To better ensure the survival of existing trees, the developer should heed the following guidelines (in addition to the mandatory requirements of Section 316):

(1) Protect trees with fencing and armoring during the entire construction period. The fence should enclose an area 10 feet square with the tree at the center.

(2) Avoid compaction of the soil around existing trees due to heavy equipment. Do not pile dirt or other materials beneath the crown of the tree.

(3) Keep fires or other sources of extreme heat well clear of existing trees.

(4) Repair damaged roots and branches immediately. Exposed roots should be covered with topsoil. Severed limbs and roots should be painted. Whenever roots are destroyed, a proportional amount of branches must be pruned so the tree doesn't transpire more water than it takes in. Injured trees must be thoroughly watered during the ensuing growing year.

(5) Prune all existing trees that will be surrounded by paving to prevent dehydration.

E–2:
Standards for Street and Parking Lot Trees

Trees planted in compliance with the requirements of Sections 315 and 317 shall have most or all of the following qualities. The trees recommended in Section E–10 represent the best combinations of these characteristics.

(1) Hardiness

(a) Resistance to extreme temperatures.

(b) Resistance to drought.

(c) Resistance to storm damage.

(d) Resistance to air pollution.

(e) Ability to survive physical damage from human activity.

(2) Life Cycle
- (a) Moderate to rapid rate of growth.
- (b) Long life.

(3) Foliage and Branching
- (a) Tendency to branch high above the ground.
- (b) Wide spreading habit.
- (c) Relatively dense foliage for maximum shading.

(4) Maintenance
- (a) Resistance to pests.
- (b) Resistance to plant diseases.
- (c) Little or no pruning requirements.
- (d) No significant litter problems.

**E-3:
Formula for Calculating 20 Percent Shading of Vehicle Accommodation Areas**

following is an elementary formula for determining the number of shade trees required in and around paved parking lots in order to presumptively satisfy the shading requirements of Section 317.

(1) Including parking spaces, driveways, loading areas, sidewalks, and other circulation areas and not including building area or any area which will remain completely undeveloped, calculate square footage of the vehicle accommodation area: _____ sq. ft.

(2) Multiply ×.20

(3) Area to be shaded = _____ sq. ft.

Add:

(4) Area shaded by existing trees to be retained in and around the vehicle accommodation area:* _____ sq. ft.

(5) Area shaded by required screening trees, if any:* _____

(6) Area shaded by required street trees, if any:* _____

(7) Subtotal = _____ sq. ft.

(If line (7) is greater than line (3), then the shading requirement has been met. If not, go to line (8).)

(8) Enter the difference between line (7) and line (3): _____ sq. ft.

(9) Divide line (8): 707

(10) Total number of shade trees required *within* the vehicle accommodation area = _____ trees

*Existing trees retained in compliance with Section 316 will be credited according to their actual crown radius. Shaded area may be calculated as follows:

$$3.14 \times (\text{crown radius})^2 = \text{shaded area.}$$

Trees planted within the vehicle accommodation area are credited with shading 707 square feet (based on a crown radius of 15 feet.) New or existing trees on the perimeter of the parking lot are credited for having only half a crown over the vehicle accommodation area (e.g., new perimeter trees will be credited for shading 354 square feet). Generally, all trees planted in compliance with the screening requirements of Article XIX, Part I, and the street tree requirements of Section 315 will be considered perimeter trees. When smaller trees such as Dogwoods are planted, the credited shading area will be adjusted downward to 314 square feet for interior trees and 157 square feet for perimeter trees. (Based on a crown radius of 10 ft.)

E–4: Typical Parking Lot Planting Islands

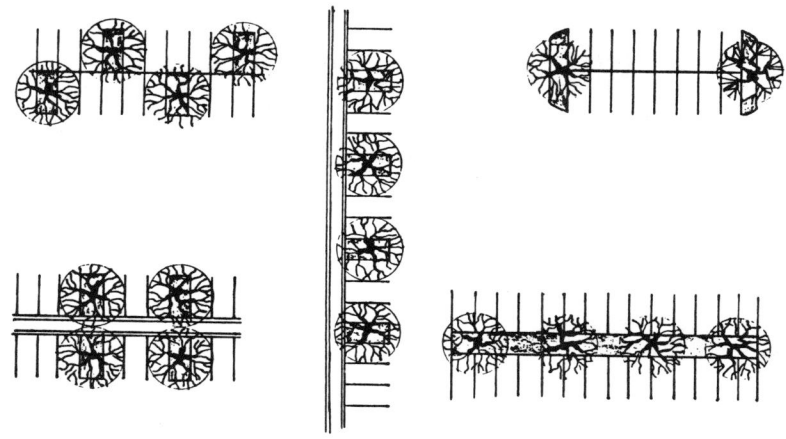

E–5: Guide for Planting Trees

The trees recommended in Section E–10 have minimal maintenance requirements. However, all trees must receive a certain degree of care, especially during and immediately after planting. To protect an investment in new trees, the developer should ensure that the following guidelines are followed when planting:

(1) The best times for planting are early spring and early fall. Trees planted in the summer run the risk of dehydration.

(2) Plant all trees at least 3½ feet from the end of head-in parking spaces to prevent damage from car overhangs.

(3) Dig the tree pit at least one foot wider than the root ball and at least six inches deeper than the ball's verticle dimension.

(4) Especially in areas where construction activity has compacted the soil, the bottom of the pit should be scarified or loosened with a pick ax or shovel.

(5) After the pit is dug, observe subsurface drainage conditions. Where poor drainage exists, the tree pit should be dug at least an additional 12 inches and the bottom should be filled with coarse gravel.

(6) Backfill should include a proper mix of soil, peat moss, and nutrients. All roots must be completely covered. Backfill should be thoroughly watered as it is placed around the roots.

(7) Immediately after it is planted, the tree should be supported with stakes and guy wires to hold it firmly in place as its root system begins to develop. Staked trees will become stronger more quickly. Remove stakes and ties after one year.

(8) Spread at least three inches of mulch over the entire excavation in order to retain moisture and keep down weeds. An additional three-inch saucer of mulch should be provided to form a basin around the trunk of the tree. This saucer helps catch and retain moisture.

(9) The lower trunks of new trees should be wrapped with burlap or paper to prevent evaporation and sun scald. The wrapping should remain on the tree for at least one year.

(10) Conscientious postplanting care, especially watering, pruning and fertilizing, is a must for street and parking lot trees. Branches of new trees may be reduced by as much as a third to prevent excessive evaporation.

E-6: Typical Opaque Screens

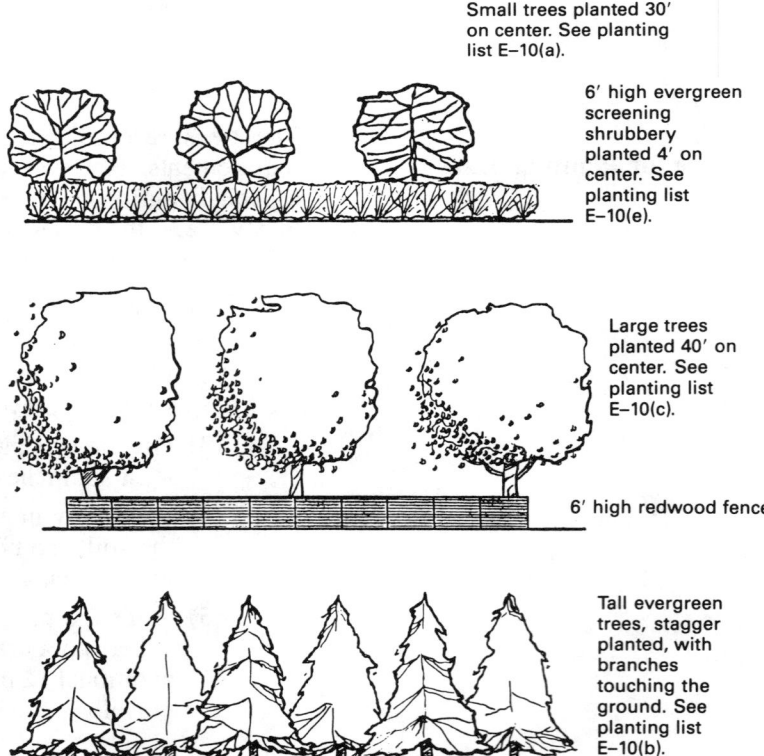

Small trees planted 30' on center. See planting list E-10(a).

6' high evergreen screening shrubbery planted 4' on center. See planting list E-10(e).

Large trees planted 40' on center. See planting list E-10(c).

6' high redwood fence.

Tall evergreen trees, stagger planted, with branches touching the ground. See planting list E-10(b).

E–7:
Typical Semi-Opaque Screens

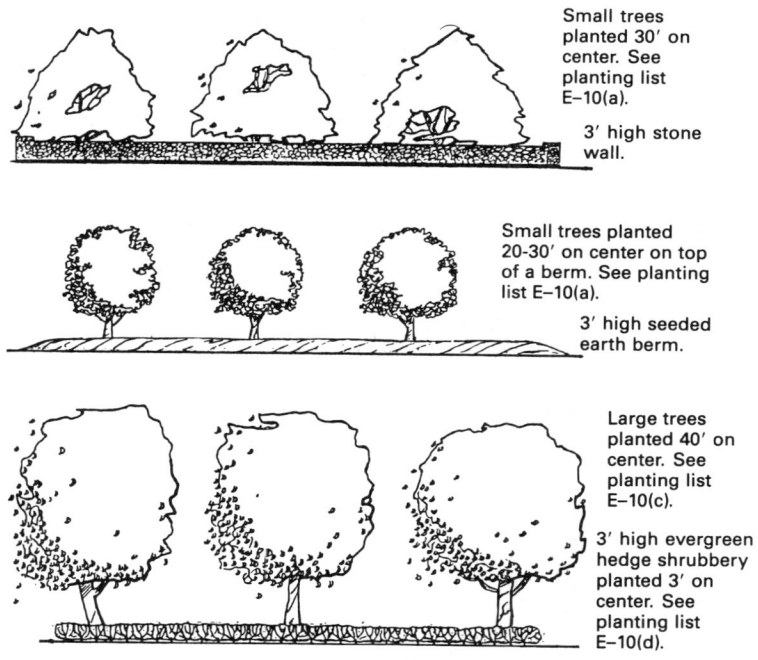

E–8:
Typical Broken Screens

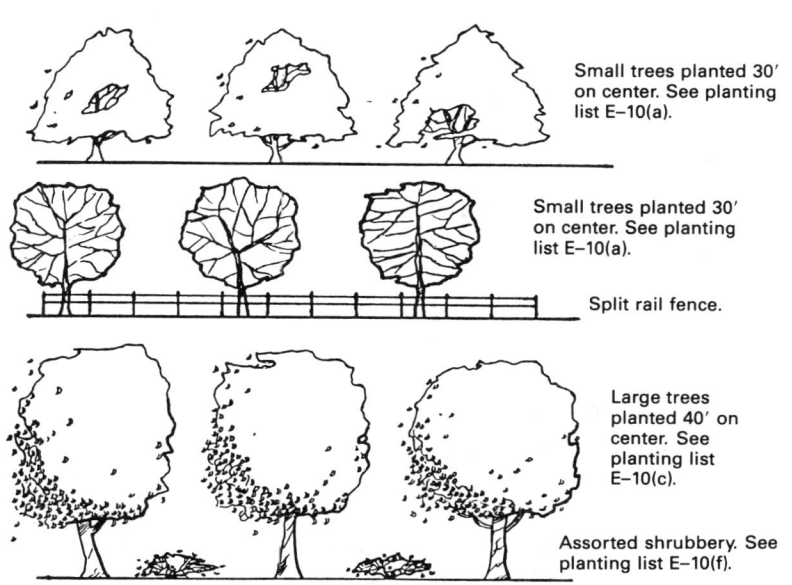

E–9:
Guide for Planting Shrubs

Shrubs planted for screening purposes should be given a proper culture and sufficient room in which to grow. Many of the guidelines for tree planting listed in Section E–5 also apply to shrubs. However, because specific requirements vary considerably between shrub types, this appendix does not attempt to generalize the needs of all shrubs. For detailed planting information on individual species, refer to:

[List one or more reliable reference sources on shrubs.]

E–10:
Lists of Recommended Trees and Shrubs

The following lists indicate plantings which will meet the screening and shading requirements of Article XIX of the land-use ordinance. The lists are by no means comprehensive and are intended merely to suggest the types of flora which would be appropriate for screening and shading purposes. Plants were selected for inclusion on these lists according to four principal criteria: (i) general suitability for the climate and soil conditions of this area, (ii) ease of maintenance, (iii) tolerance of city conditions, and (iv) availability from area nurseries. When selecting new plantings for a particular site, a developer should first consider the types of plants which are thriving on or near that site. However, if an introduced species has proven highly effective for screening or shading in this area, it too may be a proper selection.

Sections E–11 through E–16 contain descriptions of the trees and shrubs listed here.

(a) Small Trees for Partial Screening

　(1) River Birch　　　　　　(8) American Holly
　(2) American Hornbeam　　 (9) Golden Rain Tree
　(3) Eastern Redbud　　　　(10) Crape Myrtle
　(4) Flowering Dogwood　　 (11) Sourwood
　(5) Washington Hawthorn　(12) Carolina Cherry-Laurel
　(6) Russian Olive　　　　 (13) Callery Pear
　(7) Mountain Silverbell

(b) Large Trees for Evergreen Screening

　(1) Deodar Cedar
　(2) Southern Magnolia
　(3) Carolina Hemlock

(c) Large Trees for Shading

　(1) Norway Maple　　　　　(7) Sycamore
　(2) Red Maple　　　　　　 (8) Eastern Red Oak
　(3) Ginkgo　　　　　　　　(9) Willow Oak
　(4) Honeylocust　　　　　(10) Scarlet Oak
　(5) Sweet Gum　　　　　　(11) Laurel Oak
　(6) London Plane-Tree　　(12) Littleleaf Linden

(d) Small Shrubs for Evergreen Screening

　(1) Glossy Abelia　　　　　(6) Convexa Japanese Holly
　(2) Warty Barberry　　　　 (7) India Hawthorn
　(3) Wintergreen Barberry　(8) Azaleas and Rhododendrons
　(4) Dwarf Horned Holly　　(9) Japanese Yew
　(5) Littleleaf Japanese Holly

(e) Large Shrubs for Evergreen Screening

(1) Hedge Bamboo
(2) Thorny Elaengus
(3) Burford Holly
(4) Yaupon Holly
(5) Laurel or Sweet Bay
(6) Japanese Privet
(7) Fortune Tea Olive
(8) Red Photinia
(9) Lauretinus Viburnum

(f) Assorted Shrubs for Broken Screens

(1) Japanese Barberry
(2) Fringetree
(3) Border Forsythia
(4) Vernal Witch Hazel
(5) Common Witch Hazel
(6) Pfitzer Juniper
(7) Drooping Leucothoe
(8) Winter Honeysuckle
(9) Star Magnolia
(10) Northern Bayberry
(11) Judd Viburnum
(12) Doublefile Viburnum

E-11:
Small Trees for Partial Screening

The following trees are recommended for use in all types of screens. Though smaller than the trees listed in planting lists E–12 and E–13, each of these trees will reach a height of at least 20 feet. Selections marked with an (*) are also recommended as shade trees and may be credited for meeting the 20 percent shading requirement for paved parking lots.

(1) River Birch *(Betula nigra)*. Height: 20–40 feet; Spread: 8–16 feet. The River Birch is a native tree which usually grows along stream banks. In landscape design, it is adaptable to either high or low locations, but still requires a lot of moisture. This tree has an interesting papery bark and a graceful branching habit. It has no special pest or maintenance problems.

(2) American Hornbeam *(Carpinus carolinia)*. Height: 20–30 feet; Spread: 15–20 feet. This native tree has a natural yet refined appearance. It is slow growing, but at maturity it serves as an excellent small shade tree. Its fluted muscular trunk is an interesting feature. In the wild, the American Hornbeam is common in moist rich soil, yet, when used in landscape design, it is soil tolerant and does not require an unusual amount of water. It has no pests and no special maintenance problems.

E-12:
Large Trees for Evergreen Screening

The following trees are ideal for screening large scale areas such as shopping centers and industrial sites. They are also effective in combination with other smaller screening plants. Both are moderate to fast growers. They are not considered to be shade trees.

(1) Deodar Cedar *(Cedrus deodara)*. Height: 40–150 feet; Spread: 30 feet +. The Deodar Cedar is a useful and attractive evergreen. It should be allowed plenty of room in order to assume its beautiful natural form. Its pendulous branches should be allowed to touch the ground. It prefers relatively dry soils, grows rapidly, and is easy to maintain. "True Cedars" such as the Deodar are not native to North America, but they have become quite popular in the South as a landscape tree.

(2) Southern Magnolia *(Magnolia grandiflora)*. Height: 40–60 feet; Spread: 25 feet +. Magnolias are striking trees which serve well as screens when their branches are allowed to grow to the ground.

Generally, this tree does well in city conditions, but it should be planted in quite rich acidic soils and it requires a lot of moisture. Furthermore, magnolias require ample space for growth. If planted in full sunlight, they will grow rapidly. Because it drops large waxy leaves, seed pods, and flowers, the magnolia may present a litter problem.

E–13:
Large Trees for Shading

The following trees may be used for screening, but they are recommended especially for shading streets and parking lots. Unless otherwise noted, they will grow rapidly. Each species will attain a mature spread of at least 30 feet.

(1) Red Maple *(Acer rubrum)*. Height: 40–50 feet; Spread: 25 feet +. This tree is an example of a maple which is not recommended where there will be high concentrations of air pollution. However, with its excellent shading characteristics and beautiful colors, it should not be ignored. This tree grows rapidly, but, unlike the Norway Maple, it does not become brittle with age. The Red Maple is a native tree which is usually found in moist, even swampy areas, but it adapts well to a variety of situations. Although subject to maple insects and diseases, it is usually a long-lived tree.

(2) Honeylocust *(Gleditisia triacanthos)*. Height: 50–75 feet; Spread: 25 feet +. Its open, spreading form and feathery leaves may give the Honeylocust a frail appearance, but it is in fact a quite sturdy tree, notable for its resistance to storm damage. It is a native tree which is drought resistant and adaptable to city conditions. Grass and shrubs thrive beneath a Honeylocust because it casts light shade. This tree is especially useful for its ability to be transplanted at a relatively advanced age. Accordingly, it may be used for immediate effect in a landscape design. The Honeylocust has its pests and diseases, but it is fairly hardy. Thornless and fruitless varieties such as "Moraine" are recommended.

E–14:
Small Shrubs for Evergreen Screening

The following shrubs are recommended for informal (unclipped) hedges or screens. Each species grows to a height of less than six feet; therefore, these shrubs are appropriate for semi-opaque screens.

(1) Glossy Abelia *(Abelia grandiflora)*. Height: 4–6 feet; Spread: 3–5 feet. Abelia is quite common in local nurseries and tends to be less expensive than other shrubs on this list. It bears pale pink flowers throughout the summer. Although it has proven quite popular for informal hedges, it has several drawbacks. Abelia should be pruned and thinned to maintain its best form. It may drop its leaves due to low temperatures, lack of pruning, or starvation.

(2) Warty Barberry *(Berberis verruculosa)*. Height: 3–4 feet; Spread: 3–4 feet. Barberrys as a group have proven to be excellent hedge plants. With their dense, spiny limbs, they are effective barriers in public places. The Warty Barberry is a shrub with a neat, compact habit. It is soil tolerant and has no special

maintenance requirements. It grows slowly, but it will reach a height of three to four feet within five years.

E–15:
Large Shrubs for Evergreen Screening

The following shrubs are recommended for high hedges or screens. Each species grows to a height of more than six feet; therefore, these shrubs are appropriate for opaque screens.

(1) Hedge Bamboo *(Bambusa multiplex)*. Height: 10–12 feet; Spread: 4–6 feet. Hedge Bamboo grows rapidly yet is more easily confined to a limited area than most types of bamboo. It is adaptable to a variety of situations, but requires plenty of water. For best effect as a screen, Hedge Bamboo should be stagger planted.

(2) Thorny Elaengus *(Elaengus pungens)*. Height: 8–10 feet; Spread: 6–10 feet. This shrub tolerates many adverse conditions. It will grow rapidly in relatively infertile, dry soils. Its dense thorny branches form an excellent natural hedge. It is one of the most common evergreen shrubs in the south.

E–16:
Assorted Shrubs for Broken Screens

The following is a sampling of shrubbery that would be appropriate in a broken screen. Because many of these plants are deciduous, they are not suitable for opaque and semi-opaque screens. (Note: Many of the evergreen shrubs described in planting lists E–14 and E–15 are also suitable for broken screens.)

(1) Japanese Barberry *(Berberis thunbergii)*. Height: 3–5 feet; Spread: 3–5 feet. This extremely common deciduous shrub is considered to be one of the toughest members of the Barberry family. It survives drought, poor soils, exposure, and the worst city conditions. With its many thorns, the Japanese Barberry is often used as an impenetrable barrier, but it is attractive enough to stand alone as a specimen plant. It requires no special maintenance and, when planted singly, needs no pruning.

(2) Fringetree *(Chioanthus virginicus)*. Height: 10–30 feet; Spread: 8–10 feet. The Fringetree is known for its profusion of beautiful flowers. It is considered to be one of the most striking native American shrubs. It is relatively difficult to transplant, but once established it does well in cities as it endures heavy smoke and dust. The mature Fringetree's only drawback is that its leaves appear rather late in spring.

Appendix F Guide for Noise Levels

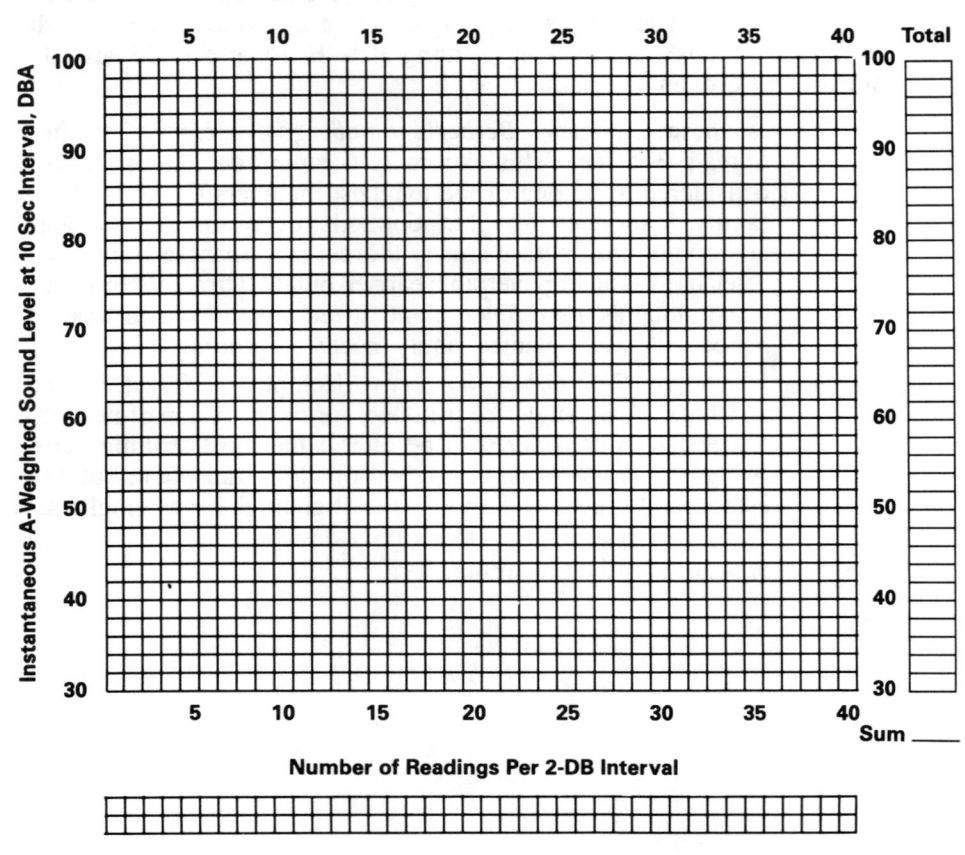

Appendix F–1
Community Noise Measurement Data Sheet

Appendix F-2
Computational Work Sheet
to Hand-Calculate L_{eq}
from Sound Level Meter
Measurements Recorded
on Data Log

A	B	C	D
Noise Level Band, dB	Count	Relative Noise Energy	Relative Total Noise Energy
100	×		=
98	×	79,400	=
96	×	50,100	=
94	×	31,600	=
92	×	20,000	=
90	×	12,600	=
88	×	7,910	=
86	×	5,010	=
84	×	3,160	=
82	×	2,000	=
80	×	1,260	=
78	×	794	=
76	×	501	=
74	×	316	=
72	×	200	=
70	×	126	=
68	×	79.4	=
66	×	50.1	=
64	×	31.6	=
62	×	20.0	=
60	×	12.6	=
58	×	7.94	=
56	×	5.01	=
54	×	3.16	=
52	×	2.00	=
50	×	1.26	=
48	×	.79	=
46	×	.501	=
44	×	.316	=
42	×	.200	=
40	×	.26	=
38	×	.0294	=
36	×	.0501	=
34	×	.0316	=
32	×	.0200	=
30	×	.0126	=

SUM B = _____   SUM D = _____
SUM D/SUM B = _____ L_{eq} = _____

Data Requirements:

- Each noise reading must be taken at a standard time interval between measurements.
- Each noise level recorded is the instantaneous level.

Step	Procedure
1	Enter number of counts per noise level in Column B.
2	Multiply the counts in Column B by the number in Column C and enter the result in Column D.
3	Add all values in Column B to determine Sum B, add all values in Column D to determine Sum D, and divide Sum D by Sum B.
4	Locate the value in Column C that is approximately equal Sum D/Sum B. The corresponding value in Column A is equal to L_{eq}. Interpolate to the nearest 0.5 dB.

Example

Given the following count data, find L_{eq}

Noise Level	Number of Occurrences
81	
82	2
80	—
78	5
76	11
74	4
72	—

Using Steps 1—4 gives:

A	B		C		D
81					
82	2	×	2,000	=	4,000
80	0	×	1,260	=	0
78	5	×	794	=	3,970
76	11	×	501	=	5,511
74	4	×	316	=	1,264
72	0	×	200	=	0

Sum B = 22; Sum D = 14,745
Sum D/Sum B = 670

L_{eq} = 70 dB

- by linear interpolation in Column C and Column A

Appendix G Worksheet

Appendix G
Conditional or
Special Use Permit
Board Consideration
Worksheet

Applicant: ....
Property Location: ....
Proposed Use of Property: ....

I. COMPLETENESS OF APPLICATION
   ☐ The Application is complete.
   ☐ The Application is incomplete in the following ways:

   ....
   ....
   ....
   ....
   ....
   ....

II. COMPLIANCE WITH ORDINANCE REQUIREMENTS
   ☐ The Application complies with all applicable requirements of the Land Use Ordinance.
   ☐ The Application is not in compliance with the following requirements of the Land Use Ordinance: ....

   ....
   ....
   ....
   ....
   ....
   ....

III. GRANTING THE APPLICATION
   ☐ The Application is granted, subject to the following conditions:
   1) The applicant shall complete the development strictly in accordance with the plans submitted to and approved by this Board, a copy of which is filed in the City Hall.
   2) If any of the conditions affixed hereto or any part thereof shall be held invalid or void, then this permit shall be void and of no effect.

   ....
   ....
   ....
   ....
   ....
   ....
   ....
   ....

IV. DENYING THE APPLICATION
- ☐ The Application is denied because it is incomplete for reasons set forth above in I.
- ☐ The Application is denied because it fails to comply with the ordinance requirements set forth above in II.
- ☐ The Application is denied because, if completed as proposed, the development more probably than not:
   - ☐ Will materially endanger the public health or safety for the following reasons: ....
   ....
   ....
   ....
   ....
   ....
   - ☐ Will substantially injure the value of adjoining or abutting property for the following reasons: ....
   ....
   ....
   ....
   ....
   ....
   ....
   - ☐ Will not be in harmony with the area in which it is to be located for the following reasons: ....
   ....
   ....
   ....
   ....
   ....
   ....
   - ☐ Will not be in general conformity with the Land Use Plan, Thoroughfare Plan, or other plans officially adopted by the board for the following reasons: ......
   ....
   ....
   ....
   ....
   ....
   ....